9-20-02

89-13479

Prefaces to Liberty

Bernard Wishy is on the history faculty of Columbia University. Born in Brooklyn, N. Y., in 1925, he attended New York City high schools, received a B.A. from Columbia College in 1948, an M.A. from Yale University in 1949, a B. Litt. from Oxford University in 1952, and a Ph.D. from Columbia University in 1958. He has had numerous articles and reviews published in *Political Science Quarterly, American Historical Review, Commentary,* and *The New Leader.*

Prefaces to Liberty

Selected Writings of John Stuart Mill

Edited by BERNARD WISHY

*"Si, enfin, la verité me paraissait
à droite, j'y serais."*—ALBERT CAMUS

Beacon Press   Beacon Hill   Boston

To the Memory of J. Bartlett Brebner

Preface

This book brings together for the first time much of the published work of John Stuart Mill relevant to the problems raised in *On Liberty*. These letters and articles have been gathered from various sources in England and the United States. The collection makes it possible to observe in one place the development of Mill's ideas on civil liberties from his earliest years to 1859, the year of *On Liberty*. The absence of *On Social Freedom* may elicit some controversy. Its authenticity has recently been challenged by Professor J. C. Rees in his pamphlet *Mill and His Early Critics*. After much hesitation I have concluded that Rees' case has been sufficiently established to abandon the claim for Mill's authorship of the little known and posthumously published essay.

Editing these selections has given me many pleasant obligations. I should like to acknowledge particularly the help of the late J. Bartlett Brebner and Robert K. Webb.

My wife Carol and my friends Moshe Decter and Anthony and Diana Wethered have most of my gratitude for their aid.

Contents

Prefaces to Liberty

Introduction

It is difficult for the sensitive visitor to England today to leave Britain without strengthened belief in the possibilities of political democracy. English government suggests moderation, intelligence, and responsibility. Universal suffrage seems easily united with sober expertness in political leadership and public administration. The calm deliberation of the English contrasts remarkably with the usual tone of politicians in America.

Admirable as these English qualities may be, they belong principally to the most recent period of Britain's long history. England began to acquire its sobriety only in the last century, particularly during the Victorian period. The man of the 1950's who could go back a century to England in the middle of Victoria's reign would find a culture which, although more cruel and crude than ours, was in many respects already accepting the disciplines of an urban, industrial, politically democratic society. If he went back to the first generation of the nineteenth century, fifty years earlier, he would be shocked at the difference in social tone and at the corruption and chaos of life.

In 1815 England was, in G. M. Young's words, "a world in which medieval prejudice, Tudor law, Stuart economics, and Hanoverian patronage still luxuriated in wild confusion." It was a decentralized society ruled by a long established oligarchy of great landed and commercial families. The open violence and cruelty of life in the countryside were appalling, and only the bravest or most foolish of men would walk in central London after dark. The most biting pamphleteer of the time, William Cobbett, called London "the great wen," a raw and ugly boil on England's face. In poli-

1

tics, no Roman Catholic could vote, no professing Jew could sit in Parliament, and only a few hundred thousand men in a population of about fifteen million were legally eligible to vote. The open venality of elections would probably shock the hardiest of modern American bosses. It would be difficult to determine whether the House of Commons or the House of Lords (then in the fullness of its powers) was more shocking for insensitivity to the sickness of English society. King George III was in the last years of his life and in the final stages of his insanity; his son, the Prince Regent, combined a high personal style with the lowest moral standards. The traffic in political patronage that flowed from the king was clogged with corruption. A senseless, archaic legal system, inherited from past centuries, was the despair of its critics. Repressive laws against free speech, a free press, and free assembly were on the books.

In social life, overpopulation on the land sent thousands of people crowding into small cities. Troubled since the Middle Ages by problems of sanitation and public safety, the towns were not equipped to cope with the large influx of new factory workers and the aggravated living conditions. Relief for the workers could not come through trade union action because unions were forbidden to organize. The seeds of evangelical religious piety grew well among the uprooted workers, and the yield was fervor against sin and a repressive moral discipline that often warred against the lures of liquor and lechery. Wealth, however, was no guarantee of social equality. Among the various disabilities they suffered, even well-to-do dissenting Protestants who might afford the costs could not enter Oxford and could not take a degree at Cambridge. These ancient universities were, in effect, closed to all who were not Anglicans. The university teachers maintained a curriculum as outmoded in many respects as some of the old buildings.

These few short lines can just suggest the harshness of the world into which John Stuart Mill was born. Few men in his time were more closely associated with the effort to take this raw, undisciplined, wasteful England and turn it irreversibly toward the rationality and order we now associate with English life and politics. Few other Victorians so skillfully read the future. None so transcended the age in laying out the agenda of democratic culture and in grasping the conflicting tendencies of democratic life.

The story of Mill's career is inseparable from an account of the ceaseless reforming ferment of his age. Even to sketch Mill's life, one must try to explain what is sometimes called "the Victorian mind"—a bold phrase that, properly used, encompasses the most contradictory moral and intellectual tendencies. A full biography would have to deal as much with the life work of the other principal Victorian writers and European intellectuals of the time as with Mill's own ideas. Some of the important facts about his private life, however, can be separated from discussion of the spirit of his age and the development of his political ideas.

Mill was born in London in 1806. His father was James Mill, then a writer for periodicals, but after 1819 an assistant to the Examiner of Correspondence for the East India Company. He was also an important democratic reformer of the first third of the nineteenth century. John Mill, in his *Autobiography*, does not mention his mother even in connection with his birth. One gathers from other sources that she was, in the stock phrase, a good and kind woman, but completely pushed aside by her husband. James Mill might as well have been the only source of John's existence, for he was the dominating influence in his son's early life.

From all accounts, the child was an intellectual prodigy. Even considering the father's great effort to train his son to be a model of intellectual clarity and scholarliness, John's childhood achievements must ultimately be traced to his extraordinary natural gifts. The father kept the boy at home, close to his side, and laid out for him a systematic course of studies starting with the classics and arithmetic. In this age of soft pedagogics, we are stunned at a child reading Greek at three and Latin at eight. Yet John Mill speaks well of this early start in intellectual life. What is really upsetting about this famous father and son was the absence of spontaneous love and uncalculated tenderness in their relationship. Later in life John would bitterly regret his arid childhood and youth under his father's impatient taunts and demanding supervision. He would resent the affront to his emotions, to his "moral sentiments," and to his imagination implicit in his father's concentration on intellectual analysis. James Mill was not a cruel man; he was simply too self-disciplined and hostile to expressions of feeling to be able to show warmth and affection for his boy. Correction and catechism rather than loving concern were his usual habits with the child. John, as a result, was deeply devoted to his father but could not really love him.

What food for imagination there was in John's early years came from his books of history and biography and from those poets for whom James Mill had use. These books seem to have brought John the excitement and relief of belonging to "the other culture"—the land of imagination—of whose valuable place in education Lionel Trilling has spoken so well.

While John was still an infant, his father met the great philosopher Jeremy Bentham. From that time forward James Mill was the center of the various reform movements sponsored by Bentham's followers. Bentham had proposed that the archaic English law and chaotic public administration be made more rational, that they be based not on fictional justifications but on what he considered a scientific reckoning of pleasures and pains. Government was to aim at securing the greatest happiness for the greatest number; the test of all private and public actions was general happiness, not religious truth or abstract right. The Benthamites' attack on social abuses through the steps of investigation, propaganda, reform legislation, efficient administration, and honest inspection laid the basis for modern English political practice. Such work took up much of the public life of both Mills, and it was John Mill who helped give this influential philosophy its name, Utilitarianism.

The younger Mill's formal studies were supplemented by close acquaintance with the Benthamite world. He knew intimately Bentham himself and the brilliant economist, David Ricardo, among others. By the age of twelve Mill moved from the classics to the study of formal philosophy and economics. At fourteen he traveled abroad to France to live with Bentham's brother and to continue his education. At fifteen, back in London and anticipating a career at the bar, he studied law with the future great jurist and Benthamite, John Austin. At about the same time, he was introduced to the study of psychology. Recalling this awesome course of studies, Mill tells us that Sundays were not exceptions and that play with other children was frowned on. Yet sympathy for him should not obscure his intellectual achievement. Although this boyhood constantly at lessons helped bring on a severe neurotic condition at about the age of twenty, it also produced what was potentially one of the finest minds of the age.

In 1822, at about the age of seventeen, Mill became his father's assistant at the East India Company. The job, he claimed, gave him a strong sense of practical affairs and was a relief from intellectual labors. By 1856 he had worked his way up to the second highest position in the organization. The famous books, the many pamphlets, the constant letters to the newspapers and journals, the reports, the book reviews —all those earlier writings for which Mill is remembered— were products of off-hours and spare moments, which, fortunately, were ample. From the very beginning of his clerkship, Mill was also writing, organizing, and campaigning for reform. Benthamism, he tells us, became his "religion" and the democratic reform of English society and government his principal objective. Study groups, editorial work, and debating societies were started before he was twenty. All this time, he continued his constant reading and devouring of ideas; the toll on his emotions was prohibitive.

In the fall of 1826, while in "a dull state of nerves," Mill asked himself: "Suppose that all your objects in life were realized; that all the changes in institutions and opinions which you are looking forward to could be completely effected at this very instant: would this be a great joy and happiness to you?" When he found himself answering "No!" everything he had been taught to esteem collapsed. (Mill seems to have identified strongly with his father before his "mental crisis." Beyond that we can say very little about his unconscious mind.) The passages in the *Autobiography* describing his unhappiness are deeply moving. Mill believed that neither his friends nor his father could begin to understand his troubled state of mind, let alone counsel him. His description of what was wrong comes down to the starvation of his feelings. He first turned, as he had as a boy, to "the other culture," to "those memorials of past nobleness and greatness from which I had hitherto drawn strength and animation." These failed. Sentence after sentence in Mill's description of 1826-27 mentions "pleasure," only to note its absence in his life. His passions could no longer be satisfied by his goals.

Just as suddenly as this severe depression came on him, it lifted. Reading a moving passage in a book about the death of a father and the succession of his son to his powers, Mill began to weep. The tears helped him to recover; from that moment his burden grew lighter, and gradually the clouds withdrew. He decided that he could not live directly for the happiness of others (the Benthamite creed) or even deliberately for his own happiness. He looked instead for those goals in life that he found brought him happiness as a by-product. Mill's start on steady reading in the poetry of Wordsworth and Byron was a deliberate attempt to fulfill his sensual needs directly. These palliatives were helpful for the next four years, but they soon assumed second place to the influence of his future wife, Mrs. Harriet Taylor.

For the man called by Gladstone the "saint of rationalism," Mill's private life was extraordinarily marked by recurrent rebellions of his nonrational nature. Most powerful rationalists, however, are suppressed romantics. The boy's love of the splendor and glory of the ancient world, his delight in natural scenery, his great attraction to poetry, his

"mental crisis"—all suggest that his passions demanded more
than merely to serve his intellect and the great Benthamite
cause of "utility." His relations with Mrs. Taylor intensified his pleasures in poetry and in the "cultivation of the
feelings."

Mrs. Taylor had a "rich and powerful" nature; she was
married to a well-to-do, admirable merchant. Mill was
twenty-five when they met in 1830; Mrs. Taylor was a little
younger. They quickly developed what Mill called "my
most valuable friendship"; and for nearly twenty years Mr.
Taylor made no moves toward divorce as the couple became
deep friends and collaborators. Almost from the beginning
Mill seems to have been in love with her and, soon, Mrs.
Taylor with him. Yet such was the nature of the friendship
that there is little reason to believe that the pair ever became
lovers before marriage. The very fact that Mrs. Taylor was
already married might have been attractive to Mill, saving
him from accepting the sexual responsibilities of marriage.
Nevertheless, as Mill and Mrs. Taylor gradually became
linked together in the public eye, her husband's situation became impossible. Mrs. Taylor eventually separated from her
husband; she continued to see him and to travel with him,
but lived alone until Taylor died. Two years later, in 1851,
she and Mill (then 45) were married.

Whatever the hidden and mixed motives that kept
them together, there can be no doubt that the match was
ideal and the marriage supremely happy. Harriet's sudden
death in Avignon, in the south of France, in 1858 was a stun-
ning blow to Mill and perhaps accounts for his elaborate
praise of her virtues in his later works. What scholars cannot
yet agree on is her precise intellectual influence on Mill. Although he extolls her virtues and her contributions to his
writings, Mill says that she produced no revolution in his
thought. She confirmed and strengthened his tendencies
away from abstractions and rigid system toward a greater
respect for the complexity of fact and an awareness of the
attractions of competing intellectual possibilities. He alleges that she made him more skeptical about generaliza-

tions. She seems also to have stood somewhere behind such specific changes as Mill's lessened enthusiasm for democracy and his conversion to a quasi-socialism.

In 1858, the same year Harriet died, the East India Company was dissolved. Mill then chose to use all his time for his writing. For the next fifteen years, except for a three year service in Parliament, he was producing most of the major works in politics and philosophy for which he is remembered. He also maintained a large flow of letters, reviews, and articles. His worldwide reputation as a sensitive liberal intellectual had by now become so much the public mark of the man that George Eliot, the great novelist, expressed fears that he might lose his intellectual independence when he was nominated by the Liberals for Parliament in 1865.

His parliamentary career was, however, a fine and unusual one. He refused to run unless he were allowed to ignore party lines after election. Once in the House of Commons, he brought his great gifts into constant, although at first unpopular, use. His speech in favor of extending the suffrage to the working classes was called epochal, and he helped prevent working class violence, perhaps even revolution, during the agitation for wider suffrage in 1866. He also pushed along many of the Liberal reforms of the next few years and led what was in effect a filibuster against a government bill to close public parks to political meetings; the bill was not passed, and the now famous area for debating unpopular opinions in Hyde Park, London, was assured. Mill also introduced in Parliament for the first time provisions for proportional representation and votes for women.

Despite this record, Mill had made many Liberal and Tory enemies, and he was not re-elected. From 1868 on, he spent much time in Avignon in the company of his stepdaughter, Helen Taylor, who tried to take her mother's place as Mill's critic. Although he finished a number of essays, including the *Autobiography*, the only major piece he saw through publication was *The Subjection of Women*, an attack on those prejudices and laws that, in his opinion had kept Harriet Taylor from the public eminence he thought she deserved.

Mill died suddenly in May 1873 and was buried with his wife at Avignon.

Had Mill taken stock of England before he died, he would have noticed great changes in his lifetime. By extremely hard work and good luck, the English had created what was in effect a new civilization. Despite widespread misery and glaring social inequalities, England was a healthier, more democratic, and more humane society. Factory and city, although still grim and heartbreaking, had taught men new routines that promised future wealth and leisure. Conscious attempts to improve urban life were being made all over England. Police, fire service, better public and private sanitation, and street lighting were appearing everywhere. Free elementary education for all children was spreading and a national education act was passed by Parliament in 1870. Oxford and Cambridge had revised their curricula, had dropped their religious barriers, and were entering one of those brilliant ages that are recurrent in the history of great universities. Many new colleges, universities, and technical schools had also been founded. Religious tests for voting and for seats in Parliament had been removed.

Amid grave fears that democracy would prove a disaster, the urban working class had been given the right to vote in 1867. The modern party system, civil service, and dignified parliamentary procedure were well established. The corruption of public life had declined remarkably; indeed, administration had become so honest that English observers of the United States (then in the throes of the Grant administration scandals) seemed to assume that England had never known anything but a scrupulous regard for the general good among its political leaders and royal family. In short, by 1873, England had squeaked through to the beginning of modernity without social revolution. The middle-class reformers of John Stuart Mill's youth had achieved most of their principal objectives.

II

The history of the years 1815-1873 is the story not only of these changes in institutions but of a marked shift in the temperament of reform. In 1815, most of the institutions we now associate with a liberal society were still in the future. The favorite defense offered by conservatives in 1815 was that zealous reformers were asking England to move toward untested ideals and questionable innovations. Men like the Duke of Wellington, who helped lead the battle for "our perfect British constitution" against the demand for reform of Parliament, did seem to have history on their side. The great historic institutions of church, crown, and aristocracy—the classic foundations of England's and Europe's life for centuries—still had honest and deep claims on men's loyalties. Despite the French Revolution and the threat that the fight for Liberty, Equality, and Fraternity might break out again, conservatives could still believe that the revolutionary ideas that had kept Europe at war for over a generation could be checked or even crushed. The ancient privileges and proprieties of European life might be saved.

Their liberal critics seemed principally to be appealing to abstract notions of freedom or equality that were opposed by the whole grain of history. The classic case against reformers had been formulated for conservatives by Edmund Burke, the foremost eighteenth century English critic of the French Revolution. Burke called the leaders of 1789 mere "men of mind"—"sophisters, economists, and calculators." He made them seem half-mad creatures possessed by abstractions and generalities. In the name of untried principles, these reformers seemed to Burke to be bent on destroying the great and luminous fabric of European civilization. Whatever ideals they professed, in their all conquering empire of Reason, at the end of every vista he saw not justice but the gallows. However wrong Burke was in his assessment of the actual events of 1789, he was an accurate prophet of the end of the old order of European life. He expected, however, blood and frustration from the new so-

ciety and foretold the secular absolutism and political terror
that, in fact, appeared with the Jacobins of 1793-94 and recur in the totalitarians of our day.

Even if reformers could show the mass misery under the
old European order, could the program of 1789 be justified
on grounds other than "mere principle"? Could belief in a
new future for mankind be other than a faith? Liberals,
unlike Tories, did not have the strength of accepted social
practice behind them. As time passed, reformers would
learn how to combine the call to principles of freedom and
equality with appeals to existing interests, to fear of revolution, and to the possibilities of bargain and compromise.
They would even learn how to use the favorite conservative
weapon, an appeal to history. Professor Stanley Mellon has
recently demonstrated that between 1815 and 1830 French
liberals did in fact try to capture "history" from their opponents. In 1820 the great French historian François Guizot
reminded conservatives that the French Revolution of 1789
had become history, a fact. It could not be reversed and had
somehow to be accepted. At the same time, he tried to
dignify the liberal cause by discovering deep in the French
past a long tradition of popular freedoms and resistance
against tyranny. He urged liberals to abandon or modify
abstract defenses of human rights inherited from the philosophers of the eighteenth century and to construe their
struggle for freedom since 1789 as deriving from ancient
traditions worthier than those of the conservatives. In England, attempts similar to Guizot's were to be made by
essayists and historians. In his famous *History of England*,
Thomas Macaulay envisioned an English past in which the
struggle for Magna Carta in the thirteenth century and the
fights against Charles I and James II in the seventeenth century were, by implication, the dignifying predecessors of
the struggle for middle-class reform in his own time.

In 1815, however, an appeal to "history" still meant
to many liberals, "Beware! Torys at work!" For the Benthamite reformers, including the younger Mill, "history"
was what Bentham had called one of the "false methods of

reasoning on the subject of legislation." "The antiquity of a law," Bentham wrote, "may create a prejudice in its favor; but in itself it is not a reason." Bentham also rejected arguments for laws based on the authority of religion, of metaphors ("a man's house is his castle"), of fictions ("divine right," "social contract"), of fancies ("the rights of a father"), and of imaginary laws ("natural law" and "natural rights"). He claimed that law should be judged only by its effects, and that the effects were calculable in advance by measuring pleasures and pains. This appeal to a "moral arithmetic" as the basis for reform was attacked by conservatives as another dangerous effort by "men of mind" to legislate for mankind, guided solely by abstractly defined notions of happiness. However much the Benthamites loved music and poetry privately, their political and moral theories give weight to the conservative criticism.

Political changes, however, rarely come directly from the efforts of professional reformers, whatever their philosophy. It would be naïve to think that the walls of old England fell only at the blast of Bentham's horn or after an Amen of the other equally powerful group of reformers of the time, the evangelical Protestant sects. Indeed, there are Englishmen today who claim that many of the walls of privilege still stand—in education, the armed services, the church, and professions.

Led by men like James Mill, the first stage of the long struggle for democracy came to a climax in the Reform Bill of 1832. This brought only a modest change in the voting strength and representation in Parliament of the urban middle classes, and the middle class victors soon forgot their pledges to lower class leaders. The bill was more important for destroying the Tory claim that the British Constitution was finished and perfect than for any substantial advance toward democracy. For the first time also, according to Mill, opposition to public abuses was expressed in concrete detail on the floor of the House of Commons and in the press. Mill attributes the prominence of the Benthamites in the agitation to the general public excitement and to "the regular appearance in controversy of what seemed a new school of writers, claiming to be the legislators and theorists of this new tendency."

Implicit in the Benthamite work were two themes that dominated English reform for a generation: "the condition of England question" (as it was to be called) and "the new society." Through their influence on parliamentary committees and Royal Commissions of Inquiry, the Benthamites, along with the private insurance companies and new statistical societies, built an impressive mass of facts about the daily conditions of English life. After the Benthamites drafted a new national code for relief of the poor in 1834, charitable institutions, factories, sanitation facilities, the burial of the dead, water supply—the list is endless—all came under careful scrutiny. England, says G. M. Young, was passing "from humbug to humdrum."

There was slightly more agreement among the diverse groups of reformers about "the condition of England" than about what form of "new society" England ought to adopt. The public was assailed with facts about the present and with countless blueprints for the future. Utopian Socialists might disagree with those who called for more laissez-faire, and democrats could argue with paternalists, but over most of the great debates of the age hung a mood of absolutism and abstraction that touched the Benthamites as well as other "schools" of reform.

In many respects, the specific proposals of Mill and his associates came close to being the prototype of a modern democratic program. In politics, says Mill, they had "an almost unbounded confidence in the efficacy of two things: representative government, and complete freedom of discussion." Extension of the suffrage and parliamentary reform were to be accompanied by free universal education; most Benthamites believed that character was formed by circumstance and that decent education and tolerable living conditions would soon disprove the charge of paternalists or reactionaries that the mass of men were inherently too stupid or too depraved for self government. Some of the Benthamites also wanted the end of the established church and asked for votes for women.

The other chief Benthamite proposal, for an economy free from government intervention, would strike later critics as undercutting the plans for political democracy. The Benthamites did not then appreciate the extent to which the "natural" operations of the market could lead to concentrated economic power and social privilege that would, in turn, weaken the effectiveness of popular institutions. The young Mill thought that a free economic life would be self-adjusting. Let there first be honest and good government, and then let each man judge and pursue his own self interest, and general well-being would follow. In England's nascent industrial society, there were many fiercely competing small firms working close to the margin, with little excess capital and with no provisions for limited liability. The free-market ideals of the day, therefore, could seem plausible.

The classical economists as well as the factory owners are usually held responsible for the miseries of the working classes. The greatest of these economists, David Ricardo, had accepted but misconstrued the arguments of Rev. Thomas Malthus that rapid, unchecked breeding by laborers would act continuously against working class betterment. The general argument was that to pay much more than a subsistence wage would be to encourage earlier marriages, thus more children and the consequent sinking of living conditions back to a subsistence level. The Benthamites, however, had correctly understood Malthus' intentions and disagreed with Ricardo. By practicing birth control, principally in the form of "moral restraint," the workers could restrict the labor supply. Employers would then have to pay the higher wages that make for better standards of living. Mill and his friends were astute enough to understand that social misery and democratic government could not go hand in hand.

The enthusiasm of the Benthamites for all these schemes was unbounded. Scientific legislation was to create a balance of interests in society and clean up the legal and administrative mess. Thereafter, it was assumed, men could be free to follow their own interests, needing the state merely for *ad hoc* adjustments. The agitation for these and other reforms generated a heated ideological atmosphere. In the two generations after 1815, panaceas ranged from mesmerism and phrenology to free trade and votes for women. Some of these great enthusiasms had justice and wisdom behind them; others were mere fads and silly; a few were dangerous. Together, they helped make early Victorian reformism doctrinaire. Mill says of himself and his associates that they were filled with a "youthful fanaticism" and "sectarian spirit."

One major source of enthusiasm for the redemption of England was the attempt of the evangelical Protestant groups to drive sin from English life. Another source, however, was the collapse of traditionalist Christian society in England under the twin blows of industrialization and liberalism. Men raised in a society in which all things seem to impinge closely and directly upon each other, in which the room for individual maneuver and personal choice is limited, tend to be conservative. Let one sin be committed or one link in the social chain be broken, and people expect the heavens to fall. Such men will live with or find ways to go around incredible abuses, providing that there is little hope for change. But let the possibility appear of sweeping all restrictions away—let traditional social ties be weakened, as they were in England around 1800 by the French wars, by population growth, by technological innovation, by new ideas —and all that hunger for life, damped down by the old society, will come rushing out in reformers dressed initially in the bravest colors and making the most extravagant pretensions to a new heaven and a new earth. Such were the conditions under which the first liberal and democratic programs for the "new society" were formulated. It was against their pretensions to being total or final truths that Mill rebelled in the 1830's.

As we have seen, Mill's reaction against the sectarianism, the spirit of system, and the rationalism of his Benthamite youth was primarily personal and temperamental. As his feelings about himself changed, Mill placed higher value upon the personal wish, the private pleasure, the seemingly eccentric feeling. Along with this growing sense of his own resistance to general rules for life, Mill became increasingly sensitive to the complexity of social questions and, as he read more widely, to the virtues of his opponents' ideas. As early as 1830, Mill was moving toward a political pragmatism and pluralism that were not to become more general in England until the 1860's. Thus, in Mill's own career, we have exemplified part of the history of the liberal temperament: its origins in a sectarian spirit with high hopes and great schemes, and its progress toward more realistic and less demanding claims on life. The impressive thing about Mill was that, although he developed a strong sense of the limitations of liberalism and democracy, he still worked wholeheartedly for liberal and democratic improvements. He was one of those exceptional intellectuals for whom political action did not require absolute sanctions.

It is common to take the early reform mood of men like Mill as one basis for what is called Victorian optimism. Certainly there was confidence, even smugness in him and in many Englishmen. But an air of doubt and fear also hung over Victorian society, particularly among intellectuals, as the century advanced. In the fifty years after Waterloo, England came perilously close to revolution several times. The wrench to settled opinions and habits in creating the "new society" we now take for granted must have been formidable. It is probably safe to assume that, sometime around the middle of the century, Christianity rapidly lost its prestige and authority for many leading intellectuals. Clear notes of anxiety and skepticism about the future recur among many of the chief writers of the Victorian age, particularly those who had suffered "a crisis of faith." As the doctrines of reformers like Mill became less rigid, a sense of struggle took precedence over buoyant optimism. Where optimism did exist among the Victorians, it often came as a whistle in the dark and with a sense of "we may just about make it."

The middle classes had held on to law and order for dear life. They had tried to create, by the self discipline and sobriety that we call Victorian morality, an example for the working classes and a call to responsibility for the aristocracy.

Gradually, also, as the nineteenth century wore on, the old society of privilege and status slowly gave way. Benthamite method and reform schemes became social practice and law. When victories were won, the reform banners had to be furled and the barricades dismantled. Winning liberals and radicals who kept faith were given the keys to the cheerless offices, piled high with documents, where the "new society" had to be given life. The victory of reform movements made liberals face up to a daily round of administration given mostly to answering petty questions and complaints about matters like poor lighting in public buildings. The world of programs and the world of power were not the same. By 1839, Mill had already lost many of his former associates to respectability or irresoluteness. Democratic leadership passed down into the lower ranks of the middle classes; as it did, Mill drew further back from a full commitment to democracy. By 1870 the amiable intoxication of reformism had given way to the first "morning after."

The three notable political works published in England in the 1860's are Mill's *Considerations on Representative Government* (1861), Walter Bagehot's *The English Constitution* (1867), and Matthew Arnold's *Culture and Anarchy* (1869). Each of these works is concerned with different questions, yet they share common assumptions and attitudes. Their mood is a sense of plight, rather than of progress. The victories of liberalism and democracy are assumed; but skepticism, a sense of danger and difficulty, and a feeling of doing as well as one can are dominant themes. Each writer is alarmed at the resistance of liberalism and democracy to the claims of intellect and excellence. The contrast with the "almost unbounded confidence" of the young men of the years after Waterloo could not be more striking.

III

In Mill's time, intellectuals were generally not super-ficial, even when they were versatile. By the time of his death, Mill had published impressive major works in poli-tics, logic, economics, ethics, psychology and sociology. The weakest of these was merely astute; the best were works of genius.

It is difficult to assess precisely the great influence of his astonishing production. The many reprintings of books like *A System of Logic* (1843) and *Principles of Political Economy* (1848) only begin to suggest his popularity. Men like Leslie Stephen, one of the leading liberal intellectuals of the generation after Mill, testify that at Cambridge Uni-versity in the 1840's and 1850's Mill's *Logic* had great pres-tige, that this work, more than any other book of the time, helped turn young men like Stephen away from Christianity and toward rationalism. The most famous of Mill's later books are *On Liberty* (1859), *Considerations on Represent-ative Government* (1861), *Utilitarianism* (1863), and his *Autobiography* (published posthumously in 1873).

Of all these works, the most influential is still *On Liberty,* the famous attempt to define the limits of freedom and authority in the modern state. *On Liberty* stands at the heart of modern liberalism, and Mill is most remembered today for his plea for social diversity and individuality. His other writings on freedom and authority, however, are not at all well known. In part to commemorate the centenary of *On Liberty* in 1959, it was decided to bring together a wide selection of these other pieces for the first time. By starting with his letters on freedom of discussion, written when he was only seventeen, and ending with *On Liberty* nearly forty years later, the development of Mill's views on toleration and civil freedom can be fully traced. We can perceive the actual complexity of Mill's thought about social diversity and recognize that his writings do not define liberal doctrine so much as they epitomize liberal dilemmas. Mill became

increasingly alert, as the years passed, to the conflicts of individuality with convention and law, of egalitarianism with
excellence and privacy, and of the pluralist's sense that no
general rule is likely to fit the world with his realization that,
nevertheless, there must be rules.

None of the issues Mill raises in these selections should
be considered only in the light of general political theory.
His ideas are closely connected with events in his private
life—with his "mental crisis," for example, or his relations
with Mrs. Taylor. They represent not only political doctrine,
but also Mill's attempt to define his place in a society in
which the role of the intellectual was rapidly changing.

In the last century there has grown up an extraordinary
self-consciousness among intellectuals about the nature of
the life devoted to the pursuit and use of ideas. Mill was a
prototype of the modern liberal intellectual. He strikingly
epitomizes the intellectual's feeling for or, as we say, commitment to ideas. For Mill, existence seems inconceivable
without the fullest involvement in ideas of what life is and
ought to be. In politics, religion, education, and sex; in the
largest and smallest matters of private taste and public opinion—ideas did not merely analyze or give guidance for the
world; they tended to assume an existence of their own, so
great were the joy and exhilaration they inspired. Mill's
persistent interest in issues like freedom of discussion is as
relevant to his private life and to the emergence of the modern intelligentsia as it is to general problems in democratic
political theory.

Keeping in mind this role of ideas in Mill's life, but
shifting to their content as doctrine, let us examine Mill's
views on personal liberty expressed in this volume. The
first group of selections belong to that period of Mill's life
when he was a radical democrat and a Benthamite enthusiast. Although Mill's "mental crisis" occurred in 1826,
there was no dramatic or immediate change in his published
political opinions. In fact, he was always to be known as a
liberal and a democrat. The initial effect of his crisis on

him was, again, primarily private and temperamental. The
rebuilding and repair of his emotional life came first; the
changes in his political opinions followed.

All the selections preceding the essay *Civilization* were
written in the 1820's, that is, before the Reform of 1832.
These were the years in which the first great wave of nineteenth century reform agitation was building up. England
was still the old society of privilege and mess. For Mill and
his friends, the primary threat to the freedom of the individual was bad government—that is, irresponsible or dishonest administration, unfair courts, and the many political
and social inequalities of the generation before Queen Victoria. "It was a time . . . of rapidly rising Liberalism,"
Mill wrote, and "the tide began to set for reform."

In April 1824, the Benthamites brought out the first
issue of *The Westminster Review,* a magazine primarily
political in purpose and radical in tone. It was the first of
several journals to profit from Mill's close collaboration; it
was also one of the greatest and longest lived of modern
journals of opinion. In the 1820's, the chances that its pub-
lishers would be prosecuted under the libel laws and for
political heterodoxy were very real. Mill and his father did
yeoman and brave work in launching and sustaining the new
magazine, and it played a large role in the radicalism of the
day.

Among the London daily newspapers, *The Morning
Chronicle* was a Benthamite favorite and a leading responsible voice of radical sentiments. Mill wrote more extensively for it than for any other newspaper in his early years.
His far-ranging contributions suggest both the scope of the
assault of the reformers on corruption in the 1820's and his
own initial pre-occupation, not with the limits of democracy,
but with the problems of undemocratic government and its
effect on individual liberties. Besides the pieces on civil
liberties reprinted here, Mill wrote between 1823 and 1830
on such issues as the iniquities of government intervention
in economic affairs, on law reform, on the responsibility of
judges to the aristocracy rather than to the people, on send-

ing thieves to punishment on the treadmill, on absentee landlords in Ireland (a lifelong interest), and on the government's failure to balance the budget.

One theme was constant: the English constitution was not perfect and balanced, as the Tories claimed. The interests of the vast majority of English citizens were not safeguarded by "virtual representation" (the Tory sophistry that Parliament, however elected, spoke not for a class but for the entire nation). Injustice and misery, not harmony and order, were the major facts of English political and social life. The attack came all along the line. Give the people their voice directly; let the government drop its controls over speech and press; reform the law; improve education—and then see if popular institutions and civil freedoms do not vindicate themselves.

Implicit in all these proposals was a dilemma that Mill never solved, although he became increasingly concerned with it. The issue is as complex as it is obvious: *what are the limits of majority rule over the individual?* This problem has troubled modern democratic theory since the end of the seventeenth century, when John Locke left the issue unresolved in his famous *Second Treatise on Government,* which argued that the will of the majority must be the test of legitimate government. So long as unjust kings and insensitive aristocracies existed, the virtues of democracy could seem to far outshine its imperfections. But what effective appeal would exist for the individual in a society in which the majority rules and public opinion is king? While societies remained decentralized and no one group was near a monopoly of power, the harried citizen could often find protection among his oppressor's rivals. As the power of the central state advanced, however, and as it joined eventually with the force of majority rule, the possibilities of escape— the choice of alternatives—seemed significantly limited.

Mill's experience during his "mental crisis" of the way in which his happiness conflicted with the happiness of others was the real starting point of his later doubts about his democratic radicalism. Immediately after his crisis, he still had

no serious doubts that the victory of the Benthamite proposals would bring all the individual freedom that he had
hoped for. But soon a fresh interest in the critics of rationalism and democracy brought him new ideas about the relation of the individual to society. These ideas played on and
strengthened his growing alienation from a sectarian or
dogmatic use of the democratic prinicple of "the greatest
happiness for the greatest number." Although the Benthamites emphasized the greatest happiness as well as the greatest number, and recognized that the greatest happiness
must include that of the minorities, they paid little attention to the possible conflict between majorities and minorities, and they never settled the limits of majority rule. Once
Mill caught the problem, he returned to it countless times in
his career. He never found an answer that would satisfy
the demands of a pure political theory, but he performed
great services in laying out the problem in many of its rami-
fications.

Shortly after his crisis, Mill became a friend of John
Sterling, a devoted follower of Samuel Taylor Coleridge,
the Christian and conservative poet, critic, and philosopher
who greatly influenced many English writers in the nineteenth century. In 1840, Mill was to publish an appreciative
essay on Coleridge that helped alienate him further from
Benthamite enthusiasts. Coleridge, as Mill observed, was at
the opposite pole from Bentham. He was a sensitive Tory,
who opposed the Reform of 1832. He believed that truth
could be found through intuition and imagination, and
scoffed at what he considered the arid rationalism of the
Benthamites. He was the most powerful English defender
after Burke of the role of tradition in giving shape and vitality to a civilization. Originally an enthusiast for the
French Revolution, he turned against it with the rise of
Jacobin tyranny; yet he remained a constant critic of English
imperfections and held church and state, aristocracy and
democracy up to his absolute standards of ideal excellence.

John Sterling had become one of his followers, and
about 1830 Mill gradually moved into Sterling's circle and

away from the Benthamites. Mill never accepted Coleridge's idea that there were transcendent absolute standards of morality and justice to which all good societies and virtuous men conformed. Mill always believed that all knowledge had its basis in experience: intuition and imagination could suggest or support an idea, but its ultimate test was compatibility with facts and reason. He agreed with Coleridge, however, that institutions and laws should satisfy private or poetic standards of excellence as well as general utility. As Mill knew, the happiness of many people did not necessarily guarantee that of any one individual.

Coleridge thus represented for Mill the claim of those nonrational aspects of politics and morality that the Benthamites had neglected or dismissed as unscientific. From him and from Goethe, whom he read at about the same time, Mill began to develop his own version of what Goethe had called "many-sidedness," a sense of the mysteries and imponderables in life and a belief that no one system of thought was likely to do justice to the actual variety and complexity of the world. This awareness in Mill of the limitations of rigid logic helps account for the complaint of people like Harriet Martineau, the radical journalist and essayist, that Mill was untrustworthy because he was always changing his principles. Mill's own analysis of his temperament in the 1830's was, "If I am asked what system of political philosophy I substituted for that which, as a philosophy, I had abandoned, I answer, no system; only a conviction that the true system was something much more complex and many-sided than I had previously had idea of . . ."

The influences of Coleridge and Goethe came at about the same time that Mill was reading the theories of the French writers, St. Simon and Comte. These men were important figures in a revolt against eighteenth century rationalist thinkers, who, they argued, had given insufficient weight to the effects of history on human development. Many aspects of the schemes of St. Simon and Comte were sentimental: they promised a new mankind through brotherly love. Other parts of their philosophy, such as plans for a

female goddess to head their cult, were bizarre. Their followers were usually well-intentioned fanatics. When Au-
guste Comte published his final blueprint for the new society
some years later, Mill was horrified at the tyranny Comte's
speculations had led to.

What most attracted Mill to the St. Simonians of 1820
was their theory of history. Their idea of successively al-
ternating ages of faith and criticism, leading to ever advanced creeds, was one of the attempts to find a new complete philosophy of history, as Christianity, losing its influence, left an ardor for alternative absolutes. It would be
difficult to accept the St. Simonian theory (since all ages
are marked by *both* strong belief *and* skepticism), but the
lessons for Mill were important. He concluded from his
study "that the human mind has a certain order of possible
progress, in which some things must precede others, an order
which government and public instructors can modify to
some, but not to an unlimited extent: That all questions of
political institutions are relative, not absolute, and that different stages of human progress not only *will* have but *ought*
to have, different institutions . . ." From this, another
blow against Benthamite and other absolutes followed: "I
obtained a clearer conception than ever before of the peculiarities of an era of transition in opinion, and ceased to mistake the moral and intellectual characteristics of such an era,
for the normal attributes of humanity." It followed that
democracy itself was not an absolute, but only an attractive
option that would work under certain conditions and not
under others.

A personal crisis leading to a strong sense of individualism; a call from the Coleridgeans and others to ideals of excellence not necessarily found in the standards of the majority; and St. Simon's implication that democracy was not
a universal or scientifically demonstrable truth, but only an
historically appropriate form of government—all these prepared Mill for the most important book about democracy
that he read after Bentham, Alexis de Tocqueville's *Democracy in America* (1835).

No book of Mill's time or ours examined the influence of democracy on ideas and morals in such detail as did Tocqueville's study of American culture. The author was a young French aristocrat. Worried about his future during the political upheaval in France in 1830, Tocqueville used the occasion to visit America, ostensibly to investigate its prison system. He arrived in 1831 and stayed for a year, making extensive journeys into all sections of the country. Like hundreds of European visitors before and after him, Tocqueville put his observations about America into a book, which is, unchallengeably, the most imaginative and fruitful study of the United States ever made by a foreigner, or even by an American.

Tocqueville dealt not only with American politics but also with what we have come to call the "democratic way of life." His book was not intended to be a catalog of curiosities about the United States. It is consciously a study of the culture of the Western world at the dawn, as Tocqueville saw it, of a new democratic age. America was Europe's future.

Although deeply committed to the old aristocratic virtues of individuality, high personal honor, and intellectual and artistic excellence, Tocqueville believed that the age of aristocracy was giving way to a new culture with charms of its own. Genial, comfort-conscious, practical, democratic— the culture nevertheless had its own conceits and weaknesses that Europe should be warned about in advance. Tocqueville believed that nothing could stop the coming of democracy; that is, a society with majority rule and social equality. Democracy appealed to two of the strongest human passions, the desire for justice (which for Tocqueville was democracy's vindication) and to feelings of low envy for the gifted or powerful individual. Democratic citizens would be particularly susceptible to flattery of their commonest images of themselves. What was immediate, easy, accessible to most men would tend to become the common standard. Self-discipline and intelligence, on which democracy really depended to make good its promise of a good and virtuous life for all men, would often be discounted; in the haste and heat of daily life, not excellence but money and ease would become the tests of success. The master passion of democracy, the desire for equality, could become so self confident and vulgar that it might turn against the individualism it originally promised to liberate. Solidified public opinion and majority control of the state might create what could be called a soft totalitarianism, depending less on terror and physical force than on sapping the "undemocratic" desire— the urge to resist what was simple or to test the real worth of "what most people want." Although democracy would worship man in general and would speak in Promethean terms about men's collective power and wisdom, the single citizen might find his powers of individual choice and personal judgment constantly lessening.

Tocqueville analyzed these tendencies in an astonishing variety of subjects. His book was the first full study of democratic life and a handbook on democratic style—in oratory, poetry, sculpture, warfare, and dozens of the commonest pursuits of daily life. To counter the dangers of democracy, Tocqueville suggested decentralization; a strong feeling for law; the growth of private groups organized for the particular needs of individuals; and Christianity, which, by reminding men of their fallibility and mortality, might prevent democrats assuming they were gods.

Mill read and reviewed Tocqueville's volumes enthusiastically, and he and Tocqueville later became correspondents and personal friends. In his *Autobiography,* Mill credits Tocqueville with taking him from an enthusiasm for pure democracy to "the modified form of it which is set forth in my *Considerations on Representative Government.*" Mill had already anticipated this change himself in his essay, *On Genius* (1832), in which he compared English "cram" unfavorably with the Socratic education in critical inquiry. In this work, published three years before Tocqueville's, Mill doubted that the "march of mind" and mass education would supply the inspiration for real individuality. He wondered whether a democratic future would be dominated, not by intellectual giants, but by "an increasing multitude of dwarfs." From 1835 on, however, Mill's growing belief that diversity and individuality were the best tests of civilization became predominant in his political writings. Behind all his later political works were the continuing influences of what he had read in Tocqueville and of Mrs. Taylor's own strong beliefs about individual freedom and social diversity.

"Civilization—Signs of the Times," published in *The Westminster Review* in 1836, was Mill's first major independent essay in which the influence of Tocqueville can be traced and in which Mill went into detail about the dangers of mass society. In his reviews of Tocqueville, Mill had observed that many of the tendencies of American society which Tocqueville attributed to the effects of equality could be found in England of the 1830's; yet in England equality was not a powerful force. Mill agreed that the rule of the masses was the common future of Europe and America, yet he thought that other forces must be at work besides the desire for equality if both undemocratic England and egalitarian America were moving in the same direction. These other things he now called "civilization."

As social and economic life becomes more complicated, Mill explained in this essay, the sheer pressure of living together forces upon men a degree of social cooperation unknown in the past. A paradox of modern society is that its aim of greater individual freedom and choice depends on increased cooperation to make available the goods, services, ideas, and wealth on which a worthy individualism depends. The necessity for working together more closely and more cooperatively breeds overdependence on the group and timidity about largely private destinies. The individual tends to become lost in his public roles. At the same time the democratic and modern virtues of comfort, tolerance, leisure, and ease can also sap the will or obviate the need for doing or thinking what is painful or disagreeable. The amiable and humane take precedence over the heroic.

Grant these premises, and the consequences for democracy become apparent. Individuality and variety, Mill's two criteria of a high civilization, are endangered not only by democracy's vices (as Tocqueville had noted) but by her virtues as well. The liberation of human powers that civilization and democracy promise depends on lively minds and disciplined imaginations. The threats against these appearing in sufficient abundance are "the decay of individual energy" from within and the pressure to be overcooperative from without. It was typical of Mill to prefer dealing with the limitations of a virtue rather than with the obviousness of a vice. When so many of his contemporaries were attempting to prevent democracy from harming the old European order, Mill was a century ahead of them in trying to prevent democracy from harming itself. In our age of "the lonely crowd" and "the organization man," Mill's essay seems disconcertingly prophetic.

Mill himself reports that, after the influence of Tocqueville, his political opinions underwent no serious change. For the next forty years he sought to reconcile democratic power with those freedoms essential both to democracy's own well-being and to the development of individual happiness and excellence. Late in life, he thought that proportional representation and extra votes for the educated would give minorities and men of intelligence a voice that majoritarians could not ignore. Always active in him at the deepest level, however, was hostility to absolutism, whatever its name or promise. As the pieces between *Civilization* and *On Liberty* show, Mill spoke continuously as a liberal and as a friend, but not a zealous partisan, of democracy.

Given Mill's inability to embrace any moral or political view as final, his commitment to liberalism and democracy troubled his more consistent contemporaries. They were probably astonished and dismayed at his defense of the Puseyites, the reactionary reform group in the Church of England of the 1830's and 1840's. It would be hard to imagine two people intellectually more opposed to each other than Mill and John Newman, the young leader of the Oxford religious reformers. Newman was as gifted in his defense of dogma and religious authoritarianism as Mill was in his fight for a liberal, dogma-free society. In his letters on the Oxford Movement, Mill made clear his doctrinal disagreement with the Newmanites. As in the case of Coleridge, however, he welcomed such gifted and honest spokesmen for the other side. In the debate about church and state that Newman and his friends precipitated, Mill hoped for a real clarification of issues and more precise statements by all parties about their ideas, for an invigoration of English religious life, and for a more honest and thorough settlement of disputes than might come from a discussion among bland men who occupied only various middle positions. The parallel today would be for liberals to welcome the rise of a vigorous intellectual conservatism in America because it would force liberalism to give a better account of itself than it does without an opposition.

Mill's notion that progress depends on the freest and most vigorous debate was the basis for his defense of the Puseyites. This generous assumption—that free discussion brings as much truth as men are likely to get—had been continuous in Mill's thought since his first publication at the age of seventeen. He spelled out this theory of emergent social truth as part of a general theory of knowledge in *A System of Logic* (1843), a landmark in the history of philosophy.

Mill's general intention in this work was to place all knowledge on an empirical and inductive basis. In the physical sciences, observable facts and experiment lead to generalizations that are continuously tested against new facts. These generalizations or laws are used to advance men's understanding and control of nature. Mill argued that a parallel science of society could liberate men from ignorance and oppression, and provide a more humane and happier existence than mankind had ever known. To help make life better and come to terms with the great social changes of modern times, one had to understand how institutions worked. For that knowledge men needed disinterested, thoroughgoing analysis of society; but that, in turn, required the fullest possible exchange of opinions and ideas.

An adequate science of society could be built up only

by the slow accumulation of knowledge and by constant testing of various hypotheses about every aspect of existence.
No one "science," such as political economy or ethics, could
get at all the facts. Throughout history theological and metaphysical notions had been used to explain human events that,
in the future, would be put on a precise natural and empirical basis. The one thing Mill was willing to gamble on as his
own contribution to understanding the laws of society was
his conviction that the cause of social change had been man's
mind. All history was conceived as a continuous conversation
among many disputants, each of whom offered some different
explanation or point of view. By keeping the debate open,
by trial and error, by the dialectic among ideas, men would
move slowly but constantly toward more adequate knowledge
of themselves. If any contributor to this civilizing colloquium
were silenced, society might be denied an opinion that would
help in its eventual liberation. To Mill, intellectual and
civil liberty and the widest diversity of opinions were prag-
matic necessities if human progress was to be achieved. Mill
anticipated that, at some distant time, man would have
enough knowledge and verified beliefs to become the real
master of his destiny.

The modern phrase, "the search for truth," characterizes what Mill had been trying to express in his continuous
pleas for free discussion. Together with his interest in the
fullest and freest development of individual potentialities
and in promoting the social diversity that widens the range
of human choice, "the search for truth" was a major theme
implicit in Mill's most famous work, *On Liberty* (1859).
Both his dedicatory page and other evidence suggest that
Mrs. Mill played a large role in composing the essay, but the
question of who wrote *On Liberty* must always be subordinate to what it says.

Mill's first letters on free discussion had appeared in
1823. *On Liberty* was published in 1859. Mill had thus been
debating these issues and had been redefining and adjusting
his position for more than thirty-five years. Harriet Taylor
had perhaps inspired Mill to think more about modern con-

ditions of individualism and diversity, but Mill's original deep interest in freedom of opinion preceded her influence. *On Liberty* is not, then, a sudden effort *de novo* to analyze certain aspects of freedom and authority in the coming age of democracy. Nor is it, as too often assumed, a logical theory or clear definition of the limits of individual freedom and social power. By the time Mill published *On Liberty,* he had become so sensitive to alternative views of the relation of the individual to society that a theory of individual liberty consistent with all recognized possibilities seemed impossible. Rather, he takes up many lines of attack. In pursuing a seemingly fruitful argument (for example, that opinion should be free and only actions limited) he will suddenly come upon an attractive side path or hit a roadblock. When he returns to his main road, after taking a detour, his argument has shifted so as to include the new information from his foray. New terms, new definitions, new nuances have entered that do not fit the categories with which he started. *On Liberty* thus epitomizes the very process by which Mill believed civilization advanced. The play of mind back and forth over competing ideas defines the issues and reveals the choices and possibilities open to men, with their advantages and their costs.

It is true that Mill starts *On Liberty* with an implied promise to define "the nature and limits of the power which can be legitimately exercised by society over the individual." In his effusive dedication to his wife, Mill indicates that the volume was revised "in a very insufficient degree" because of her sudden death. Some critics believe that Mill should or could have published a piece with fewer ambiguities and contradictions; a few others find no final satisfactory "position" in *On Liberty* at all and put it aside as a valiant but fruitless attempt to get at an important question.

Those who are aware of the difficulties of *On Liberty* have suggested several explanations for them. Among some philosophers, Mill is treated as a gifted but confused logician who stumbled upon more good mistakes than bad answers. A few critics think he was trapped by what is called the "Victorian compromise" between the claims of an older aristocracy and the demands of emerging democracy. Mill, according to this view, could neither abandon his attraction to an aristocratic individualism nor reject social and political equality. A most familiar position is that Mill's early Benthamite belief in "the greatest happiness for the greatest number" was never reconciled with his later strong attachment to romantic individualism that came from reading Wordsworth, Goethe, Coleridge, and others.

However much can be said for these theories, we cannot overlook the extent to which Mill's errors in logic, his lack of final clarity, and his uncertainty and contradictions were from another point of view, the virtues of his temperament. Mill was too conscious of many positions; when they seemed half valid, he was quick to grant points to his opponents. He moved too knowingly among attractive but opposing possibilities to relish a systematized politics.

Granting these splendid gifts of temperament, we can accept *On Liberty* as it stands. The contradictions of this work are its position. If we make politics into an absolute and demand rigorous theories, we shall find, as Mill did, that theoretical justifications of individualism or collectivism lead to paradoxical conclusions; in practice, they will compel us to sacrifice more individual freedom or social well being than we are prepared to give up. A thorough theory of individualism may approach philosophic anarchism, and a fully consistent defense of the needs of society implies authoritarianism or totalitarianism. But in pure logic, there may be no choice between these extremes; in theory, we cannot have it both ways.

A civilized society, however, could be profitably conceived as one that refuses to push such ideals as "majority rule" or "supremacy of conscience" to extremes. As Mill follows out his arguments for individualism, he nears a point of distressing clarity and backs away toward confusion and ambiguity. Similarly, as he examines fully society's stake in individual opinion and actions, he approaches an authoritarianism that he dislikes, and draws back. The rigid theor-

ist demands that he go forward; those who follow Mill stand
at the middle (more mindful than Mill, one hopes, of the
extremes) and accept contradiction and ambiguity as the
price of civilization. *On Liberty* is, as its critics charge, ambiguous and contradictory. But it is truer to a tolerable life
than is the pure logic that, in politics, maims and kills. *On
Liberty* and its reception are an obvious fulfillment of Mill's
statements that he had no system and that any adequate system would have to be more manysided than we can yet conceive.

I

On Religious Persecution

1823

More than mere bigotry lay behind the disabilities suffered by English Roman Catholics, Jews, and non-Anglican Protestants until the nineteenth century. Throughout Mill's life, the ancient image persisted that England was both a nation and a church. During the English Reformation, three centuries earlier, Richard Hooker had provided what was to become the classic formulation of the Anglican theory of church and state: any man born in England was to be regarded as both a citizen of England and a member of the Church of England. This idea fit well a society that tended to esteem stability and order more than experiment and social pluralism. Moreover, religion as the revealed word of God, affecting every aspect of human existence, seemed too serious a matter to be left to private judgment. On doctrinal as well as practical grounds, therefore, those who were not Anglicans —that is, members of the officially established church for whose support all Englishmen were taxed—had no secure place in society. They were, in effect, social outcasts, in disagreement with the major articles of Anglican belief and without the organic ties to the body politic that had been sanctioned by centuries. Those who were not of the Anglican faith could not really be regarded as completely English.

As Christian fervor declined as a dominant influence in men's lives, and as different faiths learned to live together, religious and political life in England began to draw apart. By 1815 toleration and tolerance had increased, but more in practice than in law; James Mill still had to warn his son to keep his opinions about religious matters to himself as much as possible. Several times during the nineteenth century there were violent outbreaks of anti-Catholic feeling. The political and social disabilities of non-Anglicans were only gradually chipped away.

This letter on religious persecution, taking issue with the traditional claim that "Christianity is part and parcel of the law of England," is both youthfully arrogant and Benthamite in tone. Mill tries to deflate a "high-sounding maxim" by logic, and he offers a Benthamite definition of law that may reflect his legal training by John Austin, Bentham's friend and the future, famed jurist. Mill implies that opinion and human character by their very natures can not be regulated by law, a line of thought that he seldom uses again.

A LETTER FROM *The Morning Chronicle*
OF JANUARY 1, 1823

SIR,

I beg leave to submit to you some observations, which may, perhaps, appear too obvious to be deserving of insertion. The importance, however, of the subject, and the state of vagueness in which everything connected with it has been hitherto suffered to remain, must plead my apology for intruding upon your notice.

The late persecutions for matters of opinion have frequently been defended, on the ground that "Christianity is part and parcel of the law of England." This sentence, put together by a Judge, passed from Judge to Judge with solemn and appalling gravity, will be found, on examination, to be, like the many other high-sounding maxims with which our law abounds, utterly unmeaning and absurd. This is so evident, that nothing but the extreme vagueness of the language in which this doctrine is conveyed could have protected it from detection and exposure.

A law is a precept, to the non-observance of which, pains and penalties are attached by the Government. Against this

definition, I apprehend, no objection can be brought. And
the law of England, collectively considered, is a collection of
the precepts, thus sanctioned by legal authority.

Having thus settled the meaning of one of the words
employed, let us pass to the other. Christianity then consists
of two parts—a collection of precepts and a collection of opinions. When we speak of the spirit of christianity, of its morality, &c., we allude more particularly to the precepts. When
we speak of the doctrines, the dogmas, the truths of christianity, this is with reference to the opinions which it inculcates.
This division appears to me to be complete. No one can mention any thing connected with christianity, which is not either
matter of precept, or matter of opinion.

Now when it is asserted by Judges that christianity is
part and parcel of the law, is this meant of the *precepts* of
christianity?—No, certainly: for if so, it would mean that
every moral duty is enforced by the law of England, of the
impossibility of this, it is scarcely necessary to produce any
illustration. Not to notice the frequent admonitions which
we find in the Gosel for preserving *purity of heart,* it will
not be denied that sobriety and chastity are among the first
of moral duties. But what would be the consequence of erect-
ing them into a law? It is enough to say that it would be necessary to place a spy in every house.

But if not the *precepts,* perhaps the *opinions* which
christianity inculcates, may be said with propriety to be "part
and parcel of the law." And how? The law is a collection of
precepts. In what sense can an opinion be part of a collection
of precepts?—Surely this maxim, which has been made the
foundation of proceedings such as we have lately witnessed,
is either palpably false, or wholly without a meaning. Unfortunately the protection, as it is sacrilegiously termed, of
the christian doctrines, by the persecution of those who hold
contrary opinions, is part and parcel of the law. But this, the
only intelligible sense in which the maxim can be taken,
ought not thus to be made a foundation for itself.—The
Judge argues as follows:—I punish infidelity, because chris-

tianity is part and parcel of the law. This is as much as to say, I punish infidelity, because such punishment is part of the law.—This may be a very good defence for the particular Judge who pronounces the sentence, but is it not absurd to give it as a justification of the persecuting law?

AN ENEMY TO RELIGIOUS PERSECUTION

2

On Free Discussion

1823

These three letters were published in the same month as the foregoing letter against religious persecution. Mill had actually written five letters, but two were not printed because they were too vehement; the danger of prosecution was always present. Mill signed the letters with the pseudonym Wickliff, after the famous fourteenth century pre-Protestant religious reformer. (He evidently did not know how very far Wickliff was from being a friend of toleration.) The background of these letters is an interesting chapter in the history of English radicalism.

Richard Carlile was a lower-middle class London radical and newspaper editor, not overscrupulous about the truth. A zealous follower of Thomas Paine, he called his paper the *Republican*. Carlile had been imprisoned in 1819 for his free-thinking opinions, but the *Republican* continued to appear. The government pursued him with vengeance: an old fine against him was called up, and his property was seized in payment. He received three more years in jail; his wife, sister, and shopmen were prosecuted as his accomplices; and the Duke of Wellington headed the public fund for their indictment and trial.

The Benthamites had no great taste for Carlile personally or for his theories of natural rights, but they did care about free discussion in the press. James Mill had just published a well-received analysis of freedom of the press, and John Mill was indebted to his father for some of his ideas. His three letters were part of the campaign on Carlile's behalf and, as

39

such, a small skirmish in the larger battles of the reform enthusiasts of the 1820's.

In recounting the great dangers of the government choosing opinions for the people (for that is what the alternative to free discussion in religion came down to) Mill has in mind the corrupt and oligarchic government of the day.

In these letters Mill tries to disprove the common assertions that religious infidelity prevents truth-telling and undermines private morality. He is, in effect, trying to weaken the claims that support the Tory order. He seems to assume that freer formulation of public opinion will serve truth and that public opinion will be predominantly benign in its effect; there is no worry here about the tyranny or corruption of public opinion nor any sign of his later skepticism about "truth." As he began to understand the weaknesses of the "new society," public opinion would satisfy him less, because of its tendencies to vulgarity and arrogance rather than to truth.

A LETTER FROM *The Morning Chronicle*.
OF JANUARY 28, 1823

LETTER I

SIR,

At a time when the question of free discussion on religious subjects is agitated with unusual perseverance, and is therefore peculiarly interesting, I think it highly useful to call the public attention to the nothingness of the arguments which have been brought against unlimited toleration; arguments which, though they have been refuted many times already, are daily repeated, and by a very common artifice represented as never having been answered.

I shall first observe, that as it is generally allowed that free discussion contributes to the propagation of truth, and as this assertion is never controverted on the great majority of subjects, it is incumbent on those who declare against toleration to point out some reason which prevents the general rule from being applicable to this particular case; to shew that free discussion, which on almost every other subject is confessedly advantageous to truth, in this particular case unfortunately contributes to the progress of error. If they cannot produce any satisfactory reason, the general rule ought unquestionably to be observed; and that, even if it were not necessary to employ fine and imprisonment in support of the exception; much more when so great a mass of evil is produced by it.

The puerility of the reasons which have hitherto been brought against religious toleration, is perfectly surprising, and proves most satisfactorily that the cause in support of which they are brought is a bad one. The most common of all is the worn-out fallacy, that there is greater danger of mistake on these subjects than on others.

This assertion, it is to be observed, is wholly destitute of proof. In a subsequent letter I will endeavour to prove, not only that the danger of mistake is not *greater,* but that it is much less in the case of religion than in any other. Admitting, however, for the present, that there is greater danger of mistake, I shall proceed to shew, that if free discussion be excluded, the danger is greatly increased.

For if you determine before-hand that opinions shall be promulgated only on one side of the question, in whom will you rest the power of determining which side shall be chosen? The answer is, in those who are most enlightened and best qualified to judge. But there are no determinable and universal marks by which wisdom is to be known. To whom will you give the power of determining what men are the most enlightened?

What is meant, though it is not openly avowed, by the assertion that the wisest men shall chuse opinions for the people, is that the Government shall chuse them. But if the Government is allowed to chuse opinions for the people, the Government is despotic. To say that there is no danger in permitting the Government to chuse religious opinions for the people, is to assert what is notoriously untrue; since there is no conceivable opinion, true or false, which may not, at some time or other, be made a religious doctrine. There is scarcely a single improvement, either in physical or in political science, which has not at one time or another been opposed by religion. The Ptolemæan astronomy was at one time a part of religion. A professor was imprisoned within these last two years at Rome for maintaining the truth of the Newtonian system, which is still condemned by the Papal Court. The doctrine of passive obedience and non-resistance was generally a religious doctrine, and is still that of the pre-vailing party of the Church of England.

But if you exclude discussion on any one doctrine of religion, you must, by parity of reason, exclude it on all. It is in vain to say that Atheistical opinions shall alone be ex-cluded. What reason is there why this more than any other subject should be prevented from undergoing a thorough examination? There is, if not a reason, at least a cause, why Atheism now undergoes that persecution to which other less obnoxious doctrines were formerly subjected. But this cause is merely that the persuasion of its falsehood is more general than in the case of any other obnoxious opinion. To bring this as a reason for preventing discussion, is to say that the people are better qualified to judge before discussion than after it: which is absurd, since before discussion, if their opin-ions are true it is only by accident, whereas after it they hold them with a complete conviction, and perfect knowledge of the proofs on which they are grounded.

That the evils incurred by permitting any person or persons to chuse opinions for the people are evils of the greatest magnitude, is evident from the arguments which I have adduced. This subject is developed in the most satis-factory manner in Mr. Mill's invaluable Essay on the Liberty of the Press, forming an article in Napier's Supplement to the Encyclopædia Britannica.

The only other argument of any plausibility which the anti-tolerationists adduce in favour of the present persecu-tions, is the incalculable mischievousness of the doctrines persecuted, which they conceive to outweigh the evil we have proved to arise from allowing the Government to chuse opinions for the people.

I, therefore, propose to examine whether the mischievous effects of these doctrines are so great as to justify persecution; secondly, whether there are not many other doctrines attended with mischiefs infinitely greater, and which, nevertheless, it would be reckoned, and with justice, highly improper to persecute; thirdly, to prove that there is scarcely any kind of mischievous opinion, be it what it may, which the ignorant are not more likely to adopt, if it be tolerated, than atheism and deism; and lastly, to refute some of the minor fallacies which have been brought in defence of persecution.

These four objects I shall endeavour to attain in as many letters, if they should be thought worthy of insertion in your admirable paper, which, in addition to the other benefits it is continually rendering to mankind, has uniformly stood forward in a most manly and most Christian manner in defence of free discussion.

WICKLIFF

A LETTER FROM *The Morning Chronicle*
OF FEBRUARY 8, 1823

LETTER II

SIR,

In my first letter I endeavoured to give a general conception of the plan which I intend to pursue in advocating the cause of free discussion. This plan I will now endeavour to carry into execution.

Persecutors do not usually attempt to justify their intolerance under pretence of avenging the cause of God. The absurdity of this pretension would be too obvious, since it would imply that God is unable to avenge his own cause; and since it is also evident, that Christianity rejects this method of defence. If there was any reason which could justify persecu-

tion in the eyes of a man of sense, that reason must be its utility to man; and it is upon this circumstance accordingly, that
the greatest stress has been laid. By permitting the propagation of infidel doctrines, you destroy, it is said, the principal
security for good judicature, and for the practice of private
morality.

How far this assertion is true it shall be our business to
inquire; and first as to judicature—among those requisites
without which good judicature cannot exist, the principal is
true and complete evidence. A great part of the evidence delivered in a Court of Justice consists in the testimony of witnesses. To secure veracity on the part of witnesses is therefore one of the most important ends to which the Legislator
can direct his endeavours.

For insuring the veracity of witnesses, among other securities the ceremony of an oath has been resorted to. That
the desired effect is attained in a very considerable degree is
certain—that this beneficial result is to be attributed to the
ceremony of swearing, is by no means a legitimate conclusion.
There are several motives which tend to produce veracity on
the part of witnesses. Even those who attribute the effect
principally to the ceremony of swearing will admit, that the
fear of punishment and the fear of shame in this instance co-
operate with the religious inducement.—Since, then, it is allowed on all hands, that the veracity of witnesses is the joint
result of several causes, it is for them to shew why it is to be
attributed to one of these more than to another.

When a number of different causes co-operate in the
production of a given effect, it is often a matter of some difficulty to determine which of the causes is principally instrumental in bringing it about. This difficulty, however, is removed, if an opportunity presents itself of examining the effects produced by each of the causes, taken separately. If we
find that one of the causes, when unsupported by the others, is
not followed by any degree of the effect in question, we shall
be intitled to conclude, that in all those cases in which the
effect really takes place, it is to the other causes, and not to
this one, that it ought to be attributed.

This opportunity fortunately presents itself in the case we are considering. There are several instances in which, although the ceremony of an oath is employed, neither the laws nor the popular voice enforce observance of it. If it should appear that in all these cases truth is uniformly and openly violated, then we ought to conclude, that whenever judicial mendacity is prevented, we owe this benefit to the laws and to popular opinion, not to the ceremony of swearing.

I. It is notorious, that from motives of humanity, but in defiance of the strongest evidence, Juries frequently condemn a criminal to a milder punishment than the laws have appropriated to his offence, by finding him guilty of stealing under the value of 40s. Here the oath of the Jurymen is flagrantly violated. They have sworn to judge according to the evidence; but humanity, which dictates the perjury, also prevents public opinion from censuring the perjured Jurymen. This instance, therefore, makes it apparent, how slender is the security which an oath affords, when unsupported by, or at variance with, public opinion.

II. Another most striking instance of the inefficacy of oaths is, the abuse which is made of them at the Custom House. So notoriously does every merchant, who imports or exports goods, swear falsely to their quality and amount, that Custom House oaths have almost passed into a proverb. This perjury, indeed, has for its object to evade certain laws, which are so admirably contrived for the purpose of fettering commerce, that if they were rigidly enforced, certain commodities could not possibly be exported or imported. From the acknowledged absurdity of the laws, this perjurious evasion of them is not reprobated by public opinion.

III. Every young man, at his admission into the University of Oxford, swears to obey certain statutes, drawn up by Archbishop Laud for the government of the University. Now it is well known that no one of these students ever bestows a single thought upon the observance of these statutes. The cause of this non-observance is, that from the uselessness and absurdity of the statutes, public opinion does not enforce obedience to them. If, however, the ceremony of an oath was of any efficacy in preventing mendacity, this efficacy would shew itself even in a case where the obligation is not sanctioned by public opinion. The violation of the University oath, in every case where its observance interferes in the slightest degree with the convenience of the swearer, is a complete proof that the ceremony of swearing affords no security whatever for veracity in any other case, and that whenever witnesses speak the truth, it is not because they have sworn, but because they fear punishment and shame.

The inefficiency of an oath is practically recognized by English Legislators, and by English Judges, when they admit persons of all religious denominations to give evidence, after taking an oath according to the form prescribed by their own religion. For there are some religions which are acknowledged to have little or no efficacy in preventing mendacity. Yet we do not find that, *ceteris paribus,* less reliance is to be placed on the oaths of one set of religionists, than of another.

But the law is not even applicable to all Christians, which amounts to an admission of the inefficacy of oaths to secure good evidence. The respectable sect of Quakers is freed from the necessity of swearing, and yet it is always understood that there is proportionably less false evidence on the part of the members of that body, than on the part of the members of any of the swearing sects.

Having thus made it appear that it is not to the influence of religious motives that good evidence is to be attributed, we might conclude from analogy that the security we have for useful actions is chiefly referrable to other sources. This conclusion is farther supported by the frequency with which dueling and fornication are practised, notwithstanding the positive manner in which they are forbidden by Christianity. They are practised merely because public opinion does not, in these instances, support the dictates of religion. The drinking of wine in Mahometan countries is another equally striking instance.

From the considerations which we have adduced, all of them notorious results of experience, it is evident how ill-founded is the argument of those who defend persecution on the ground which we have combated.

In my next I will endeavour to shew that persecution is not necessary for the support of Christianity.

WICKLIFF

A LETTER FROM *The Morning Chronicle*
OF FEBRUARY 12, 1823

LETTER III

SIR,

I shall now endeavour to prove that persecution is not necessary for the preservation of Christianity.

The Christian Religion may be contemplated in two points of view. We may direct our attention to those peculiar characteristics which distinguish it from all other doctrines, true or false; or we may consider it with reference to those properties which it has in common with all true doctrines, as contradistinguished from false ones.

Not one, but many, arguments might be adduced to prove that Christianity, considered merely as a true doctrine, could not, under the influence of free discussion, fail of prevailing over falsehood. This ground, however, has already been gone over by far abler pens than mine; and a truth which has been maintained (not to speak of other writers) by Divines so eminent as Tillotson, Taylor, Chillingworth, Campbell, Lardner, Lowth, Warburton, Paley, Watson, and more recently by Hall, cannot stand in need of such feeble support as I can afford.

In the present Letter I shall therefore confine myself to the consideration of those qualities peculiar to Christianity, which render persecution even less necessary for its support than for that of any other true doctrine.

And first, let me observe, that the only supposition on which persecution can be defended—by such of its advocates,

I mean, as are Christians—is that of the utter incapacity and incorrigible imbecility of the people. That infidels should think persecution essential to the being of Christianity, can be matter of no surprise; but one who believes in the truth of the doctrine he supports, can not for a moment entertain any such opinion, unless he believes what no man, whose judgment is not biassed by interest, can believe, that the people are incapable of distinguishing truth from falsehood.

The fact, that the utility of persecution rests on such a basis, would alone induce every reasonable man to scout the idea of it; but, even though we were to allow the incapacity of the people, to admit the truth of all which their worst calumniators have ever imputed to them; it would not be less true that Christianity can support itself without persecution, nor, consequently, would the arguments in favour of toleration be a whit less conclusive.

If a true proposition, and the false one which is opposed to it, are presented at the same time to the mind of a man who is utterly incapable of distinguishing truth from error, which of the two is he most likely to embrace? This question will be found to admit of an easy answer. If he was before prepossessed in favour of either opinion, that one he will still continue to hold. If both were equally new to him, he will choose that which is most flattering to his prevailing passion.

All the prepossessions of those whom it is wished to protect by persecution from the danger of becoming infidels are uniformly and confessedly favourable to religion. No where is education, even partially, in the hands of infidels. There is no place where religion does not form one of the most essential parts of education. It is not, therefore, upon this ground, that persecution can be justified.

To counteract the effect of early impressions, it will, no doubt, be affirmed that infidelity is peculiarly flattering to the passions, and that those who wish to throw off the shackles of morality will be glad, in the first instance, to emancipate themselves from the salutary restraint which religion imposes.

It was partly with the intention of obviating this objec-

tion that my last letter was penned. There is no use in representing the evils of infidelity as greater than they really are:
nor does a disposition to do so evince, on the part of him who
shews it, any very great anxiety to vindicate either himself or
his religion from the imputation of want of candour. That
infidelity excludes us from the blessings of a future life,
would surely be a sufficient reason to induce every reasonable
man to reject it. I have endeavoured to shew that even if
(which God forbid) all sense of religion were to die away
among men, there would still remain abundant motives to
ensure good conduct in this life. The passions, therefore, are
not interested in throwing off religious belief, or all our ethical writers have been employing their labour to very little
purpose.

Nor is this all. Infidel doctrines are peculiarly ill fitted
for making converts among that portion of mankind who are
most in danger of mistaking falsehood for truth. They bear
a greater analogy to general abstract propositions in metaphysics than to any thing which can immediately affect the
sensitive faculties. Besides, they superinduce what, to all men
not convinced of the necessity of it by the habit of scientific
disquisitions, is the most painful of all states of mind, a state
of doubt. On the other hand, one of the strongest feelings
in every uneducated mind is the appetite for wonder, the
love of the marvellous. Witness the rapid progress of so many
religions, which we now think so unutterably absurd that we
wonder how any human being can ever have given credit to
them. This passion is gratified in the most eminent degree
by the Christian religion; for what is there in Christianity
which is not in the highest degree sublime and mysterious?

Against so general and so powerful a feeling, what has
scepticism to oppose? It is not peculiarly fitted to take hold
of the imagination; on the contrary, it is eminently and almost universally repelled by it. If, then, it had not been evident before, I trust that the considerations I have adduced
will suffice to make it so, that of all the doctrines which the
invention of man ever devised, none is so little likely to prevail over the contrary doctrine as religious infidelity.

Doctrines which, if left to themselves, have no chance of prevailing, may be saved from oblivion by persecution. The advocates of infidelity are active and fearless; no persecution can daunt, no ignominy can restrain them. By persecution they are raised to an importance which they could never otherwise have attained: by ignominy they are only advertised that it is impossible for them to retreat. To prevent them from diffusing infidelity through the whole kingdom, what has been done by our well-paid divines? I am not aware that they have yet employed any other weapon than vague and declamatory abuse. Books indeed there are; but, alas! what avails a mass of ponderous volumes, written in a style as little suited to the capacity, as the price at which they are sold is to the purses, of those for whose use they are principally required? It is true abuse is far easier, and requires less time and application than argument. But unless my knowledge of the duties of Christian Clergymen is very imperfect, they do not receive one-tenth of the produce of the soil in order that they may attack infidels by coarse and disgusting abuse, but that they may bring them back by gentle persuasion within the pale of the Church.

WICKLIFF

3

On Persecution and Unjust Punishments

1823

Richard Carlile's wife, Mary Ann, was tried as his accomplice, found guilty, fined and imprisoned. Joseph Hume, one of the foremost radical spokesmen in Parliament and a close friend of James Mill, presented to the House of Commons a petition for her relief. There were two issues in the case: the alleged immorality of the Carliles' opinions, and the injustice of their punishment. Hume defended the Carliles, as did Mill, on the grounds that free discussion would aid, not weaken, Christianity and that morality was compatible with infidelity and with belief in religions other than Protestantism.

Hume also said that Carlile was "one of the best moral characters in England." In fact, Carlile was not a fully responsible person, and many of the Benthamites knew that. The danger represented in Hume's defense is the tendency of defenders to endow an unpopular figure—John Brown and Captain Dreyfus are examples—with personal virtues he does not own. The difficulty, of course, is that candour would throw trumps to the persecutors. But, as Mill shows, Carlile's character need not have entered the argument.

What was actually at stake for "the Ministerial Benches" was much more than Carlile himself. There was the persistent idea that an organic Anglican society such as England had no place for those opposed to its basic beliefs. Free-thinking opinions like Carlile's aroused fears of Jacobinism and of renewal of the Revolution after thirty years of European war and social unrest. More than anything else, there was the desire to stamp down, wherever it appeared, criticism of the old England. The

Six Acts of 1819, which curtailed civil liberties, and societies like
the Constitutional Association were attempts to fight by law,
propaganda, and heresy hunts those calling for basic changes in
English life.

In this newspaper article "Mr. Owen" is Robert Owen, the
well-to-do manufacturer and Utopian Socialist. "M. de Chateaubriand" is the famous French Catholic essayist. "Addison" is
Joseph Addison, the eighteenth-century writer and journalist.
"Bishop Sanderson" and "Warburton" are famous theologians.
"Mr. Denman" and "Mr. Lennard" are leading House of Commons members. "John Wesley" is, of course, one of the founders
of Methodism.

An Article from *The Morning Chronicle* of May 9, 1823

We are not of the number of those who have no praise
but for the times that are past. We think, on the contrary,
the present time, on the whole, better than any former time.
There are, for instance, unquestionably a much greater number of intelligent and enlightened men in this country now
than it has ever contained at any former period. But while
we willingly admit the general superiority of the age, we are
not blind to its defects. There is, in particular, one feature
belonging to it which we cannot contemplate with satisfaction. We allude to the mental cowardice which prevents men
from giving expression to their conviction, and the insincerity
which leads them to express what they do not think. A certain assembly has fully its share of this want of singleness of
heart and pusillanimity. No man who knows any thing of
the world can listen for any length of time to the language
used in the assembly in question, without perceiving that
the fear of offending in this quarter, and the desire to please
in that, rather than conscientious conviction, too often ac-
tuates the speakers. There are certainly some distinguished
exceptions, who scorn to sacrifice on the altar of timidity or
machiavelism, and of these we think Mr. Hume unques-

tionably one. The unshrinking firmness with which he grapples with the subjects that come before him, without turning to the right hand or the left, has indeed not been lost, either on the country or on the House. We doubt, for instance, whether another Member of any standing in the House could have been found to present and enforce the Petition from Mary Ann Carlile which he brought forward some weeks ago, though the grounds on which he supported that Petition were such as to make a strong impression on the House, and a still stronger on the country. But taking counsel only from his own conscience, being actuated by a sincere desire to rescue that religion of which we deem him a sincere believer and friend, from the odium which false or less judicious friends were throwing on it, and listening to the counsel of the most eminent advocates of Christianity, the most illustrious ornaments of the Church of England, when its higher places were not deemed the almost exclusive portion of the Nobility, he hesitated not to raise his voice in favour of equal law and free discussion, which were wounded in the case of this individual. The result proved, that it was a mere phantom, at which others had taken fright, and the advocates of persecution and of partiality were found unequal to a contest which only exposed them to ridicule.

Last night he presented a Petition from Richard Carlile, an individual whom an injudicious activity has of late brought so much into notice. Alluding to the prejudices against this man, he stated as the result of his inquiries respecting him, that "he was one of the best moral characters in England," that "his religious opinion might differ from that of some other persons, but that that did not affect his moral character; and he would dare any one to contradict him, when he said that as a husband, as a father, as head of a family, and as a neighbour, Mr. Carlile might challenge calumny itself." This was cheered by the Ministerial Benches, not probably because they who cheered knew whether Carlile was a moral or immoral man, but because they thought Mr. Hume had got on ticklish ground, by allowing the probability of a notorious infidel being moral. But we are not to hold religion in less esteem, when we find that faith does not uniformly produce good works, any more than we are to deem it unnecessary to the support of morality, because we find occasionally moral individuals without a due sense of religion. "An unbeliever (says Bishop Sanderson), awed sometimes by the law of natural conscience, may manifest much simplicity and integrity of heart; and the true child of God, swayed sometimes with the law of sinful concupiscence, may bewray much foul hypocrisie and infidelity! It is only injuring the cause of religion to attribute more either to it, or to the absence of it, than is consistent with the truth; and the most respectable Christian writers, though they justly observe that religion and honesty are most frequently found together, are ready at the same time to allow that they are sometimes found separate. We never for instance heard it questioned, that Mr. Owen of New Lanark is a very moral man. On the other hand, we have doubts whether M. de Chateaubriand was a much more honest man when he brought water from the River Jordan for the baptism of the King of Rome, or is so even now, than when "shocked at the abuse of some of the Institutions of Christianity and at the vices of some of its professors, he suffered himself to be misled by sophistry and gave way to declamation."

It is curious to see what very different notions have prevailed on this subject within a comparatively short period. Addison thought Catholicism worse than infidelity, because the former was incompatible with morality, while the latter was not. Bishop Sanderson seemed to think the Atheists, whom he supposed to be more numerous than either Papists or Sectaries, principally dangerous from the possibility of their joining the Catholics. "Neither," says he, "will the supposed (and I fear truly supposed) greater number of Atheists, than either Papists or Sectaries, be any hinderance to the Papists for finally prevailing. Because it is not for the interest of the Atheist and his religion (pardon the boldness of the catachreses) to engage either for or against any side farther than a jeer, but to let them fight it out, keep himself quiet till they have done, and then clap in with him that getteth the day. He that is of no religion can make a shift to be of any rather than suffer. And the Atheist, though he be in truth and in heart neither Protestant nor Papist, nor any thing else; yet can he be in face and outward comportment either Protestant or Papist, or any thing else (Jew or Turk, if need be) as will best serve his present turn." If Catholicism were incompatible with morality, we should be rather in an awkward plight in the present day, for notwithstanding the aid which infidelity has received of late by the publicity given to it at the expence of the Constitutional Association, we suspect (so much has Atheism gone down since the worthy Bishop's time, that the Atheists are now less numerous than even the Priests of the Catholics, leaving out of the account the flocks. We say nothing of the number of the other sectaries, as this is a much sorer point than that of the number of Atheists, from which we believe no Church Establishment will ever be in much danger.

The question of last night, however, was not so much free discussion itself, as the injustice which had been committed under a sentence levelled against it. On the subject of the severity which had been displayed, Mr. Lennard forcibly observed "that the supporters of the Six Acts, having failed in their efforts to procure the punishment of perpetual banishment, as was contemplated, had still continued through the agency of the Judges to supply that deficiency by sentences which amounted to perpetual imprisonment." Mr. Denman, indeed, offered an apology for the Judges that "had they been aware of the inability of Mr. Carlile to pay the fine at the time judgment was passed, he was sure they never would have passed it." But this apology does not, at all events, apply to the case of Mary Ann Carlile, with respect to whose means to pay the fine imposed on her there never could be the smallest doubt.

Religion disclaims those who would advance her cause by the mean expedients to which Mr. Hume alluded last night. Let good ends be promoted by fair and upright means. The equal administration of law is due to the Infidel as well as to the Christian. Give not to the Infidel any advantage from your disgracing a good cause by disreputable means. In the words of Bishop Warburton, "Can any but an enthusiast believe that he may use guile to promote the glory of God— the wisdom from above is without partiality and without hypocrisy. Partiality consists in dispensing an unequal measure in our transactions with others; *hypocrisy in attempting to cover that unequal measure by prevarication and false pretences.*" And in the words of a man less learned, perhaps, but not less upright than Bishop Warburton, we mean the worthy John Wesley, "no man living is authorised to break or dispensed with in breaking any law of morality."

The discussions have done, and will do, good, and we trust Mr. Hume will return to the subject. The Courts of Law must profit by them. "Shame, albeit the daughter of sinne, becomes sometimes the mother of conversion; and when all good motions else seem mere strangers, this one is admitted as a profitable, though unwelcome guest."

4

On the Rights of the Press in Courts

1823

This letter, protesting the barring of reporters from a court, is another indication of how far from fact were English claims about equal justice. The judge's prejudices, his deference to the higher rank of the complainant, and his arbitrary powers undercut the fair administration of justice. Had Mill written this a little later, he might have been less sanguine about the disinterestedness of public opinion, which he here envisions as a correcting force on the judiciary. Mill had not yet faced the less attractive features of democratic public opinion. Had he lived to see the corruptions of the popular democratic press, he might have welcomed the stringent controls over information about trials that English newspapers must now accept.

A LETTER FROM *The Morning Chronicle*
OF AUGUST 20, 1823

SIR,

Among the numberless blessings which we are continually told that we owe to our glorious Constitution, a good administration of justice has always been considered as the most valuable. While the judicature of every other nation is corrupt, profligate and oppressive—a ready tool in the hands of power; it has been our boast that ours alone is pure and undefiled; that it gives ear alike to the rich and to the poor, that neither the interests nor the prejudices of rank and station ever divert our Judges from the straight path of equity and impartiality.

A practical illustration of this inestimable blessing occurred some days since at the Queen-square Police-office; and although several papers, and you, Sir, among the rest, have taken up the subject, far too little stress has, in my opinion, been laid upon it.

A servant of a lady of rank presented herself at the office, to complain of ill-treatment received from her Ladyship. Her statement appeared in the papers. A day or two after the husband of the lady appeared, and denied the story told by the servant. So far both parties stood upon the same ground. On one side was the woman's affirmation; on the other, that of her master. The woman's story was probably false: that is not the question. It is not sufficient that it should be *presumed* to be false; there ought to be *evidence,* and *conclusive* evidence of its falsehood, before a Magistrate, who sits to act as a Judge, should take upon himself to reject her application. Observe now the conduct of Mr. White: not only does he without farther inquiry pronounce in favour of the gentleman, *upon his own affirmation* only; he does more—because the newspapers *inserted* the woman's story, being equally ready to insert that of her master, he declares that reporters shall be no longer admitted into Court.

That defect of publicity should occasion defect of evidence against criminals, by preventing many persons from hearing of the trial, who would otherwise have come forward as witnesses, is the least of the mischiefs which will arise out of this precedent. The impunity which it will secure to a corrupt Judge, is the greatest.

Although it is the prevailing cry of the English Aristocracy that the Judges are immaculate, and although a deluded people have too long given them credit for any quantity of virtue which they think fit to claim, the public now at length begin to learn that it is absurd to expect from men the qualities of angels. To make a man a Judge, does not change his nature. Judges, like other men, will always prefer themselves to their neighbours. Judges, like other men, will indulge their indolence and satiate their rapacity whenever they can do it without fear of detection. The judicial office offers not fewer, but more numerous, and far more immediate temptations, than one who is not a Judge can easily be subject to. Allow any man to profit by injustice, and it is not the name of Judge which will shield the people from his oppression. When we see how soon almost any virtue yields to continued temptation, there needs little to persuade us, that if every Magistrate were to follow the example of Mr. White, and administer justice with closed doors, Magistrates would ere long be again what they were in the time of Fielding and of Smolett—leagued with every thief in London.

To illustrate the tendency of the precedent, I will put a case; and it is one which might easily have occurred—Suppose that the woman's story had been correct, and that of her master false; it will not be denied that *there are* masters who would not scruple to tell a lie, if they knew that, as in this case, their simple affirmation would put an end to the dispute. But it is only a rich man; it is only a member of the aristocracy, whose word is to be taken as conclusive evidence in his own cause. Thus then, whenever a rich individual and a poor one contradict each other on a matter of fact, the poor man is to be disbelieved, and the rich man suffered to carry off (perhaps) the wages of mendacity. And, to crown all, this iniquity is to be covered with the veil of secrecy. Then, perhaps, other motives than aristocratic sympathies may mix themselves in the decision of causes; again, perhaps, we may see a judicial controversy transformed into a competition between the purses of the parties, which can best satisfy the rapacity of the Judge.

Mr. White may derive a precedent, though not an excuse, for the violation of almost the only security we have for the purity of judicature, from the example which has been set by higher authorities, of prohibiting the publication of trials, until the whole of the evidence shall have been given,*

* The proprietor of *The Observer* Newspaper was reprimanded by the Court, for publishing one part of the trial of Thistlewood and others, before the trial was closed.

for the benevolent purpose, forsooth, of preventing *ex parte* statements from going forth to the world, and giving a false impression of the state of the case. I am not aware that it is a recognised maxim of jurisprudence, however frequently it may be acted upon in practice, that occasional and partial evil shall preponderate over universal good. There might be some reason indeed, for preventing *ex parte* statements from going forth, if the Judges could invent any method of hearing both parties at once. Until, however, some such method shall have been discovered, I shall continue to think that if Juries, who are taken from among the public, can hear first one party, and then the other, and yet decide justly, there cannot be much danger in presenting the evidence to the public, in precisely the same order as it comes before the Jury.

A Judge must always have much to gain by injustice: and if due securities are not provided, he will do injustice. The only efficient security which our Constitution provides is publicity: it is the disgrace which a Judge incurs by an unjust decision. This disgrace is greater or less, according as the public attention is more or less drawn to the case. Now it is well known that after a cause is decided, the interest taken in it to a great degree subsides. The prohibition of *ex parte* statements is, therefore, a contrivance to avert the public attention from abuses of judicial authority: to protect the Judges from that odium which their conduct may deserve.†
Encouraged by the success of this *indirect* attack upon the only security for good judicature, Mr. White, more boldly, has cut the Gordian knot, and destroyed that security altogether.

This is not, however, an affair to be passed over in silence. The securities against abuse, which, in the present state of our Government, we possess, are not so numerous that we can afford to lose one, and that one the most important of them. He is not a lover of good judicature, or he is a very blind one, who does not cry shame upon Mr. White, for

† That they may be themselves *bona fide,* and may not *think* they deserve odium, does not affect the question. The *consequences* to the public are the only thing which deserves attention.

setting a precedent so destructive of all security for justice; that if he himself were deliberately planning the most flagrant abuses of power, he could not have hit upon an expedient better calculated to serve his purpose.

A LOVER OF JUSTICE

N.B. Since writing the above, I have had the pleasure to learn that Reporters still continue to attend the Office, notwithstanding the injunction of Mr. White.

5

On the Justice of Religious Oaths

1823

The case Mill refers to in this letter came up in an Irish court. Mill had a lifelong interest in "the Irish question" and was constantly at work for religious, political, and social justice for Ireland. He was one of the most consistent critics of absentee landlordism and a fighter for Irish land reform.

The requirement of religious oaths, which gave bigots an opportunity to screen their real prejudice, was one of the most persistently vexing problems in nineteenth-century England. Mill helped point the way to using *actions,* such as actual perjury or false testimony, rather than *creed* as the basis for taking a man's word or admitting him to first class citizenship. His principle was that men should be judged as individuals, not as members of groups or by mere labels. This shift to judgment on the basis of actions, rather than opinion, was not merely a sign of growing intelligence and rationality. It symbolized the passing of a traditionalist and corporate society, in which individual identity was discounted, and the emergence as a practical social proposition of the ancient notion of the worth of the individual.

In his last paragraph, Mill points to one of the later paradoxes of liberal society—the extent to which humane and decent English politicians were responsible for or remained insensitive to shocking injustices committed under the English flag overseas. As George Orwell was to remind English opponents of the empire in the 1930's, the wealth and progress of English society depended on the exploitation of subject nations for cheap raw materials.

A Letter from *The Morning Chronicle* of August 26, 1823

SIR,

I observed in your Paper of Friday last, a conspicuous instance of the mischiefs of judicial oaths. These mischiefs you have frequently adverted to, but I question whether so glaring an instance of them ever yet presented itself to your notice.

A man was called to give evidence at a Court of Justice in Ireland on a cause of no extraordinary interest. He declined taking an oath on the ground of religious scruples: upon which Mr. Baron Pennyfather fined him £100.

Either this man was conscientiously averse to taking an oath, or he wished, under that pretext, to evade the necessity of giving testimony.

On the former supposition, every discerning lover of justice must lament that, by the imposition of a ceremony which (as we see in the case of Custom-house and University oaths) adds no security whatever, the testimony of a highly conscientious witness should have been excluded.

This supposition appears the most probable, as persons appeared to certify that the witness was known to have these scruples. But even if he really wished, under this pretence, to frustrate the ends of justice, the consequence is not less deplorable. If he had avowed his determination not to give evidence, he would have incurred the infamy which so pernicious a resolution deserves. By covering the wickedness of his intention under the cloak of religion, he screened himself from well merited disgrace.

If there were nothing more, therefore, than the exclusion of his evidence, this were surely enough: but when to the exclusion we add the fine, it ought to inspire every man with serious reflections. It will stand upon record that in the nineteenth century, a fine of £100 was imposed upon a man because his religious opinions differed from those of Mr. Baron

Pennyfather. I blame not the Judge, but the law, for exclud-
ing the witness. The glory, however, of the fine, belongs
wholly to the Judge, who, instead of labouring to effect the
amendment of a law which excludes the conscientious while
it lets in the unprincipled witness, took upon himself to im-
itate the Court of Ecclesiastical Commission, and punish
Heresy with a fine of £100.

The lawyers may quibble—they may say that he was
fined, not for heresy, but for contempt of Court. Contempt of
Court is a mere cant phrase, and, in most instances, a phrase
employed for the worst of purposes. On this principle, the
Judges under Charles II. might be justified, who repeatedly
fined the Jury because they would not condemn those whom
it suited the "Court" and their employers to oppress. All the
quirks with which the English law, more than any other,
abounds, will not alter the fact, that a man has been fined one
hundred pounds *for his religious scruples;* not for refusing
to give evidence—he did not refuse this. He never hesitated
to give a *solemn affirmation* of all which he knew; he scrupled
only the oath. The Judge had not power to dispense with the
ceremony, but he was under no obligation to impose on a
pawnbroker, not likely to be in very opulent circumstances,
a fine which may amount to the ruin of all his prospects in
life.

When I consider that the class to whom Mr. Baron Pennyfather belongs, are continually holding up the importance
of encouraging the spirit of religion among the people, continually lamenting the little influence which religious motives
exert over human conduct, I cannot help thinking that they
should be the last to impose a ruinous fine upon a man on
account of the peculiar strength of his religious principles,
and thus hold out encouragement to the disregard of those
principles.

In discussing this subject, I have avoided considering
the question whether oaths are or are not consistent with
Christianity—for even supposing the witness to have been in
error, a man is not to be fined £100 for being in error.

The administration of justice in Ireland has so long

been a scene of all which is unjust and oppressive, that an occurrence, which, if performed at our doors, would have excited attention, may, perhaps, be passed over, when happening amid so many others still more atrocious than itself. But the law is the same in England as in Ireland. In both countries the lawyers are equally ignorant and equally prejudiced; and what has happened in the County of Cork, may, ere long, perhaps, he imitated in that of Middlesex.

THE CENSOR OF THE JUDGES

6

On Religious Prosecutions

1824

This article advocating the removal of restraints on free expression of religious opinion, together with the subsequent essay on freedom of the press, are the most substantial of Mill's early efforts to deal directly with the problem of toleration. Arguing by implication against Tory authoritarianism, his emphasis here (as in his other early writings) falls more on the state policy called toleration than on the public attitude called tolerance. Although toleration and tolerance are closely related at all times, Mill focuses on them separately. His first concern was to obtain legal safeguards for free discussion by destroying the arguments of those who wished the state to use its power to maintain religious uniformity. Later, as liberal guarantees in law were won, Mill turned to the more complex problem of tolerance—the social costs of intolerance and the arguments in favor of diversity of opinion.

As Mill observes in this essay, the militancy of society and state about beliefs was not constant. Eighteenth-century religious life in England had conflicting characteristics. Established and respectable religions, like Anglicanism, became increasingly benign, rationalistic, or torpid, while the growth of the evangelical sects—and of a general evangelical fervor that was to touch all Christians—made for growing hostility against rationalistic religion and greater militancy about religious and moral life. Although the rise of evangelicalism long preceded the outbreak of the French Revolution, the Revolution sharpened its attack on infidelity, religious sloth, and rationalist optimism. Especially in its Jacobin phase (the Reign of Terror and the

66

Committee of Public Safety), the Revolution was interpreted as the disastrous natural culmination of atheism, materialism, and deism. The general reaction which set in extended well beyond the Protestant sects. In the general upset and threatening atmosphere of 1789–1815, however, a stricter and militant religiosity seemed a bulwark against Jacobinism. Dixon Ryan Fox, an American historian, has well characterized the American phase of this revival of religious orthodoxy as "the Protestant Counter-Reformation," the enemy being men like Tom Paine and Rousseau. Fox's phrase could be applied equally well to England.

Persecution for heterodoxy was intensified. In view of the irresponsibility of judges, the vagueness and generality of the libel laws, and the Tory desire to stamp out any source of reform or criticism, the results were what might be expected. The persecution of Richard Carlile was only the most egregious of many attempts to suppress heresy and infidelity. Mill chronicles these in part and offers several arguments against the repressions of dissent.

In all his arguments, Mill avers that he regards Christianity as "the only true faith." It is not fully clear in what sense he means this. Mill had been educated without any religious opinions whatever; and at this time, he was near the height of his devotion to Benthamite rationalism. We can only assume from biographical evidence and from his writings that for Mill Christianity meant only the morality of the Gospels, not metaphysics or theology. Without consciously wishing to mislead people, he may have adopted his opinion about the truth of Christianity to ease acceptance for his view that Christianity itself requires and demands toleration. He may have thought of himself as a Christian in the same sense that humane modern secularists associate themselves with a "Judaeo-Christian tradition."

Assuming that Christians are possessors of the truth, Mill asks them "to act as if there remained the possibility of their being in the wrong." They can act tolerantly toward falsehood, from strength rather than weakness. But in a society which claims that there is no final moral or religious truth, that we can never really know what is right or wrong, how can there ever be heresy or falsehood? Indeed, how can we act intelligently at all, since all actions should be premised on beliefs that we feel are true? These questions Mill had to face later, after he lost his Benthamite certainty that moral right and wrong could be scientifically calculated.

AN ARTICLE FROM *The Westminster Review*
OF JULY, 1824

"About this time there arose a set of men who denounced the prevalent system of religion as superstitious and idolatrous; who believed themselves destined to be its reformers, and aimed at reducing it to certain simple principles; who pursued this object with fearlessness and perseverance, although they had to encounter the opposition both of public opinion and of the constituted authorities; and many of whom, when tried for blasphemy, scrupled not to repeat, in the face of their judges, the obnoxious expressions for which they had been arraigned, and were about to suffer. They gloried in addressing themselves to the multitude; and the sympathy, which was excited by the proceedings against them, induced many to listen with a favourable ear to their opinions."

In looking over the manuscripts of a person lately deceased, a slip of paper dropped out, containing the above passage. There were no marks by which to ascertain whether it was original, or an extract; and much speculation was immediately excited among the persons present, about the parties to whom it referred. One said, without hesitation, that it described the first Christians; another contended for the authors of the Reformation from popery; a third held that it was a correct notice of Carlile and his deistical associates; and a fourth observed that it applied alike to all, and that so nearly allied, in one point of view, were glory and infamy, saintship and criminality, the Catholic Calendar and the Newgate Calendar, a niche in St. Peter's Church and a dungeon in Dorchester Gaol.

It is assuredly no recommendation of the recent prosecutions of unbelievers in Christianity, that their occasion, their object, the manner in which they have been met, and the effects which they have produced, are capable of being described in terms which accurately narrate the conduct, sufferings, and success of those who are so deservedly the objects of veneration and gratitude. Christianity can be under no obligations to those who, while they profess to support her cause, enable her enemies to say, as she recounts the tale of her early struggles with persecution, *mutato nomine, de te Fabula narratur.*

Yet if such prosecutions be necessary for the well-being of the community; if the prosperity of England require that some martyrs should be made *by* the religion *for* which so many have been made in former times; then, by all means, let them continue, and be multiplied, and let Christianity, which benefits the country in so many other ways, also benefit it by the sacrifice of its own character for mercy, toleration, and consistency. It is, however, well worth considering whether we be reduced to this dilemma.

Does the welfare of a country indeed demand that attacks upon the prevalent religion of that country should constitute a legal offence? Of course we mean by "attacks," speaking or writing against it, and not molesting the persons, invading the property, or interrupting the worship, of its professors. The Christian, whether Catholic or Protestant, cannot answer this question in the affirmative; for even if he should go so far as to say of those who accomplished the subversion of Druidism, or the reformation from Popery, that they were criminal, although, out of their evil, Providence educed the good of making him a Christian and a Protestant, neither of which he could else have been; yet must he allow that the apostles preached and wrote against Judaism, as taught by the rulers of the Jews, and against that idolatry which was the established religion of the Roman empire. He cannot maintain that they were rightfully incarcerated; or that the suppression of their doctrine, had it been practicable, would have been a public benefit.

The legislators of England cannot answer this question

in the affirmative; for, by voting grants, or affording facilities to societies for propagating the gospel in foreign parts, to missionary societies of various descriptions, and to Bible societies (for what is the Bible but a continued denunciation of idolatry in all its forms?) they are lending their sanction to attacks upon the prevalent religions of half the nations of the earth. This is not done as a mode of annoying countries with which we are at war; as the forgery of assignats may have been rewarded, while that of Bank notes brought men to the gallows. It is considered a moral and philanthropic act; not a suborning of crime, or a violation of the law of nations. A British subject would be punished for firing into a Turkish vessel; but he is not punishable for attacking the captain and sailors with Bibles or Tracts, which, if they read and believe, will make them apostates from the faith of Mahomet, and blasphemers of the Koran. While on terms of amity with the Sublime Porte the laws of England restrain us from despoiling them of their property, but not from despoiling them of their religion.

Whoever believes that Christianity is of divine origin, and consequently more benignant in its tendency than any other religion, must also believe it to be for the interest of a large majority of the inhabitants of the earth, that their present religious systems should be assailed and overturned, for that to be planted in their stead.

Unless men had acted on this principle, the most absurd and debasing superstitions which have existed must have been perpetuated; and unless they continue to act upon it, those which now exist must be perpetuated. An eternal limit is fixed to the progress of the human mind, in reference to the most important subject upon which it can be exercised. All unchristian countries are condemned to remain unchristian, and the introduction of that which we esteem our own best blessing is declared worthy of punishment at their hands, as an invasion of their safety and their happiness.

The existing religion of any country either is, or is not, susceptible of improvement. If the former, allowing it to be the province of the government to decide what is an improvement, and how it should be made, the freest discussion of its merits should be authorized as the best mode of furnishing materials for a reformation. Only thus can be ascertained what will, and what will not, abide the test of reason and utility, and where alteration, omission, or addition is expedient. And if the latter, if it be already absolutely perfect, still should the attempt to controvert it be lawful, for the result can only be a more general and vivid perception of its worth, and consequently the strengthening and extension of its influence.

External conformity with the requisitions of a religious system is the utmost that can ever be enforced; and, constituted as men are, it is all the uniformity that is ever likely to exist, except in the very lowest stage of mental cultivation. How much it costs to produce this uniformity, and what it is worth when produced, are points pretty well ascertained by history; and so ascertained as to render argument unnecessary.

The question may then be narrowed to, whether Christianity be an exception to the general rule? Is it, upon the whole, for the good of the community that the denial of the truth of Christianity should be an offence against the law?

Nothing can be more desirable, nothing could be more felicitous, than for every member of a civil community to be completely under the influence of Christian principles. If every one loved his neighbour as himself, and did unto others as he would that they should do unto him, and practised that universal benevolence which beholds a brother in every human being, whatever his colour, country, or religion, the result would undoubtedly be a sum of happiness immensely larger than any nation ever has realized, or perhaps ever will. But whatever Christianity may be in the New Testament or may have been in its earlier days, this is not the practical Christianity of our age and country. The church of England, the most approved manufactory of believers, turns out few finished specimens of this pure workmanship. Our spiritual machinery produces, in general, a very inferior article; and still less can be expected from the power which is merely temporal. Penal laws can have very little efficacy for such a purpose. They may make the "outward sign" imperative, but they never can bestow the "inward grace." An act of parliament for the abolition of human depravity would have very little chance of being carried into execution. This species at least of radical reform is remote and chimerical. It is useless to legislate for an object which the very nature of things renders unattainable. Whether we take the theological or the philosophical estimate of man, it is alike hopeless to speculate, even with the wisest employment of all the powers of church and state, on annihilating unbelief, and making every Christian a paragon of goodness. Legislation must proceed on the supposition that, do what it may, the country cannot be made completely Christian, however devoutly to be wished may be that consummation.

The effective prohibition of a public denial of Christianity, and the prohibition if made at all is meant to be effective, is then morally certain to produce a quantum of hypocrisy commensurate with the infidelity which it coerces into outward conformity. How this hypocrisy should improve the national character, or increase our national prosperity, or in what way it is more to be desired than so much open and honest unbelief, is out of our power to imagine. Several reasons may be assigned for regarding it as the greater evil of the two. First, granting that in some instances a defective faith may be the source of vicious conduct, still hypocrisy is a vice in itself, a mean, detestable, and polluting one, and to the full as likely as unbelief to generate a brood of vices with all the rapidity of the geometrical ratio. The avowed unbeliever may become a bad man; the hypocrite *is* a bad man. Had Sheridan made Charles Surface a sceptic, he still would not have levelled him with Joseph. It is pleasanter to see people's faces, though they be ugly ones, than always to meet them in masks; and more comfortable for them as well as for ourselves. Sincerity is one of the last things on which penalties should be levied. The great spiritual physicians who would vaccinate the nation with hypocrisy to prevent the eruption of Infidelity, are not acting on a true Jennerian analogy. The preventive disease is too loathsome to be voluntarily induced for any such purpose. Again, the prohibition of avowed unbelief increases the most tangible evil ascribed to infidelity, viz. that it enfeebles, or destroys the security of an oath. "Where," demands Mr. Whitehead, "among such as have abandoned the gospel, are we to look for the binding sanctity, and the security of those oaths which depend entirely upon a reverential belief of it in the persons who take them? How could public justice ever be safely administered with the aid of the gospel sanction alone, between the assertions of infidel and of believing witnesses?" There are not many witnesses, we apprehend, the credibility of whose testimony is much enhanced by the introductory ceremony so irreverently performed in our courts of justice, and in other places. A character for veracity, and a safe passage through the perils of a skilful cross-examination, would be satisfactory make-weights with an intelligent jury, for an unsworn infidel testimony against an unsupported Christian deposition. Let it be, however, that the oath of an unbeliever is worth no more than his word, and that his word is worth but little; surely the ends of justice are most in danger from a system which, by making avowed unbelief an offence, keeps both judge and jury in the dark as to what class of witnesses they have to deal with. In proportion as the difference is magnified which believing that Christianity is true or false makes in the value of men's testimony, exactly in that proportion is it desirable that a conviction of its falsehood should, where it exists, be legally avowed. The unbeliever would then come into court *quasi* unbeliever, and experience would soon ascertain whether any, and what deduction from his credibility should be made on that account. And, if unbelief be so intimately connected with vicious conduct as is represented, then, to identify its votaries with Christians by the penal suppression of their dissent, must tend to lower the practical standard of Christian morality, both in appearance and in reality. If Satan be numbered among the sons of God, we shall strike a lower average of the moral worth of the assembly. The evil communications of the hypocritical few will corrupt the good manners of the believing many. Christianity will obtain a less triumphant verdict when judged by its fruits; and the leaven which it covets will leaven the whole mass with an immoral taint. The interdiction too of open denial and direct attack will compel unbelievers to employ that insidious and undermining system which is so much more dangerous, because it is less obvious, and more difficult to encounter. The man who buys a book professedly deistical, which carries hostility to Christianity on its title page, and goes manfully into the arguments against revealed religion, knows what he is about. He reads it with his mind on the alert; and if he make a parlour guest of such a book, it is because he thinks it not dangerous for his family; and not because both he and they are imposed upon by specious appearances, and a forged letter of introduction. The case is very different when the history, the novel, the poem, the metaphysical essay, the scientific treatise, are employed as vehicles of Scepticism; here distorting a fact, there neutralizing an argument; never avowing the object, but always pursuing it; sapping the foundations of faith without noise, and leaving the building to fall of itself; ("thou canst not say, I did it";) leading the reader, almost unconsciously, to the relinquishment of opinions, without having ever gone into a full investigation of their evidence, because that evidence has been frittered away in detail without having ever been fairly met, and avowedly controverted. Against this no vigilance can guard, and it greatly augments the difficulty both of escape and refutation. This is not the best form of that hostility which will exist in some form or other. There is little wisdom, little friendliness to religion, in making its adoption compulsory on the unbeliever. If his flag were recognized, he would be much less disposed, if at all, to fight under false colours. And finally, unless the effective prohibition of a denial of Christianity be accompanied with an equally effective suppression of any diversity of interpretations of Christianity, the evil is probable of a great corruption of Christian doctrine. It is useless to say, that the whole shall not be controverted, if every part may, separately, be assailed and destroyed. The conflict will, in many cases, be transferred from the evidence of Christianity to the meaning of Christianity. The hostility which must not vent itself in contradicting a proposition, will be exercised in the perversion of that proposition. Should avowed infidelity be slain by the sword of the law, a thousand heresies would soon swarm in its carcase.

Were infidelity effectively prohibited, a very wholesome check upon the conduct of the professors of Christianity, and especially upon that of the clerical order, would be removed. Whatever influence upon the mind may be ascribed to the future judgment of a superior Being, it cannot be denied that the present judgment of our fellow-creatures has an effect too salutary to be despised, or lightly parted with. A zealous writing and publishing unbeliever is as formidable to a bishop as an attorney-general to a political libeller. The honour of the church is better looked after when all her faults are "set in a note-book, learned, and conn'd by rote, to cast into her teeth." Whatever contempt may be poured upon the assailant, the highest dignitary or the poorest methodist parson, if the attack be on the score of immoral conduct, would rather that it were not made, and will sacrifice something to prevent its being made with justice. Men linked together by a common profession are, by that very fact, rendered more liable to degeneracy. We continually witness the perpetration of iniquities by bodies of men, from which the individuals of whom they are constituted would shrink with abhorrence. There is also a conventional sanctity about the priest, an ex-officio purity, which is very apt to satisfy his own conscience, and dim the observance of his followers, and which requires, for the good of both, that some who are untouched by the spell should overlook their proceedings, and report things as they are. Christianity originally discharged this useful office for Heathenism, and made it much more moral in self-defence. Protestantism stood in the same relative position towards Popery. There was a great reformation amongst those who remained in the old church as soon as a new church sprung up to watch and accuse it.

The new church begins to grow old, and may not be the worse for a flapper. The service is not the less valuable even should it be rendered in a less amiable temper (if that be possible) than heretofore. The morally deformed may still be transformed, though by the agency of an evil spirit. If it be good that there should be the devil as an "accuser of the brethren" in the other world, by parity of reasoning it must be good that there be the infidel to accuse them here. Whatever be the character of his vocation, it is for the public interest that he should labour in it. The abuse is easily prevented, as bearing false witness may be punished, without suppressing bills of indictment. The toleration of a variety of Christian sects may perhaps be alleged, as sufficient to provide this wholesome stimulus to good works in each and all. Their hostility is undoubtedly keen enough to make them pretty severe censors upon each other. But common faults may produce mutual indulgences, which the unbeliever would not feel, and out of which they may be shamed by his exposure. With all the uniformity and indivisibility of the Catholic Church, there were plenty of parties in it before the reformation, but their beneficial agency, in this particular, was very feeble compared with that which was afterwards exercised by their common enemy. It would be some benefit to Christian sects should the presence of avowed unbelievers only teach them to moderate their mutual animosities, and estimate more correctly their common principles; but we are much mistaken in the perfection to which the christian world has attained, if it would not do more than this, and lay open some common failings also. Besides, the general denial of the truth of Christianity can only be prohibited on principles which imply the expediency of not tolerating sectaries. Very many heresies are "blasphemous and damnable," as well as infidelity. They are, on the authority of the ablest and soundest divines, as pernicious to the morals here, and to the soul hereafter, and their open toleration, consequently, as inconsistent with the well-being of a state. All the reasoning against the denier of Christianity applies equally to the denier of its essential doctrines; and what are essential doctrines depends upon which sect is uppermost. The lowest grade of heresy, whatever it may be, succeeds to all the antipathy which else would light upon infidelity. When faith had sunk no lower than to the creed of the Homoiousians, the Homoousians persecuted them to death as blasphemers. That terrible term will always designate those who have least faith comparatively, whether positively it be much or little. Where such beings are allowed to exist, it means unbelievers; wanting them, it means Unitarians; wanting them, it means Arians; wanting them, it means Arminians; and wanting them, it means Protestants. It always catches those who are hindmost in the race of faith. Till Christians lose the knack of using it, there can be no toleration unless some who are called blasphemers be tolerated. When Unitarianism was unknown, Nonconformity was a crime. Till Infidelity began to assume a popular form, Unitarianism was a crime. The good policy of toleration, as to each, has only been discovered when, from an extreme party, it became an intermediate one, and the *odium theologicum* was transferred to the new-comers. So long as we keep this tyger, somebody must be thrown to it for food, and in case of need its stomach will digest a heretic as easily as an infidel.

If, then, there be no consistent medium between allowing that all theological tenets should be controverted, and prohibiting the discussion of any, the question takes a yet simpler form, and is of still easier solution. That freedom of discussion has generally, the happiest effects on the mind and manners of the people, on the progress of intellect, and the diffusion of knowledge; or, in other words, that it is a powerful means of increasing happiness, will scarcely be disputed. That all religions, unless Christianity be an exception, ought to be subjected to such discussion, if the public good be consulted, will also be allowed; or if not, the arguments have been already indicated by which, we think, that proposition is established. An exemption for Christianity can only be contended for, on one or all of the following assumptions: 1st, That it is the only true faith; 2nd, That it is the only faith by which men can be saved; and 3rdly, that it

is a faith eminently useful to society in its immediate effects.
Let us enquire how far the premises will warrant the conclusion.

Christianity is the only true faith in our opinion, and
that of the great majority of our countrymen, but the works
to which the firm and general conviction of that fact must,
in great measure, be ascribed, would never have been written
had its denial been effectively suppressed, and will cease to
be read when it ceases to be controverted. The defence pre-
supposes the attack. A Tindal produces a Leland, and a
Paine calls forth a Watson. If it be a great public good that
the multifarious proofs of the Christian religion should be
fully collected, and ably stated, and clearly arranged, and
simplified, and adapted to the modes of thinking of
all classes; and that they should re-appear from time to time,
and be read with interest, and produce that intelligent conviction, which if not alone valuable, is yet most valuable:
then is it a great public good to allow the Gospel to be controverted, for without this, little or nothing of the kind will
be done; religion divorced from reason will sink into a mere
prejudice, losing the power of truth as the proofs of its truth
are unregarded, and becoming feeble for resistance and
worthless in its influence. Such even Christianity always has
been, and always must be, where discussion is suppressed.

It is with theological truth, as with all other truth:
legislative interference can have no effect in increasing either
the extent or the force of conviction: but may have much in
diminishing both, by the prevention of that full investigation from which they result. Besides, every opinion is truth
to him who believes it. The unbeliever likes his truth as well
as we like our truth. What he reckons our error annoys him,
in like manner as what we reckon his error annoys us. He
thinks his arguments ought to convince us, as we think our
arguments ought to convert him. Now, although we are in
the right, yet experience has shown, that it is very useful even
for those who are in the right, to act as if there remained the
possibility of their being in the wrong. They are wise to
leave the means of correction in existence, even for the very

remote chance of that very improbable possibility. Such caution would have been very serviceable for many who were full as confident as we are of possessing the only true religion, but whose religion is out of fashion now. If it cannot be that we have occasion to provide against that danger, there is yet another, and that is, the assumption of our own infallibility, which is a sufficient evil, and much the same in its pernicious effects, whether our religion be true or false.

That Christianity is the only faith by which men can be saved, is a position of which we share the doubts which some divines have expressed, although they will assuredly give way to the demonstrations of the advocates of that orthodox tenet, when advanced. There is no objection to arguing the question on that principle. It is very laudable in the legislature to compel all subjects to be saved, even by the heaviest penalties; but unless a hypocritical faith be as availing for that purpose as a sincere faith, the attempt can only inflict the present evil, and not accomplish the future good. Now is it for the public weal that all men who are not to be saved, and who will not be *dungeonized* into hypocrisy, should be banished or hanged; for to that we must come at last, unless they be tolerated? Such measures would deprive the state of many valuable citizens whom it can ill afford to spare. As the law now stands in this enlightened country, reckoning the Book of Common Prayer, on episcopal authority, for "one long act of parliament," the exclusion from salvation falls not only on those who deny Christianity, but on all who deny a single iota of the Athanasian Creed. They are, of course, very bad men; they must be so, as they deserve everlasting punishment; and this circumstance confirms what we are told of the evil tendency of heresy and infidelity. Our position is only, that, however bad they may be, their badness is perfectly consistent with their being useful and excellent citizens, and therefore not of a description to be legally proscribed. Hume and Gibbon are damned, according to law; and yet it is to be presumed that they "did the state some service," for they were allowed to dip their fingers in the public purse. There was Sir Isaac Newton, mas-

ter of the mint, and the glory of our country; there was Dr.
Lardner, the Presbyterian heretic, whose "Credibility of the
Gospel History" is a kind of theological "Principia," at least
in the Deistical controversy: they too are damned according
to law, but their names and works are of great worth in
Christian orations. Then there is Mr. W. Smith, a very useful member of the House of Commons; and Mr. Robert
Owen, with his parallelograms, who though he may not succeed in squaring the circle of society, yet is the very personi-
fication of benevolence: we should be loth to spare them, or
any like them, though they have both said enough of their
opinions to shew, that they will be damned according to law.
Without, therefore, intimating the least doubt of the correctness of the information possessed by his majesty's ministers
as to the terms of final salvation, on which they have the
bench of bishops for advisers, we submit, that both beasts and
men, who will have no place in heaven, may yet be by
far too useful on earth for the nation to wish for their extinction.

The remaining plea for prohibiting a denial of Christianity is the benignant character of its temporal influence.
But we have already shown that its influence is circumscribed
and deteriorated by that prohibition. That would happen
even if the prohibition were completely effective, which it
is not in the nature of things for it to be. So far as it is effective, it makes hypocrites: when it ceases to be effective, martyrs are produced. It then becomes a powerful means for
spreading Infidelity. The course recently pursued in this
country has been the most hostile to Christianity, which
could possibly have been devised. It has elevated men from
the obscurity in which, if unprosecuted, they must have always remained, to make them the champions and the victims
of unbelief, and formidable champions only because they
were victims. It has made Infidelity more popular than it
ever was before; or than it ever can be when let alone. The
facts are a volume of argument.

Deistical works have only of late years been addressed
to the multitude, because it is only of late years that the mul-

titude has begun to read. Before the French Revolution, scepticism was one of the privileges of high life. Religion was reckoned a vulgar prejudice, much beneath the dignity of a gentleman, and utterly incompatible with the pretensions of a wit. The complete change of fashion which has taken place is chiefly owing to the alarm excited by that catastrophe. Christianity has been warmly patronised in the hope that it would help to keep people quiet, teach them to pay their taxes without grumbling, and restrain them from subverting the established order of things. This naturally drew upon Christianity the suspicions of those who were most discontented and desirous of change, predisposed them to doubt or deny its truth, and prompted them to commence a theological conflict in that public arena, where even the political conflict which already raged was a comparative novelty. To the "Rights of Man" succeeded the "Age of Reason," and with the publication of the "Age of Reason" commenced the regular Deistical persecution which has now been carried on for some years, with the usual results of persecution. A bookseller, named Williams, was prosecuted and convicted, for publishing the first and second parts of that work in 1797, soon after its appearance, and suffered twelve months imprisonment in Cold-Bath-Fields. Daniel Isaac Eaton, for publishing the third part, in 1812, was sentenced to eighteen months imprisonment, and the pillory; and in the following year, escaped another sentence, by death, for the publication of "Ecce Homo," the author of which, a Mr. Houston, was imprisoned in Newgate for two years, and fined two hundred pounds. In October 1819, Carlile was tried for publishing Paine's Theological Works, and Palmer's Principles of Nature, and condemned, for the first, to two years imprisonment in Dorchester gaol, and a fine of one thousand pounds; and for the second, to one year's imprisonment, and a fine of five hundred pounds, and to find securities for good behaviour for life, himself in one thousand pounds, and two others in one hundred pounds each. His wife and sister have both been since convicted of similar offences, and suffered heavy sentences. Upwards of thirty other persons, many of them journeymen to Carlile, and the rest small booksellers, have also been subjected to fine and imprisonment in various degrees of severity. At the late Old Bailey Sessions, there were three cases in which the punishment, for selling a single copy of an obnoxious work, was three years imprisonment in Newgate, and security for good behaviour for life in one hundred pounds. The experiment has been fully and fairly tried of the efficacy of prosecutions; the severity of the sentence has been gradually increased, and the number of indictments multiplied; and what are now the results?

One has been a tenfold, perhaps we might almost say an hundred-fold, increase of the circulation of the obnoxious publications. Notwithstanding the original prosecutions, we understand from persons engaged in bookselling that it has never been difficult to procure the Age of Reason. There was always a steady, though very limited demand, sufficient to carry off a moderately-sized edition in the course of several years. In December 1818, Carlile ventured to do that openly, which had been done surreptitiously. He brought out an edition of Paine's Theological works, with all the advantage of advertisements and placards, and a previous discussion in the newspapers. The edition consisted of a thousand copies, and was completely sold off in about two months. That is to say, *one* hundred in the month which elapsed before the determination to prosecute became known, and *nine* hundred in the month which followed. From that time to the present, the sale has averaged four thousand per annum. Now the first month's sale of a book which had been well advertised, and which had also excited a Newspaper controversy, would, in ordinary cases, be at least half its probable sale for a twelvemonth. Take it at one-fourth; we then owe to the prosecutions the circulation of upwards of twenty thousand copies of the Age of Reason; and as among the poorer classes it is notorious that there are several readers to one purchaser, it may be estimated that at least one hundred thousand persons have thus been led to the perusal of that work under circumstances highly favourable to its making an impression on their minds. What confirms our ascription of this increase solely to the prosecutions is, that there has been no such demand for Paine's Political works; but that a similar extension of the sale has taken place with every work which has been made the subject of prosecution, whether political or theological.

Another result has been, to enlist on the side of Infidelity that sympathy which human nature will generally feel with those who are, or seem to be, persecuted. People will not take their notion of the culpability from the severity of the punishment; but where the latter is striking, will be led to question whether the former was so great as they might otherwise have imagined. "Pity is akin to love"; and when their sense of injustice is roused by the treatment of the accused, they are in a fair way for regarding him as innocent, and even as meritorious. An obvious attempt to put a man down on account of his opinions, raises up for him coadjutors who would else never have thought or cared about those opinions. A little army of volunteer shopmen has kept up the sale of Carlile's publications, and still keeps it up. Every one enters the house well knowing that his next removal will be to gaol; but knowing also that he shall have a successor. The Vice and Constitutional Societies, and the Attorney General, have co-operated for a most portentous creation; they have generated the fanaticism of Infidelity. Its spirit has wholly changed, and now exhibits all the proselyting enthusiasm of a Sect. The means which have formed this power cannot be the best to look to for its destruction.

A third result deserves notice, although it is only what would be anticipated by those who have observed the tendency of violent controversies to drive the parties to extremes in their opinions, especially where one of them is backed by political authority. If a persecuted man modifies his notions it will almost infallibly be, to distance them still more from those of his persecutors. Dorchester Gaol has converted Carlile, it appears, from Deism to Atheism. The Age of Reason was his creed at the time of the trials; but now his motto is "The Politics of Paine, and the Theology of Mirabeau." So by attempting to suppress the denial of Christianity on principles which admit the existence of a God and a future state, we have occasioned the open profession and zealous promulgation of Atheism, a thing unknown in America where there are no prosecutions for blasphemy. A goodly work, indeed; and a hopeful course for those to pursue, who are really desirous to preserve and extend the influence of Christian principles.

Let the abettors of these prosecutions look, for a moment, at the *primâ facie* case which they are creating against Christianity. The history of all ages and nations shews, that man is a religious animal, and will generally have a religion of some sort or other; Christianity is allowed, even by its enemies, to be one of the best systems of religion, if not the most excellent; it descends to the present generation from their forefathers, and the rising generation is educated in its faith; it has been, and is, professed by the most excellent men, defended by the most learned, and recommended by the most eloquent; we have an established clergy of about 18,-000 educated men, for its defence, and a dissenting ministry of about 8000 more, who have, thus far, a common cause; our public seminaries are universally Christian; independently of the conditions attached to filling public offices, the state of opinion is such as to render avowed or even suspected unbelief, any thing but favourable to a man's progress in society: religious periodical publications are sent forth in immense numbers, the sale of the Evangelical and Methodist Magazines is upwards of twenty thousand each, monthly; and they can scarcely be more than a moiety of the whole: and we have Bible, Tract, and Prayerbook Societies, whose annual distribution is, literally, reckoned by tens of thousands, hundreds of thousands, and millions; it may be mentioned as a sample, that in the year of Carlile's trials, the Religious Tract Society added a million and a half of tracts to its issue, which was four millions in the preceding year; the average revenue of this Society is about £9000; that of the Christian Knowledge Society, above £50,000; and that of the Bible Society about £100,000. Now if religion with all this extensive aid, all these immense advantages in addition to its proper evidence, cannot stand its ground without prosecutions for its support, we hesitate not to say, that it ought to fall. Were it the grossest imposture that ever existed, here is force enough to enable it to fight a long and hard battle with truth and common sense. If with these fearful odds, there be the slightest occasion for penalty and imprisonment to secure its ascendancy, falsehood may be at once branded on its front. Those who contend for their infliction are the real missionaries of Infidelity, and by far its most successful propagators.

It is often said, that fair and decorous argument against Christianity ought to be allowed, but not ribaldry, contumely, reviling, blasphemy, &c. Such language, having been held in Parliament, and on the Bench, may seem entitled to some attention. If it were uniformly held, much of the foregoing argument might have been spared; but that is far from being the case. On the trial of Mrs. Wright, the Lord Chief Justice is reported to have said, "the defendant was not called on to answer any reasonable or fair discussion on the truth of Christianity in general, or any of its particular tenets. The law permitted that every subject, however sacred, should be freely, yet moderately and temperately discussed; but it would not yield its protection to gross and scandalous calumnies on the established faith." And again, "If the Jury thought these passages were only parts of a fair and temperate discussion of the sacred topics to which they had reference, they might acquit the defendant; but if they considered them as gross and indecent attacks on religion, they must find her guilty." Declarations to the same effect have been repeatedly made, during the more recent trials: yet if they rightly expound the Common Law, it is at variance with the Statute; for that of 9th and 10th William and Mary enacts "that if any person, having been educated in or at any time made profession of, the Christian religion within this realm, shall by writing, printing, teaching, or advised speaking, deny the Christian religion to be true, or the Holy Scriptures to be of divine authority, he shall &c.": nay this language is at variance with the precedent continually referred

to, of Rex *v*. Woolston, when the offence was not a direct
denial, but an allegorical interpretation of the New Testament, which, in the opinion of Lord Raymond, "struck at
the very root of Christianity"; the Court declared "they
would not suffer it to be debated whether to write against
Christianity in general, was not an offence at common law."
As this, however, was law made by the Judges, we should not
object to its being repealed, or mitigated by them; only let
them know their own minds upon the subject. Notwithstanding the legal allowance of a temperate discussion of the truth
of Christianity declared on Mrs. Wright's trial, the same
Judge had declared, on that of Carlile, that "the Court was
bound not to hear the truth of the Christian religion questioned"; and that "if the defendant wished to produce authors to shew that the Christian religion *might be denied,*
that could not be allowed." The charge on that trial completely exemplifies the vacillation we are exposing. The following passages are quoted from it in the order in which they
appear in the Times Newspaper of Oct. 15, 1819. The Lord
Chief Justice said "that he had then (during the defence)
determined, and he did not regret that determination, that
it was not competent in a Christian Court, in a court of law,
to rise up and say, that the Christian religion was not a religion of truth." Soon after this he expressed himself as follows: "another topic of defence, strenuously, and in some
degree properly, urged, was the danger of restraining free
discussion and free inquiry. God forbid that any such restraint should take place! But they had to distinguish
whether the present publication was an instance of that free
inquiry and discussion, or a work of mere calumny and ridicule." Again: "The Christian religion forming part of the
law of the land, it was not fit that he (the defendant) or any
other person, should openly deny its truth." And, to complete the second vacillation, the summing-up concluded
thus: "The whole question turned on the character of the
work, and that must now be collected from it as a whole.
Was it a fair and candid inquiry? Look at those epithets
applied to the Scriptures, "a book full of lies," "a dangerous

heresy," "an impious falsehood." These were a few specimens, and he had found none other to soften their effect, or
that indicated any other object, than to defame the Bible and
bring it into universal disbelief and contempt. So thinking,
it was his duty, sitting where he did, to express his opinion to
the Jury; and that opinion was, that this publication was a
work of calumny and scoffing, and *therefore* an unlawful
publication." We say nothing of the legal trap in which a
Defendant might complain of being caught, if he acted upon
the one set of dicta, and were condemned by the other. We
say nothing of the disingenuousness of claiming merit for
tolerating argument, while there is a prospect of obtaining
a conviction on the score of calumny, and still retaining, as a
dernier resort, the illegality of every thing which tends to
the disproof of Christianity. Our object is merely, to point
out the inconsistency and mistiness of the language held by
the highest authorities on this subject; and our inference is,
that the line between argument and reviling is too difficult
even for legal acuteness to draw; that he who disbelieves and
attempts to disprove Christianity can put his arguments into
no form which may not be pronounced calumnious and
illegal; and that therefore the only mode of securing free inquiry from that restraint, at the bare idea of which his Lordship was so laudably and piously horror-struck, is to tolerate
the one as well as the other. A conclusion which, as it may
not be generally agreeable, we proceed to strengthen by other
considerations.

To declare that an act is legal, but with the proviso that
it be performed in a gentle and decorous manner, is opening
a wide door for arbitrary discretion on the one part, and dis-
satisfaction on the other. The difficulty is greatly increased
when the act itself is offensive to those who sit in judgment
upon the manner of its performance. Suppose that it were
made expulsion from the House of Commons to address the
chair ungracefully.—What a clamour would there be for
the unconditional allowance or prohibition of speech! Could
the distinction be accurately ascertained, it would be hard to
debar the man of ungainly habits from doing that which he

might think required of him by duty to his constituents and his country. But it is infinitely more unjust to debar a man who may have a comprehensive and vigorous, though a coarse and vulgar mind, from publishing his speculations on theological topics, because his style partakes of his own rudeness, and lacks the polish of that of Hume or Gibbon. If the proposition that Christianity is untrue may be legally conveyed to the mind, what can be more absurd than to say that to express that proposition by certain undefined and undefinable selections of terms, shall constitute a crime?

So far as we can understand the distinction set up in this case between discussion and reviling, it seems to be this: the one is a mere statement of a fact or argument; the other an expression of the indignation or contempt excited in the writer's mind by the doctrine to which he is opposed. Now the reason why men dislike doctrines is, that they discern, or fancy they discern, an evil tendency in those doctrines. If such a tendency be demonstrated, to the conviction of the reader, he will participate in the writer's dislike, whether the latter have expressed it or not. And if the reader be not so convinced, all that the writer says of his own dislike will go for nothing, or more probably make both himself and his argument disagreeable. It is surely inexpedient that such an appendage should constitute all the difference between crime and no crime, the enjoyment of the common rights of citizenship and a ruinous sentence of fine and imprisonment: and the more so, on account of the extreme difficulty of avoiding some expression of feeling in the discussion of moral subjects. There is no mathematical indifference in Theological controversy. The believer has it not; nor ought he to exact it of the unbeliever. The expression of indignation at what is deemed false and pernicious should be a crime in all, or in none.

The Bishop of St. David's describes the Unitarians as "God-denying apostates and heretics," "blasphemers," "not entitled to the name of Christians," who "wilfully falsify the truth." The Book of Homilies, the yet authoritative manifesto of the Church of England, describes the Catholic worship as far exceeding gentile idolatry "in all wickedness, foolishness, and madness;" characterizes its practice as "the blasphemous bold blazing of manifest idolatry;" and wonders that its votaries should not "at the least have chosen them a time of more darkness, as meeter to utter their horrible blasphemies in." (Against Peril of Idolatry part 3). Christian blasphemers then are tolerated; as is Christian reviling. Let Justice be evenhanded.

Where the feelings are so deeply interested as they always must be on theological subjects, it will necessarily happen that the party attacked will call that reviling which the party attacking deems fair discussion. In the debate on the presentation of a petition against the prosecution of unbelievers, July 1, 1823, Mr. Wilberforce observed that, "he entirely denied the truth of the argument which the honourable member (Mr. Hume) had drawn from the employment of missionaries abroad. Those individuals never proceeded to insult the prejudices of the natives of other countries, by any gross and indecent reflections. They adduced nothing but fair and sober argument to effect their purpose." Now what think the Hindoos of these temperate and unimpeachable reasoners? In the first number of the Braminical Magazine, published at Calcutta in 1821, in both Bengalee and English, is the following account of them: "During the last twenty years, a body of English gentlemen, who are called missionaries, have been publicly endeavouring in several ways to convert the Hindoos and Musselmans to Christianity. The first way is that of publishing and distributing among the natives various books, large and small, reviling both religions, and abusing and ridiculing the gods and saints of the former." Mr. Wilberforce's character of the missionary publications is probably correct. It is looking at the same object from different positions that makes all the difference. Suppose one were to describe the orthodox party in the church of England as "a generation of vipers;" and another to characterize the established priesthood as "hypocrites," "fools and blind" men who "strain at a gnat and swallow a camel," what would Mr. Wilberforce call it? It would not be

true; but that is not the question. The object of such accusations never admit their truth; nor were similar expressions
indicted, would an English court allow evidence of their truth
to be adduced. Or suppose that in any publication of the
present day it were affirmed that, "we know that" the God of
the established religion "is nothing in the world." Would
not this be reviling? Let such men as Mr. Wilberforce reflect
on the lengths to which their principles would extend in a
different age and country, and under a different establishment.

The effect of even just censure is commonly to rouse indignant feelings, much more so of that which is known to be
altogether groundless. The more abusive an unbeliever is,
the less likely is he to make an impression even on the most
uninformed. If unable to judge of the controversy in any
other way, they will decide on the same principle as the
honest countryman, who was present at a disputation in
Latin, and knew which of the disputants had the worst of it
by his falling into a passion. Indeed, in proportion to the
want of information is generally the disposition to resent
any attack upon opinions which are held in reverence. That
disposition is sufficiently strong in all, to make every appearance of insult operate as a deduction from the force of the
argument with which it is blended. To allow the publication of infidel works, cleansed of passages which are liable to
that imputation, especially while Christian works undergo
no such expurgatory process, would obviously place unbelief
in a far more advantageous position than it now occupies. So
to contrive, that in any controversy, all the writers on one
side should publish only the effusions of pure intellect, thoroughly weeded from all indications of human frailty, of
prejudice and passion, of misrepresentation, acrimony, and
reviling, would be, to give them a most undue and undesir-
able advantage. Their arguments might be few and feeble,
but the tone of candour and moderation in which they were
urged, would give them adventitious force. They would glide
along like the American serpent divested of its rattle; no

more nuisance from their noise, but much more danger of their bite.

A libel is a crime because it tends to a breach of the peace. With personal libels this may be the case, but there is something rather preposterous in applying this position to theological discussions. Who is likely to be instigated to outrage by the publication of the Age of Reason?—The Christian, one of whose objections to that work is, that it denies the obligation of loving our enemies, and doing good to them that despitefully use us, and turning the right cheek when the left is smitten? Was it ever apprehended that any of our Bishops, Priests, or Deacons, would invite Mr. Carlile to meet them at Chalk Farm? Or is the danger on the other side, from his converts? If so, it can only be aggravated by proceedings which tend to increase their numbers, and inspire them with the zeal and hatred of a sect persecuted for its opinions. Tendencies are best ascertained by facts. The increased circulation of Deistical works commenced in 1819, and the country has certainly not been since more disturbed than in the five preceding years, nor have we heard of breaches of the peace actually traced to their influence. Were it so, government is quite strong enough to keep the peace, without resorting to the very questionable, and, on other accounts, inexpedient means of persecution for opinions.

The primary argument for these prosecutions, that they are needful to protect the poor and ignorant, has been kept in view through the foregoing remarks, and we think refuted. If their effect be, to excite sympathy with the persons, and give increased circulation to the works, prosecuted; if the poor have that ability to judge, which is implied in the enlarged supply of religious publications for their use; if the clergy, established and non-established, have any tolerable portion of that zeal, talent, and respectability of character, which is supposed in order to justify the expenditure of supporting their profession; if the poor and ignorant be not less likely than others to be irritated by the language of insult towards their opinions, and soothed by that of respect; then

are the prosecutions not necessary for their defence, nor do
they act as a defence at all, but, on the contrary, multiply the
existing perils and create new ones. If fears still remain, give
them education. Let them have it as extensively and as
rapidly as possible. Every body allows that there is no danger now to the educated class. Let there be no other class.
This may not be an immediate remedy; but it is the only
effective and permanent one. It is already in active operation, and its force must continually increase. But at the same
time that popular education holds forth a pledge of the
triumph of truth over error, the redemption of that pledge
can only be postponed and impeded by the suppression of
discussion. To give the one, and attempt by legal violence
to withhold the other; to enlighten the poor, and yet continue to treat them as if they were in the grossest ignorance,
must infallibly make matters worse. When the appetite of
knowledge is excited, to refuse its gratification is most perilous. We borrow a few sentences on this point from a work
which, on account of the continuity of the argument, can
scarcely be quoted without injury to its merits, but which
we are glad of this opportunity to notice, being convinced
that it only requires to be generally read, for its author to
take his place in the very first rank of the Intellectual Benefactors of his species. "The universal education of the poor,
which no earthly power can prevent, although it may retard
it, is loudly demanded by the united voices of the moralist
and politician. But if the people are enlightened at all, it is
unavailing and inconsistent to resort to half measures and
timid expedients; to treat them at once as men and as children; to endow them with the power of thinking, and, at the
same time, to fetter its exercise; to make an appeal to their
reason, and yet to distrust its result; to give them the stomach
of a lion and feed them with the aliment of a lamb. The pro-
moters of the universal education of the poor ought to be
aware, that they are setting in motion, or at least accelerat-
ing the action of an engine too powerful to be controlled at
their pleasure, and likely to prove fatal to all those parts of
their own systems, which rest not on the solid foundation of

reality. They ought to know, that they are necessarily giving birth to a great deal of doubt and investigation; that they are undermining the power of prejudice, and the influence of mere authority and prescription; that they are creating an immense number of keen inquirers and original thinkers, whose intellectual force will be turned, in the first instance, upon those subjects which are dearest to the heart and of most importance to society."—*Essays on the Formation and Publication of Opinions*, p. 148.

Independently of the vagueness of the law itself under which unbelievers have been tried; which law seems to be nothing more than inference from the fact, that several judges have declared Christianity to be parcel of the common law; there have been various circumstances attending its enforcement, which were ill adapted to promote the avowed object. Arguments for the truth, and panegyrics on the excellence of a system of religion, do not read pleasantly in a trial, during which the accused is authoritatively silenced, should he attempt their refutation. Not that courts of justice are meet places for theological discussion; but if they be so employed to cast odium on the opinions of a defendant, it seems reasonable to men, unlearned in the law, that he should have equal privilege of speech. Simple interruption is, however, a much less evil than that of being repeatedly fined by the judge during a defence, as was the case on Davison's trial before Mr. Justice Best. And even this is more tolerable than being tried by the very jury, which, only two days before, had convicted a defendant for the sale of the same work, as in the case of Barkley, and whose deliberating for three-quarters of an hour upon their verdict, although they had not hesitated at all upon the former trial, has very much the appearance of a conflict between what consistency was supposed to require of them on the one hand, and the effect of the eloquent and admirable plea for toleration delivered by the defendant's counsel, Mr. Hill, on the other. And this is still less offensive than the manner in which the Zetetic Society in Edinburgh was treated. That Society consisted of persons whose opinions were too free for the

Kirk, and whose habits were too orderly for the tavern. They
neither printed, sold, nor publicly delivered any thing hostile
to the religion of their country, but associated to form a library, read a philosophical or theological essay in turn, and
discuss its subject and arguments: a few strangers came to
their place of meeting, and occasionally spoke; the first
being allowed under the notion that it was not legal to exclude them, and the second, when claimed, to avoid the imputation of unfairness. Every variety of opinion was allowed; and the preservation of order, temper, and the necessary restrictions as to time, were all the restraint imposed.
Would that every infidel, and every believer too, in the British empire employed his Sunday morning as inoffensively!
Thus they went on for about two years and a half, till November 1822, when, in the middle of a debate, in rushed the
sheriff with a number of police men, took down their names,
searched them all for books and papers, seized their little
library, part of which, being, in his opinion, libellous was
never returned, and carried off the president and two members to prison, who were detained for three days and then
liberated on bail, with an accusation of blasphemy hanging
over their heads for six months. This was the more formidable as they were not aware, any more than the Lord Advocate himself, or almost any body else at the time, that the
Scotch acts against blasphemy were totally repealed by 53
Geo. iii. c. 160, although it merely altered the law, as to
England, in favour of Unitarians. The administration of
justice assumed a yet more portentous form during the recent
trials at the Old Bailey, when not only was a prisoner obliged
to close his defence prematurely, in consequence of physical
exhaustion, a few moments for refreshments being refused
him, although the Court was so fatigued as to adjourn immediately after the trial; but the sentences varied from six
months imprisonment to three years, for the very same offence, as the Court happened to be pleased or displeased with
the course of argument pursued by the defendant. But the
inflictions on Carlile himself surpass all the rest in severity.
Fines to the amount of £1,500, and imprisonment for three

years; his stock and furniture immediately seized, and, with a trifling exception, neither sold nor restored; his wife and sister suffering with him, and in addition to the privation of liberty, enduring treatment for which, if a tenth of what he says be true, brutality is too soft a term; his stock again seized as it again began to accumulate; and his imprisonment prolonged (apparently it will last for life), because he cannot pay fines when the very means for doing so have been wrested from him—Is this a process either to make him, or others, admire the benignant spirit of that religion, whose name is, we had almost said, blasphemously connected with it? This man's moral character, be it remembered, is wholly unimpeached. A public scrutiny of it has been dared, and no doubt private ones have taken place. His sole offence is the publication of two books which assail Christianity, it may be in an abusive, but therefore in an ineffective manner, and which nobody is compelled to read. Why, according to the usual treatment of offenders, Mr. Carlile might, for this amount of punishment, have revelled in crime. He might have debauched half the Ladies' boarding-schools in London by the introduction of obscene pictures. He might have committed adultery with all the tradesmen's wives in Fleet-street. He might have practised cheating and robbery in twenty different forms. He might have been repeatedly guilty of manslaughter, if the circumstances were not of a very aggravated description. In short, he might have been that nuisance to society which Divines say unbelief tends to produce; but which, if it be produced, is easily and effectively suppressed by the legislature, whose powers are vainly or mischievously exerted against mere opinion.

To this phrase, so frequently parroted, that Christianity is part, or parcel of the law of England, it is difficult, if not impossible to affix any definite meaning. We can make no sense of it, but what is fatal to the purpose for which it is repeated. Christianity consists of facts, doctrines, and precepts. A profession of belief in the divine authority of the whole, may be made part of a code; but unless belief were a voluntary act, or falsehood a Christian duty, such an enactment would be rather the exclusion than the incorporation of Christianity. Legal authority may be conferred on its precepts; at least, so far as they relate to actions; but Carlile in Dorchester gaol, stripped of his property, and after the three years of confinement, to which he was sentenced, have expired, kept there till he shall pay £1500, is rather a singular commentary upon doing as we would be done by. Is the Old Testament part of the law, as well as the New? If so, we gain a clear definition of blasphemy, and that is more than our law books can furnish. The Mosaic Code has but one clause upon this offence (Leviticus xxiv), and that restricts it to cursing the Deity; an offence presupposing belief in his existence, and malignant feeling towards him; and, therefore, an offence, the perpetration of which is scarcely possible in the present state of opinion, either by believer or unbeliever. Nor did the Mosaic Code require any belief in a future state, without which, it is now affirmed, society cannot exist. The Sadducees, who denied that doctrine, and publicly argued against it, were not only tolerated, but had their full share of the government. And because this is, in some sense or other, parcel of our law, it follows that penalties should be profusely levied on all who hold their opinions. Will intolerance fly from the Old Testament to the New? From a system of severity to one of mercy? The Author of the "Address to Deists" follows her there, and we shall give some extracts from his summary of this part of the common law of England. After commenting on the total absence, in the New Testament, of any warrant for having recourse to any other means, than those of argument and persuasion, even with the most virulent opposers, he thus proceeds:—

It is sufficient to exculpate Christianity from the charge of intolerance, to show that the New Testament contains nothing to authorize its adherents to inflict punishments on its opposers; but it is expedient to add, that if it says nothing in favour of such a course, it says much against it. To employ secular force for its advancement is equally inconsistent with the example of Christ, and with his instructions.

When the apostle Peter was representing the propriety of

suffering patiently, even when suffering for doing well, he enforced his ideas by a reference to the personal demeanour of him, who was regarded by his readers with the highest reverence. "Hereunto" says he, "were ye called: because Christ also suffered for us, leaving us an example that ye should follow his steps." And what were the particulars of that example thus exhibited for their imitation? The apostle continues thus; "who did no sin, neither was guile found in his mouth; who when he was *reviled,* reviled not again: when he suffered, he threatened not, but committed himself to him that judgeth righteously."

In his case, offences against the individual were offences against religion. Christ and Christianity are inseparable. He who reviled the Redeemer, dishonoured the doctrine which he delivered, the miracles which he wrought, and the God from whom he came. "He that despiseth me, despiseth him that sent me." But though offences against him were attended with this extraordinary aggravation, he has left us an example of the meekest endurance. Was it not, it may safely be asked of any man who has once read the memoirs of Jesus, given by the Evangelists,—was it not a trait in his character, which perpetually forced itself upon your attention, that he was remarkably patient under injuries, and ready to forgive? Was it not fact, that, "as a lamb that is led to the slaughter, and as a sheep before her shearers is dumb, so he opened not his mouth?" Did he not, even when greatly displeased at the hardness of heart, and inveterate wickedness of disposition which his adversaries displayed, withhold any vindictive exercise of the miraculous powers attributed to him by his historians; which, if real, he might have really employed against them; which, if feigned, might have been feigned for purposes of terror, as easily at least, as for purposes of kindness? Did he not, with his dying breath, offer a prayer for those, who, according to Christian belief, had committed the stupendous crime of hunting down, and through malicious misrepresentations and perjured witnesses, causing to be condemned the benevolent Jesus, the Lord of Glory? Can we imagine this same Jesus, going on a certain day to Pilate, to complain that the Rabbies had represented him as a colleague of Satan, who cast out devils by the assistance of Beelzebub, and requesting that they might be committed to prison? Can we conceive of him as sending his disciples to the Roman governor, to demand punishment on those who had spoken such blasphemous words against their Master? If such a record were found in one of the Gospels, should we not look on it with a suspicious eye, on account of its dissimilarity to the rest of his deportment?

Again:

The evangelists testify that Jesus Christ gave his disciples reason to expect, that, after his decease, their principles would be aspersed, their characters vilified, and their persons exposed to persecution. The evils which they state him to have predicted, all history assures us came upon them. Whether deservedly or not, the first Christians received from those among whom they dwelt, the most decisive tokens of enmity. Pagans were incensed against the men who impugned the deity of their gods; and Jews maddened with rage against the worshippers of the crucified Nazarene. "That worthy name by which they were called," was stigmatized in their hearing, as the symbol of whatever was to be contemned or detested; and when they delivered their most solemn and affectionate discourses, their auditors, not unfrequently "were filled with envy," and spake against the things which they delivered, "contradicting and blaspheming." Something of the spirit of Christianity towards its opponents, may be ascertained through these circumstances. If we can learn what was the duty of a Christian then, to the utterer of blasphemous speeches, we may thence infer the duty of a Christian now, to the publisher of blasphemous tracts. Now the sum of the directions given by Jesus to his Apostles in prospect of these scenes, and by the Apostles to their fellow Christians who were suffering in them, seems to be, that they should leave their cause with God as their sole avenger; and in the interim instead of retaliating on their opponents, should seek their welfare. The language of Christ was, "love your enemies; bless them that curse you; do good to them that hate you; and pray for them that despitefully use you and persecute you." The language of the Apostles to their fellow sufferers was in the same temper: "Not rendering evil for evil, or railing for railing; but contrarywise, blessing; knowing that ye are thereunto called, that you should inherit a blessing.—If ye suffer for righteousness sake, happy are ye; and be not afraid of their terror, neither be troubled; but sanctify the Lord in your hearts; and be ready always to give an answer to every man that asketh you a reason of the hope that is in you *with meekness and fear.*"

Could it have been thought that they acted in the spirit of these injunctions, had they hastened to the nearest tribunal, and there preferred accusations against their adversaries, for having ridiculed their scriptures, or reviled their master?—pp. 16, 17.

The whole of this pamphlet does credit to the writer's head and heart. While he labours earnestly, and successfully, to exculpate Christianity from the charge of countenancing persecution, he is equally solicitous to win the unbeliever to a serious examination of its evidences.

That Christians, the Author of whose religion was tried and executed for blasphemy, his own words during the trial being pronounced sufficient evidence against him by his sacerdotal judge; Christians, whose prophetic books are full of the most biting sarcasms on the gods and worship of the mightiest empires; Christians, who boast a noble army of martyrs, whose lives were the penalty of their avowed departure from the religion of their country; Christians, whose missionaries are striving in every region of the earth to bring other religions "into disbelief and contempt;" Christians, Protestant Christians, whose reformers perished in the dungeon or at the stake as heretics, apostates, and blasphemers; Christians, whose religion breathes charity, liberty, and mercy, in every line; that *they* having gained the power to which so long they were victims, should employ it in the self-same way, and strive to crush the opposition of opinion, or of passion even, by vindictive persecution, is most monstrous. The inconsistency shall not remain for want of being exposed. That indeed is certain, without our efforts. Mr. Hume has repeatedly drawn the attention of the House of Commons to the subject; and we hope will continue so to do. The disgrace is felt, and always has been felt; and had we aimed to impress by authority rather than by argument, our pages might have been filled with appropriate extracts. Archbishop Secker, Bishops Lowth, Warburton, and Watson, of the church of England; Drs. Campbell and Gerard, of the church of Scotland; Drs. Chandler, Lardner, and Kippis, of the English Dissenters, have all deprecated the prosecution of unbelievers. Their tolerant spirit, their enlightened view of the real interests of religion, is not extinct. Mr. Hume last year presented a petition to the House of Commons, and it was only by accident that a similar one was not presented to the Lords by the venerable Bishop of Norwich, signed by upwards of 2,000 members of Christian congregations, and about 100 ministers, including clergymen of the established church and dissenting preachers, and persons of the most opposite theological opinions. We heartily join in its concluding prayer, that the House would "take into consideration the prosecutions carrying on, and the punishments already inflicted upon unbelievers, in order to exonerate Christianity from the opprobrium and scandal so unjustly cast upon it, of being a system that countenances intolerance and persecution:" and not only, we will add, in order so to exonerate Christianity, but also to render equal justice to believer and unbeliever, and not add to the misfortune of Infidelity the privation of civil rights, and the endurance of legal penalties.

7

On Liberty of the Press

1825

Any documentation that might be needed to demonstrate the illiberalism of English law in the early nineteenth century is provided by the last half of Mill's essay on the law of libel. The importance of the issue of the old English libel laws cannot be overestimated. As Mill claims, there was no real definition of libel in 1825, and one of the chief means used by the English government to suppress criticism was to call any critic libellous. Without reform of the libel laws, free discussion would have been precarious or impossible.

This review-essay by Mill may seem anomalous in some respects. Mill depicts a government so irresponsible and oppressive that it would be unlikely ever to permit the publication without punishment of his radical views in *The Westminster Review* or *The Morning Chronicle*. The anomaly, however, is only apparent. Mill is describing the *law* of England. Although he shows how far the strength of the law could also extend to practice, its power was not absolute. Fortunately, the effect of public opinion and of radical voices in Parliament, the fear of revolution, and the pressure of moderates in the ministry prevented the law from making political criticism wholly impossible.

In the first part of this essay, Mill attempts to define limits for freedom of the press corresponding with those in his previous article on freedom of religion. It is essential to remember that he is arguing against what a democrat takes to be an unjust government. His conclusion that there is no mean between perfect freedom of opinion and absolute despotism may be true as a basis for a theory. He will come later to believe that "perfect freedom" is impossible, even in a democratic society.

"Under a free system," Mill writes "if error would be promulgated, so would truth: and truth never fails, in the long run, to prevail over error." Here again is one of the principal arguments that will appear later in the second part of *On Liberty*. Mill is still confident in this early essay that popular rule and free discussion will serve truth. At the same time, in discussing the psychology of the public of his day, Mill describes the influences of love of ease, of innate conservatism, of the willingness to endure evil, and of worship of rank. If the public is so slothful, how will vigorous debate and the victory of truth come about? They will come, Mill believes, "in the long run," as new habits of discussion remove ignorance, fear, and the incapacity to judge well. He does not tell us how long is "the long run" or what criteria and what authority are to be used to determine "truth" *after* free discussion.

Mill was to raise the issue of limits on free discussion within a democratic society in *On Liberty*; but he never fully envisioned the possibility of a minority in a democracy using freedom to destroy free discussion for all others. One sentence in this early essay, however, suggests both Mill's awareness of this problem and his answer: "If we were as firmly convinced that the British constitution is, as we are convinced that it is not, the best possible government, we should be willing to expose even such a government to a very considerable degree of risk, rather than support it by means, which if they may be used for the preservation of the best government, may be equally used to perpetuate all the atrocities of the worst." The important phrase here is "a very considerable degree of risk." It suggests that, under "the best possible government," the "perfect freedom" Mill asks for as the only alternative to despotism would not be permitted to destroy freedom.

AN ARTICLE FROM *The Westminster Review*
OF APRIL, 1825

*On the Law of Libel; with Strictures on the self-styled Con-
stitutional Association*. 8vo. pp. 73. London. John Hunt.
1823.

The Law of Libel. By Richard Mence, Esq. of the Middle
Temple, Barrister 8vo. 2 Vols. in one, pp. 595. London,
1824.

The two publications which we have chosen to head this
article possess considerable merit, and we do not hesitate
to recommend them to our readers, as worthy of an attentive
perusal.

The first, though no name appears in the title-page, is
the acknowledged production of a known and tried friend of
the people. It consists of a series of essays, all of which, except the last, appeared nearly two years since in a weekly
newspaper. It comprises a summary exposure of many of the
abominations contained in what is called the Law of Libel,
as well as in the administration of that Law; and a brief review of the acts of a body of men, now sunk into obscurity,
who were at one time notorious under the name of the Constitutional Association. We will not say that the author has
completely exhausted the subject; but we consider no small
praise to be his due, for having said so much, and so much to
the purpose, in the narrow compass within which, by the
original design, he was unavoidably confined.

Mr. Mence's work attracted our attention, from being
advertised as dedicated to the Constitutional Association.
What might be expected from a work, appearing under such
auspices, our readers have no occasion to be informed. We,
however, had not proceeded far in the perusal, before we
found Mr. Mence to be, not a humble aspirant after ministerial patronage, content to lend himself to the purposes of
those who would keep the human mind in perpetual bond-

age; but one who does not shrink from exposing, even at the risk of his professional success, the vices of existing institutions; one who dares give utterance to great and important truths, however little acceptable to the rich and powerful; and who would be, for that reason alone, deserving of high praise, had he executed his task with far less ability than he has displayed.

Without entering into a critical examination of the merits and defects of these two works, we embrace this opportunity of delivering our sentiments upon the highly important subject to which they refer: availing ourselves of the language of either or both of them, as often as it appears peculiarly adapted to our purpose.

We shall divide our remarks into two parts; in one of which we shall discuss the general question, to what extent restraints upon the freedom of the press can be considered as warranted by sound principles of political philosophy; and in the other, we shall take a brief review of the English Law, and of the doctrines of English Lawyers, on this subject: and we pledge ourselves to prove, that the Law of England is as unfavourable to the liberty of the press, as that of the most despotic government which ever existed; and, consequently, that whatever degree of that liberty is enjoyed in this country, exists, not in consequence of the law, but in spite of it.

The general question has usually been disposed of in a very summary way. It has, in fact, been regularly assumed, first, that to employ the press in any other than a certain manner, is inconceivably wicked; and secondly, that, for this reason, it is the duty of the magistrate to prevent it, by fine and imprisonment, if not by means still more certainly and more promptly effectual.

The author of the article "Liberty of the Press," in the Supplement to the Encyclopædia Britannica, has, however, set the example of rather a different sort of reasoning; and (what was never completely or consistently done before) he has pointed out the considerations on which this question really turns. We have no higher ambition than that of treading in his steps; and, taking his principles as our guide, we shall endeavour to unravel the sophistry, and expose the mischievous designs of the enemies to free discussion.

That the press may be so employed as to require punishment, we are very far from denying: it may be made the instrument of almost every imaginable crime.

"There is scarcely a right,* for the violation of which, scarcely an operation of government, for the disturbance of which, the press may not be employed as an instrument. The offences capable of being committed by the press are indeed nearly coextensive with the whole field of delinquency.

"It is not, however, necessary to give a separate definition of every such violation or disturbance, when committed by the press, for that would be to write the penal code a second time; first describing each offence as it appears in ordinary cases; and then describing it anew for the case in which the press is the particular instrument.

"If, for the prevention of the violation of rights, it were necessary to give a separate definition, on account of every instrument which might be employed as a means of producing the several violations, the penal code would be endless. In general the instrument or means is an immaterial circumstance. The violation itself, and the degree of alarm which may attend it, are the principal objects of consideration. If a man is put in fear of his life, and robbed of his purse, it is of no consequence whether he is threatened with a pistol, or with a sword. In the deposition of a theft, of a fraud, or a murder, it is not necessary to include an account of all the sorts of means by which these injuries may be perpetrated. It is sufficient if the injury itself is accurately described. The object is, to prevent the injury, not merely when produced by one sort of means or another sort of means, but by any means.

"As far as persons and property are concerned, the general definition of the acts by which rights are liable to be violated, has always been held sufficient; and has been re-

* Article "Liberty of the Press" (in the Supplement to the Enc. Brit. near the beginning). This invaluable essay is from the pen of Mr. Mill, the historian of British India.

garded as including not less the cases in which the instrumentality of the press has been employed, than those in which any other means have been employed to the same end. Nobody ever thought of a particular law for restraining the press on account of the cases in which it may have been rendered subservient to the perpetration of a murder or theft. It is enough that a law is made to punish him who has been guilty of the murder or theft, whether he has employed the press or any thing else as the means for accomplishing his end.†

There are some species of acts, however, of which the press if not the sole, may, at any rate, be regarded as the most potent instrument: these are, the publication of facts, and the expression of opinions; and to one or other of these heads belong those uses of the press, against which the Law of Libel is principally directed.

It is not pretended that, in the language of English Law, the word Libel is strictly confined to one meaning. It includes, on the contrary, a number of acts, of a very heterogeneous nature, resembling one another scarcely at all, except in having penalties attached to them by the authorized interpreters of the law. A threatening letter, demanding money, is a libel. An indecent picture is a libel. For the present, however, we may confine our remarks to the question regarding the publication of facts and the expression of opinions.

To begin with the latter. If the magistrate is to be intrusted with power to suppress all opinions which he, in his

† Montesquieu saw pretty clearly the only case in which the expression of opinions and sentiments could be a fit object of punishment: although he did not venture to extend the doctrine further than to the case of *words*, and even among words, only to these which are called treasonable.

"Les paroles qui sont jointes à une action, prennent la nature de cette action. Ainsi un homme qui va dans la place publique exhorter les sujets à la révolte, devient coupable de lèse-majesté, parceque les paroles sont jointes à l'action, et y participent. Ce ne sont point les paroles que l'on punit; mais une action commise dans laquelle on emploie les paroles. Elles ne deviennent des crimes, que lorsqu'elles préparent, qu'elles accompagnent, ou qu'elles suivent une action criminelle. On renverse tout, si l'on fait des paroles un crime capital, au lieu de les regarder comme le signe d'un crime capital."—*Esprit des Lois*, liv. xii. ch. 12.

wisdom, may pronounce to be mischievous—to what control can this power be subjected? What security is it possible to take against its abuse? For without some security all power, and of course this power, is sure to be abused, just as often as its abuse can serve any purpose of the holder.

It is the boast of English lawyers that the offence of treason is defined; so strictly defined, that nothing is ambiguous, nothing arbitrary, nothing left to the discretion of the judge. This, they tell us, is one of the chief bulwarks of our liberty: implying, that if it *were* left to the judge to say what should, and what should not be treason, everything would be treason which the government did not like. Yet why should definition be required in the case of treason, not required in the case of libel. Is the government less interested in misdecision? Is the judge less dependent on the government? Is a packed special jury less subservient? Or are the judge and jury angels when they judge of libel, men only when they judge of treason?

It would be hardy to assert, that to give the right of pronouncing upon libels to the judge, is any thing more than another name for giving it to the government. But there are many subjects, and these the most important of all, on which it is the interest of the government, not that the people should think right, but, on the contrary, that they should think wrong: on these subjects, therefore, the government is quite sure, if it has the power, to suppress, not the false and mischievous opinions, but the great and important truths. It is the interest of rulers that the people should hold slavish opinions in politics: it is equally so, that they should hold slavish opinions in religion: all opinions, therefore, whether in politics or religion, which are not slavish, the government, if it dares, will be sure to suppress. It is the interest of rulers that the people should believe all their proceedings to be the best possible: every thing, therefore, which has a tendency to make them think otherwise, and among the rest, all strictures, however well deserved, government will use its most strenuous exertions to prevent. If these endeavours could succeed, if it could suppress all censure, its dominion, to whatever degree it might pillage and oppress the people, would be for ever secured.

This is so palpable, that a man must be either insincere or imbecile to deny it: and no one, we suppose, will openly affirm that rulers should have the power to suppress all opinions which they may call mischievous—all opinions which they may dislike. Where, then, is the line to be drawn? At what point is the magistrate's discretionary power of suppressing opinions to end? Can it be limited in such a manner as to leave him the power of suppressing really mischievous opinions, without giving him that of silencing every opinion hostile to the indefinite extension of his power?

It is manifest, even at first sight, that no such limit can be set. If the publication of opinions is to be restrained, merely because they are mischievous, there must be somebody to judge, what opinions are mischievous, and what the reverse. It is obvious, that there is no certain and universal rule for determining whether an opinion is useful or pernicious; and that if any person be authorized to decide, unfettered by such a rule, that person is a despot. To decide what opinions shall be permitted, and what prohibited, is to choose opinions for the people: since they cannot adopt opinions which are not suffered to be presented to their minds. Whoever chooses opinions for the people, possesses absolute control over their actions, and may wield them for his own purposes with perfect security.

It thus appears, by the closest ratiocination, that there is no medium between perfect freedom of expressing opinion, and absolute despotism. Whenever you invest the rulers of the country with any power to suppress opinions, you invest them with *all* power; and absolute power of suppressing opinions would amount, if it *could* be exercised, to a despotism far more perfect than any which has yet existed, because there is no country in which the power of suppressing opinions has ever, in practice, been altogether unrestrained.

How, then, it may be asked, if to have any power of silencing opinions is to have all power—since the government of Great Britain certainly has that power in a degree—how do we account for the practical freedom of discussion, which to a considerable extent undoubtedly prevails in this country? The government having the power to destroy it, why is it suffered to exist?

Why? For the same reason, for which we have a habeas corpus act, with a government possessing the power to suspend or repeal it: for the same reason for which a jury is sometimes allowed to acquit a prisoner, whom the aristocracy wish to destroy: for the same reason for which we are not taxed up to the highest amount which could be extorted from us, without impairing our power of being useful slaves. The aristocracy do not submit to these restraints because they like them, but because they do not venture to throw them off. This is conformable to the theory of the British constitution itself.

Even a Turkish Sultan is restrained by the fear of exciting insurrection. The power of shackling the press may, like all other power, be controlled in its exercise by public opinion, and to a very great, though far from a sufficient, extent, it has been and is so controlled in Great Britain. By law, however—notwithstanding the assertions of lawyers, which assertions, when it suits them, they never scruple to contradict—liberty of discussion, on any topic by which the interests of the aristocracy can be affected, does not exist at all in this country, as we have already shewn, upon general principles, and shall prove in the sequel from the actual words of the highest legal authorities.

The preliminary inquiry, however, would not be complete, unless, having discussed the consequences of restraining the press, we were also to inquire what would be the consequences of leaving it free.

It is evident, at first sight, that, whatever might be the evils of freedom, they could not be worse than the evils of restraint. The worst that could happen, if the people chose opinions for themselves, would be, that they would choose wrong opinions. But this evil, as we have seen, is not contingent, but unavoidable, if they allow any other person to

choose opinions for them. Nor would it be possible that the
opinions, however extravagant, which might become prevalent in a state of freedom, could exceed in mischievousness
those which it would be the interest, and therefore the will,
of rulers, to dictate: since there cannot be more mischievous
opinions, than those which tend to perpetuate arbitrary
power. There would, however, be one great difference.
Under a free system of restraint, the errors which would be
promulgated from authority would be the most mischievous
possible, and would not be suffered to be refuted.

That truth, if it has fair play, always in the end triumphs
over error, and becomes the opinion of the world, is a proposition which rests upon the broadest principles of human
nature, and to which it would be easy to accumulate testi-
monials from almost every author, whatever may be his political leanings, who has distinguished himself in any branch
of politics, morals, or theology. It is a proposition which the
restrictors themselves do not venture to dispute. They continually protest, that their opinions have nothing to fear
from discussion; the sole effect of which, according to them,
is, to exhibit their irrefragable certainty in a still stronger
light than before. And yet they do not scruple to punish men
for doing that which, if their own assertions be correct, merits
not punishment, but reward.

Although, however, the worst enemies of discussion
do not deny, as a general proposition, its tendency to unveil
the truth, there is a certain number of subjects on which, if
they are to be believed, discussion tends, not to enlighten,
but to mislead. Among these are all the subjects on which
it is the interest of rulers that the people *should* be misled;
the political religion of the country, its political institutions,
and the conduct and character of its rulers.

On the first of these topics, we have delivered our opinions so fully in our third number, that we shall in the present
confine ourselves principally to the three latter: all of
which substantially resolve themselves into one.

That there is no subject of greater importance, no one
needs to be told: and to say this, is to say that there is no

subject on which it is of greater importance that the people should be rightly informed. As the stability of a good government wholly depends upon its being acknowledged by the people to be good, so, on the other hand, the reform of a bad one wholly depends upon its being believed by the people to be bad. In the correctness of the estimate which the people form of the goodness of their government, their whole happiness is involved; since misgovernment includes every misery which is capable of afflicting mankind: and misgovernment is alike the consequence, whether the people believe a good government to be a bad one, or a bad government to be a good one.

We have been thus particular in laying down first principles, because the language held on this subject by rulers implies, that it is indeed the greatest of calamities, for the people to believe a good government to be bad, but that their considering a bad government to be good, is no evil at all, or at most a very trifling one. The evil, however, as we have already observed, is in both cases the same; or rather, the one is an evil, chiefly because it leads to the other: that the people should think ill of a good government is principally to be lamented, because it may occasion their acquiescence in a worse.

If, therefore, there be any subject on which the people cannot, without the greatest danger, trust the power of choosing opinions for them out of their own hands, it is this. And if such power cannot safely be given to any one, least of all can it be given to the rulers of the country.

If the people were compelled to take their opinions implicitly from some one who might have an interest in persuading them that their government is worse than it is, the greatest evils, it is admitted, would be the consequence. To think ill of a good government, and well of a bad one, are evils of equal magnitude. If, therefore, the privilege of dictating opinions to the people, on the subject of their government, be intrusted to persons interested in persuading them that their government is better than it is, the mischief cannot consistently be affirmed to be less. That rulers are so interested, will not be denied. What inference, then, are we to draw? or rather, how can the inference be evaded, that, if rulers are suffered to choose what opinons the people shall hold concerning their government, all the evils of misrule are rendered perpetual?

Such a choice, however, is made by rulers, as often as they inflict punishment upon any person for criticizing institutions, or censuring the conduct of government: unless they are willing to prohibit, under equal penalties, the expression of praise.

To forbid the expression of one opinion, and give encouragement to that of another, is surely to make a choice. To punish censure of rulers, while praise is permitted, is to say, 'tis fit that the people should think well of their government, whether good or bad; and to take the most effectual mode of compelling them to do so.

Against this reasoning it is impossible that any rational objection can be urged. Cavils, indeed, may be brought against it: but there are few conclusions of equal importance, the proof of which affords so little hold even for cavil.

When it is asserted, that to restrain discussion is to choose opinions for the people, and that rulers, if permitted to dictate opinions to their subjects, having an interest in choosing the most mischievous of all opinions, will act as that interest directs; there is only one objection which can by possibility be raised. It cannot be said, that to fetter discussion is not to choose opinions, nor that rulers are not interested in making a bad choice. But, it may be said, that our rulers are men in whom the confidence of the people may be reposed; and that, although it be confessedly their interest to make a bad choice, they will disregard that interest, and make a good one.

To such a pinnacle of absurdity men may always be driven, when they attempt to argue in defence of mischievous power. They begin by boldly denying the possibility of abuse: when this can no longer be maintained, they fly for refuge to the characters of the individuals, and insist with equal pertinacity, that in their hands power may be trusted without fear of being abused. This is a compliment of which the rulers for the time being, be they who they may, always receive as much as they can pay for: dead rulers are not so fortunate. That all rulers in time past abused their power when they could, is allowed: but an exception is made in favor of the present. This is a species of reasoning, however, which will pass current with nobody in the present day: we cannot be forced back to the times when rulers were thought not to be made like human beings, but to be free from all the passions and appetites by which other men are misled. If uncontrolled power can exist, and not be abused, then away with the British, and all other constitutions, and let us return to the despotism of our wise and venerable ancestors. But if men will abuse all other powers, when unrestrained, so they will that of controlling the press: if rulers will avail themselves of all other means to render themselves despotic, they will not pass over an expedient so simple and effectual as that of suppressing, in as far as they dare, all opinions hostile to the extension of their authority. And perfect freedom of discussion is, as we have already proved, the only alternative.

The objections which have been urged against the principle of free discussion, though infinitely diversified in shape, are at bottom only one assertion: the incapacity of the people to form correct opinions. This assumption is indeed the stronghold of all the disguised or undisguised partisans of despotism. It has been the unremitting, and hitherto, unhappily, the successful endeavour of rulers, to make it be believed that the most dreadful calamities would be the effect of any attempt to obtain securities that their power should be employed for the benefit, not of themselves, but of the community. With this view, it has been their uniform practice to vilify those whom they are striving to enslave. If the people were permitted to choose opinions for themselves, they would be sure, it is alleged, to choose the most mischievous and dangerous opinions. Being utterly incapable either of thinking or of acting for themselves, they are quite sure, unless kept in awe by priests and aristocracies, to become blind instruments in the hands of factious demagogues, who would employ them to subvert all establishments, and to throw every thing into the wildest anarchy and confusion. This language, by the way, is a practical illustration of the impartiality of the Law of Libel. It restrains all declaration, even of unfavourable truth with regard to the aristocracy: it gives full indulgence, and there is plenty of encouragement, to the propagation of all manner of unfavourable lies against the people. The conspiracy have thus all that is necessary for their purpose. Give a dog a bad name, and hang him: so they try with the people. Whether the object be to coerce them by standing armies, or to muzzle them by libel law, the motive always is pure loving-kindness, to save the unoffending, that is, the aristocratic part of mankind, from the jaws of those ravenous wolves and tigers, the people.

Such a language is calculated to act upon men by their fears, not by their reason: otherwise a little reflection would show, that the incapacity of the people, were it admitted, proves nothing, or, at least, nothing to the purpose. The practical conclusion would be the same, even if the people were so destitute of reasoning power, as to be utterly incapable of distinguishing truth from falsehood: since there is no alternative, but to let them choose their own opinions, or to give the choice to persons interested in misleading them.

An ignorant man, even if he decide at hap-hazard, has at least a chance of being sometimes in the right. But he who adopts every opinion which rulers choose to dictate, is always in the wrong, when it is their interest that he should be so, that is, on the most momentous of all topics.

Another question, which it does not suit those who make the ignorance of the people a plea for enslaving them to put, is, why are they ignorant? because to this question there can be only one answer, namely, that if they are ignorant, it is precisely because that discussion, which alone can remove ignorance, has been withheld from them. And although their masters may find it convenient to speak of their ignorance as incurable, we take the liberty of demurring to this conclusion, until the proper remedy shall have been tried. This remedy is, instruction: and of instruction, discussion is the most potent instrument. Discussion, therefore, has a necessary tendency to remedy its own evils. For the evils which spring from an undue veneration for authority, there is no such cure: and the longer the disease continues, without the remedying influence of discussion, the more inveterate it becomes.

But, the assertion itself, by which so many terrors have been conjured up—the incapacity of the people to choose correct opinions—upon what evidence does it rest? Upon history? No: for history proves, that just in proportion as the people have been permitted to choose opinions for themselves, in that proportion have they been moral, intelligent, and happy: and it is precisely in those countries in which the greatest pain has been taken to shut out discussion, that the people, when once roused from their habitual apathy, have proved themselves to be most ignorant and ferocious. No people which had ever enjoyed a free press, could have been guilty of the excesses of the French Revolution. By what artifices, then, have governments contrived to spread a vague apprehension of danger from discussion so widely among the unthinking part of mankind? By availing themselves of that universal law of human nature, by which men are prone to dread whatever they do not understand, and they who foresee the least, uniformly fear the most. The evils which they endure, habit has rendered tolerable: but change, because they cannot foresee its consequences, is the object of their terror and aversion. And though history does not prove that discussion produces evil, but the contrary, there is abundant proof from history, that it produces change: change, not indeed in any thing good, but in every thing that is bad, bad laws, bad judicature, and bad government. That it leads to such changes is the very reason for which it is most to be desired, but it is also the reason why short-sighted persons hold it in terror.

Nor it there any difficulty in convincing the understanding of any one who will coolly apply his attention to the subject. The real difficulty is, to quiet fears. We cannot confide in persons whose fears appear to us to fall always in the wrong place. Nothing is more to be feared than a habit of fearing, whenever any thing is proposed for the good of mankind. The man who is always fearing evil to the many from the many, never from the few, appears to us an object of very rational fear.

The ignorance of the people is a mere pretext for a line of conduct which would have been equally pursued without any such pretext. This appears from the little regard paid to it in the practice of rulers themselves. The proper course in regard to ignorant persons, they say truly, is to guard them against deception: now, as rulers dare not openly lay claim to impeccability, they cannot deny that there may be deception on both sides: on the side of praise, as well as on the side of blame. To praise, however, both of rulers and of institutions, the most unlimited latitude has been given: censure alone has been restricted. Every one is free to represent the government and its functionaries as better than they are; and that to any extent: but woe to him who presumes, with whatever truth, to cast any blame upon either! Does this look as if it were believed that the people are ignorant? No! it looks as if it were feared that they would be too clear-sighted.

It seems not very consistent, in those whose case rests wholly upon the people's incapacity of judging, to propose as a remedy for that incapacity, that nothing but an *ex parte* statement should be presented to them. Is incapacity to judge cured by hearing only one side? Is ignorance remedied by placing it in a situation where the most perfect wisdom could scarcely escape being misled? To make the ignorance of the people a pretext for refusing them the means of judging, when it is precisely on account of their ignorance that they stand most in need of those means, would excite laughter, if it did not excite indignation. In other countries, it is maintained that the people ought not to judge of public affairs. To prevent them from hearing evidence, therefore, is, at any rate, consistent. In this country it is admitted that the people should judge; and it is, nevertheless, asserted, that they should hear only one side!

To support this monstrous absurdity, there is, in addition to the grand assumption of the incapacity of the people, another question which it has been customary to beg. This is, that the people hate their rulers, and are strongly disposed to judge unfavorably, both of them and of their actions. So utterly false is this assumption, that, on the contrary, there is no fact to which the testimony of experience is more unvarying, than to the strong disposition of the people, to think much better of their rulers and of their institutions than they deserve. The love of ease, perhaps the strongest principle of human nature, and beyond all comparison stronger, in the majority of mankind, than the hope of any remote and contingent advantage, is constantly urging them to avoid innovation, and rest satisfied with things as they are: with what success, every one has it in his power to observe. Who is there that has not seen a hundred instances of evil needlessly endured, for one of good wantonly abandoned and evil adopted? Is there, then, no inconsistency in supposing that in public matters the case is directly reversed? Nor is the love of ease the only principle which is constantly in operation, to warp the judgments of the people in favour of their rulers. He must have looked at mankind with a resolution not to see the truth, who can be blind to the excessive veneration of the poor for title, rank, and riches, a veneration arising from the habitual propensity of mankind to over-estimate advantages which they do not possess; and which was enumerated by Adam Smith among the most fertile sources of false judgments in morality which could be named. With these two principles strongly on one side, and nothing but reason on the other, knowledge must be far advanced among the people before they learn to venerate rulers only as far as they deserve veneration. Accordingly, all history bears testimony to the constancy with which the most dreadful mis-government has been suffered to prevail in almost every country of the globe: but the advocates of restriction may safely be challenged to produce one instance from history, in which the people have risen against a good government and overthrown it.

So strong, and so durable, is the veneration of the people for their rulers: nor has it ever yet been eradicated by anything short of the most grinding oppression. What epithet, then, can be too severe for the conduct of those who would prevent this feeling from giving way, like all other mischievous feelings, with the progress of civilization; who would deny a hearing to opinions and arguments which tend to weaken the inordinate reverence of the people for every ruler, good or bad, and give free scope to those which tend to render that blind reverence, and all its consequent miseries, everlasting!

Although our sentiments on the subject of free discussion in religion have already been fully stated, we will quote one passage from an essay to which we have before referred: merely to show that the same arguments apply to religion, which we have already stated with a more immediate reference to politics:

"Religion, in some of its shapes, has in most countries been placed on the footing of an institution of the state. Ought the freedom of the press to be as complete with regard to this, as we have seen that it ought to be in regard to all other institutions of the state? If any one says that it ought not, it is incumbent upon him to shew, wherein the principles which are applicable to the other institutions, fail in their application to this.

"We have seen, that, in regard to all other institutions, it is unsafe for the people to permit any but themselves to choose opinions for them. Nothing can be more certain, than that it is unsafe for them to permit any but themselves to choose for them in religion.

"If they part with the power of choosing their own religious opinions, they part with every power. It is well known with what ease religious opinions can be made to embrace every thing upon which the unlimited power of rulers and the utmost degradation of the people depend. The doctrine of *passive obedience* and non-resistance was a *religious doctrine*. Permit any man, or any set of men, to say what shall and what shall not be religious opinions, you make them despotic immediately.

"This is so obvious, that it requires neither illustration nor proof.

"But if the people here, too, must choose opinions for themselves, discussion must have its course; the same propositions which we have proved to be true in regard to other institutions, are true in regard to this: and no opinion ought to be impeded more than another, by any thing but the adduction of evidence on the opposite side."

The argument drawn from the unsafeness of permitting governments to choose a religion for their subjects, cogent as it is, ranks only as one among a host or arguments, for leaving the people to follow their own reason, in matters of religion, as in every thing else.

In an age when the slightest difference of opinion on such a subject was deemed a perfectly sufficient reason for bringing the unhappy minority to the stake, it was not wonderful that Infidelity also should be considered a crime. But now, when a Churchman no more thinks of persecuting a Calvinist, or a Calvinist of persecuting a Churchman, than we think of punishing a man because he happens to be taller, or shorter, than ourselves; it is truly strange that there should be any one who can so blind himself as not to see, that the same reasons which make him a friend to toleration in other cases, bind him also to tolerate Infidelity.

The expression of opinions having been disposed of, it remains to be considered, whether in any case there is sufficient reason for placing restrictions upon the statement of facts. It must be admitted that the case of facts, and that of opinions, are not precisely similar. False opinions must be tolerated for the sake of the true: since it is impossible to draw any line by which true and false opinions can be separated from one another. There is no corresponding reason for permitting the publication of false statements of fact. The truth or falsehood of an alleged fact, is matter, not of opinion, but of evidence; and may be safely left to be decided by those, on whom the business of deciding upon evidence in other cases devolves.

It is maintained, however, by lawyers, that there ought to be other restrictions upon the statement of facts, besides the punishment of falsehood: there being some facts, as they allege, which, even if true, ought not to be made public. On this it is to be observed, that the same reasoning which proves that there should be perfect freedom of expressing opinions, proves also that there should be perfect freedom of expressing true facts. It is obviously upon facts, that all true opinions must be founded; if rulers, therefore, have, on any subject, on their own conduct, for example, the power of keeping from the knowledge of the people all facts which it does not suit them to disclose, they do, in fact, choose opinions for the people on that subject, just as completely as if they assumed the power of doing so, by a positive enactment.

There is one case, and only one, in which there might appear to be some doubt of the propriety of permitting the truth to be told without reserve. This is, when the truth, without being of any advantage to the public, is calculated to give annoyance to private individuals. That there are such cases must be allowed; and also that it would be desirable, in such cases, that the truth should be suppressed, if it could be done by any other means than law, or arbitrary power. It must, however, be borne in mind, that, if there are cases in which a truth unpleasant to individuals is of no advantage to the public, there are others in which it is of the greatest; and that the truths which it most imports to the public to know, are precisely those which give most annoyance to individuals, whose vices and follies they expose. Tory lawyers, indeed, for whom no doctrine is too extravagant which tends to uphold their power, or that of their employers, have asserted that one man has no right whatever to censure another: that to do so is an act of judicial authority which no individual is entitled to exercise: and that to expose vices and follies, instead of being one of the most important of all services to mankind, is a gross and unwarrantable usurpation of superiority. We hope that none but Tory lawyers are hardy enough to profess concurrence in doctrines like these. Since, then, there is no one who can be trusted to decide which are useful, which the unimportant truths; and the consequences of suppressing both would, beyond comparison, exceed in mischievousness the consequences of allowing both to be heard; the practical conclusion needs not to be stated.

We have yet to notice a shift, to which recourse has frequently been had, since the spread of liberal opinions has rendered it scarcely safe to acknowledge the same degree of enmity to discussion, which was formerly avowed. We allude to the doctrine, that *calm* and *fair* discussion should be permitted, but that ridicule and invective ought to be chastised.

This is so much the doctrine which has been fashionable of late, that most of our readers probably believe it to be the law: and so, according to the *dicta* of judges, it is: but according to other *dicta* of the same judges, it is also the law, that any discussion, unless it be all on one side, and even a bare statement of acknowledged facts, is a libel.

The doctrine, however, being as we have said, a fashionable one, it is necessary to say something on it; and we observe, in the first place, that if argument may be permitted with safety, there can be little hazard in tolerating ridicule and invective; since, on all questions of importance, it is, in the long run, the balance of argument which always determines the decision of the majority. First, from the very nature of the weapons themselves: the operation of invective and ridicule being in a great measure limited to those whose minds are already made up. They may stimulate partizans, but they are not calculated to make converts. If a man does not renounce his opinion from conviction, it is scarcely by hearing himself laughed at, or reviled for holding it, that he will be prevailed upon to give it up. Such means usually have no effect but to make him adhere to his opinion still more pertinaciously than before. And secondly, because ridicule and invective, if they may be used on one side, may be used also on the other; and against falsehood, for obvious reasons, with greater effect than against truth.

In the next place, if exclusion is to be put upon ridicule
and invective, why is it not impartial? If any advantage can
be derived from the employment of such weapons, why is it
permitted to one set of opinions, withheld from another? Or
is it that ridicule and invective then only tend to mislead,
when they are employed on the side adverse to rulers? To
deny any advantage to censure, which is extended to praise,
is the same thing, though in a less aggravated degree, with
the total prohibition of censure. Its effect, in as far as it has
any, is to give an undue preponderance to praise: its tendency
is, to make the people think better of their rulers than they
deserve; and, to that extent rulers are enabled to oppress
with impunity.

Suppose, for instance, that a writer is permitted to say,
in as many words, that ministers or parliament have acted
improperly, have engaged, for instance, in an unjust war;
but, if he says this, and moreover expresses indignation that
it should be so, he is punished. By expressing indignation, he
gives it to be understood, that the evil, in his opinion, is great,
and its authors deserving of punishment. If he refrains from
expressing indignation, he virtually says, that the evil is not
great, and its authors not deserving of punishment. Is it of
no consequence, then, that the public should be informed,
whether an evil is great or small? whether its authors are
criminal, or the reverse? We fully subscribe to the manly
and liberal sentiments of Mr. Mence on this subject. "It is
not only no crime, but a positive duty, never to state crimes
drily and coldly, and without the language of just and honest
indignation. And our law, or supposed law of libel, by repressing the exercise of this duty, ministers to and encourages every kind of vice; and corrupts and undermines the
manners and morals of the people." i.162.

Great as are these evils, they are not the greatest which
the prohibition of ridicule and invective carries along with
it: nor is it for the mere purpose of securing exclusively to
themselves any advantage which such weapons can bestow,
that rulers cling so closely to the privilege of putting them
down. It is because they know well that, if they are permit-

ted to suppress ridicule and invective, they have it in their power to suppress all unfavourable representation. Who is to judge, what is invective, and what is fair and temperate discussion? None but rulers themselves: for no line can be drawn. All censure is invective. To censure is to ascribe misconduct. Even error is misconduct, in those to whose management the great affairs of a community are intrusted. When to err is to put to hazard the welfare of a nation, it is a crime for those who cannot avoid error to remain at the helm. To impute even error, therefore, is equivalent to invective, and might be construed as employing it. The mere statement of a great crime is itself invective. It implies, and is meant to imply, moral guilt: if it fails of doing so, the statement is so far imperfect. It is impossible, therefore, to prohibit invective, without prohibiting all discussion, or leaving it to rulers to decide what sort of discussion shall be punished, and what left free.

"The question is, whether *indecent* discussion should be prohibited? To answer this question, we must, of course, inquire what is meant by indecent.

"In English libel law, where this term holds so distinguished a place, is it not defined?

"English legislators have not hitherto been good at defining; and English lawyers have always vehemently condemned, and grossly abused it. The word 'indecent,' therefore, has always been a term under which it was not difficult, on each occasion, for the judge to include whatever he did not like. 'Decent' and 'what the judge likes,' have been pretty nearly synonymous." And while *indecent* discussion is prohibited by law, they always will be synonymous.

The doctrine which we have now exposed, is merely one of the shifts to which English rulers, from their peculiar situation, have been compelled to have recourse.

In other countries, where the system to be upheld is one of undisguised despotism, the utter incapacity of the people to judge rightly, and the unspeakable wickedness of their presuming to judge at all, on the subject of government, are the avowed doctrines of rulers. The people, it is there contended, have no business to form any opinion on the acts of government. They have nothing to do with their rulers except to obey them. The magistrate, as he ought to have absolute control over the actions of all under his dominion, ought likewise to have power equally unlimited over their opinions. And this doctrine, if it has no other merit, has at least the recommendation of consistency.

The language of English rulers, down to the Revolution in 1688, was precisely similar. At that period, however, a new government was established; and this government, having come in upon the popular ground of resistance to kings, could not avoid admitting, that the people ought to be permitted to judge both of rulers and of institutions; since to deny this, would have been to give up the principle upon which its own dominion was founded. At the same time, having the same interests as any other government, it was desirous of suppressing, as far as possible, all censure upon its proceedings. Accordingly, the course which, since that time, it has pursued, has been one of perpetual compromise. It has admitted, in the fullest and most unequivocal terms, that discussion on all subjects of government and legislation ought to be free. It has even maintained, that the privilege of canvassing the acts of their government, is the birthright of Englishmen: that we owe to it all that we hold dear: that, without it, there can be no security for good government. At the same time, in the teeth of these large professions, it has maintained, that censure of established governments ought not to be permitted; and it has assumed to itself, in practice, the privilege of visiting such censure, as often as it has thought fit, with some of the severest penalties of the law.

In this see-saw, English rulers have been followed by English lawyers. We shall select our first instances from Mr. Holt's celebrated treatise on the Law of Libel: a work which, having been declared by the late lord Ellenborough from the bench to contain an accurate expression of his own sentiments, and being now generally received among lawyers as one of their standard works, may be considered unexceptionable authority, both for the law itself, and for the sentiments of rulers upon it. Observe what he says of the unspeakable importance of free discussion:

> Our constitution, in fact, as it at present exists, in a church reformed from the errors of superstition, and in a system of liberty equally remote from feudal anarchy, and monarchical despotism, is almost entirely, under Providence, the fruit of a free press. It was this which awakened the minds of men from that apathy in which ignorance of their rights, and of the duties of their rulers, left them. It was by these means that moral and religious knowledge, the foundations of all liberty, was refracted, multiplied, and circulated; and instead of existing in masses, and in the single points of schools and universities, was rendered the common atmosphere in which we all live and breathe. It was from the press that originated, what is, in fact, the main distinction of the ancient and modern world, public opinion. A single question will be sufficient to put the importance of this subject in the strongest point of view. In the present state of knowledge and manners, is it possible that a Nero or Tiberius would be suffered to live or reign.—1st ed., pp. 39, 40.

Judging from this passage, who would not conceive it to be the doctrine of English lawyers, that mankind are indebted for all that is of greatest value, to censure of existing institutions: such censure as tends to produce the most radical changes, both in church and state, and even the dethronement and destruction of a bad sovereign?

Now mark the language of the same writer, only a few pages afterwards.

> In *every society,* therefore, the liberty of the press may justly be restricted within those limits which are necessary to maintain the establishment, and are necessary to maintain its exercise.—p. 45.

"Every society" admits of no exception. It includes the worst governed, as well as the best. According to Mr. Holt, therefore, in this passage, all governments, no matter how bad, should be maintained. They are establishments, and that alone is a sufficient recommendation. It is to a free press, indeed, that we owe "a church reformed from the errors of superstition, and a system of liberty equally remote from feudal anarchy and monarchical despotism;" but as these were obtained by overthrowing a former system, and as "the limits necessary to maintain the establishment" are by no means to be passed, the writings which led to the Revolution ought to have been suppressed, and that great event, with all its glorious consequences, ought never to have been suffered to take place.

The difference, therefore, between the doctrine of rulers in England, and that of rulers elsewhere, exists only in name; and is not indicative of any difference in their real sentiments, but only in their power of giving expression to them without danger.

If there be any truth in the great principles of human nature, or any validity in the reasoning, upon which the British constitution is founded, there is no ruler who would not, if he could, suppress all censure of himself, of his measures, or of any of the arrangements which contribute to his authority. The British constitution supposes, that rulers always wish to abuse their power, and, of course, wish to remove every check which has a tendency to prevent them from abusing their power. But the great check to abuses of all sorts, is a free press. It is of the utmost importance, therefore, to observe, that all rulers have the strongest possible interest in destroying the freedom of the press: that they are under an absolute necessity of hating it; and that although they may not, at any one moment, have a fixed and regular plan for effecting its destruction, they are obstinately averse to any, even the most trifling, extension of it; and are eager to seize every opportunity for restraining it within the narrowest practicable limits.

The necessity for veiling this disposition by the tricks of language, has taught our rulers to devise a number of artful phrases, by the help of which they contrive, in the same breath, to give and take away the right of free discussion, and which, as often as they have occasion for the punishment of an obnoxious writer, serve them to beg the question in favour of their object. A trick of this kind, which has done them much good service, is the well-known profession, that they are friends to the *liberty* of the press, but enemies to its *licentiousness*.

Let us examine what this means. The liberty of the press, we are told, is good; that is, as we suppose, discussion, if not in all cases, at any rate in some cases, ought to be free. But the licentiousness of the press, it seems, is an evil; which we must presume to mean, that there are certain other cases in which discussion ought not to be free: but what cases? Of this we are not informed; for the word licentiousness, far from marking the distinction, is merely a vague epithet of blame. Their meaning, therefore, must be, that they are to judge what is the liberty of the press, and what is licentiousness. But this is to have the whole power of choosing opinions for the people. Allow them to decide what is, or is not licentiousness, and every thing will be licentiousness which implies censure of themselves, which involves any doctrine hostile to the indefinite increase and perpetual duration of their power. With them, indeed, to use the language of Mr. Mence, "the liberty of the press is a liberty of flattering, fawning, trifling, prosing, but not of writing freely, or fairly, or usefully, or in a way to engage attention, or have a chance of exciting interest, upon men or manners, or upon political, or legal, or religious, or moral subjects."—i. 206.

It now remains to exhibit the actual state of the law of this country, with respect to the liberty of the press.

It is proper here to take notice of a very elaborate attempt made by Mr. Mence, to prove that the law really is not so unfavourable to free discussion as is commonly supposed.

The whole of the law by which the offence of libel is created, exists only in the state of common or unwritten law, of precedent, or custom. But this circumstance is so far from being peculiar to libel, that more than one half of the law of England exists in no other shape.

Mr. Mence alleges, and endeavours to prove—perhaps (for we shall not enter into so unimportant an inquiry) he has succeeded in proving, that the precedents on which the law of libel is founded, are not older than the star-chamber (printing itself, indeed, was not older); and from this he infers, that they are not, to use a legal phrase, *good law;* that there is, therefore, no law of libel, and that the punishments

which have been inflicted upon alleged libellers are illegal.
Mr. Mence, however, is not the interpreter of the law. It belongs to the judges, and to them alone, to say what is, and
what is not law. It is true, that the instances of omission are
far more numerous than the instances of execution, and in the
eye of reason, are equally entitled to be considered as precedents. It is true, that the judge hears a case, or refuses to hear
it, as he pleases, and, therefore, makes the law, *toties quoties*,
under the guise of declaring it. Nothing, indeed, can be
more shocking, more grossly inconsistent with all ideas of
good law, or good judicature, than this; but it is an evil inseparable from a system of common law, and if the law of
libel be not, technically speaking, good law, we can scarcely
be said to have any law at all, since even statutes are for the
most part built upon the common law, and taking the offence
for granted, confine themselves to regulating the punishment.

It is of little importance in itself, what the law is, if the
practice be bad: but it is of the greatest importance that the
public should not be made to believe that the law, if it were
executed, would afford a security, when in reality it would
afford no security at all; and it is because Mr. Mence has
taken, as we conceive, so erroneous a view of this question,
that we think it necessary to caution our readers against being
misled by an author, from whom, in other respects, they may
derive so much information.

Our own view of the state of the law will be collected,
partly from Mr. Holt's work, which is a digest of the cases,
and which, as we have already observed, carries with it all
the weight of lord Ellenborough's authority, partly from the
dicta of judges themselves.

The object being to ascertain, what meaning the English
law attaches to the term libel, it is natural to begin by asking,
what definition of libel it affords? To which we answer,
none: nothing which deserves the name of a definition ever
having been adduced.

Mr. Holt says, "A libel is a malicious defamation, expressed either in printing or writing, or by signs, pictures,

&c., tending either to blacken the memory of one who is dead, with an intent to provoke the living, or the reputation of one who is alive, and thereby exposing him to public hatred, contempt and ridicule."—p. 50.

What can be more absurd than to put forth such a definition as this, with great parade too of exactness, and fortified by references to no less than six legal authorities; and in the very next sentence, enumerating the species of libel, to talk of libels against *religion,* against *morality,* against *the constitution.* Mr. Holt's definition, by whomsoever devised, was obviously intended only for private libel; and if applied to any thing else, is unintelligible. It necessarily supposes a person libelled. Religion, morality, &c. are not persons, either dead or alive, but abstract terms. Considered only as a definition of private libel, it is abundantly mischievous, since it informs us, that to give publicity to vice, in other words, to take the only effectual security against its overspreading the earth, is, according to English law, a crime. And this doctrine, Mr. Holt, in another place, does not scruple openly to avow.

This is, at any rate, an attempt to define. In most law books, if we look for a definition of libel, we find nothing but a fiction. Libel is punishable, we are there told, because it tends to provoke a breach of the peace. The person libelled, may, out of resentment, commit the crime of assault against his accuser: it is fit, therefore, that the law should extend its protecting shield over the libeller, and save him from the chance of a broken head, by inflicting upon him a year's imprisonment. A tweak by the nose, according to this doctrine, should be more criminal than any libel, for it is certainly far more likely to provoke the species of retaliation alluded to. Miserable as this fiction is, it has served as a foundation to lawyers for building up the excellent law maxim, "the greater the truth, the greater the libel." A bad man, it is alleged, is more easily provoked than a good man! and a true accusation being usually more cutting than a false one, exposes the accuser to a greater hazard of being knocked down!

"One might almost as reasonably contend," says Mr.

Mence, "that it ought to be criminal in point of law for any person to carry money about him, lest it should tempt some scoundrel to pick his pocket or knock his brains out. The punishment in such a case, as the law now stands, would fall upon the thief, instead of the tempter. And the peace would be at least as well secured, and the interests of morality much better consulted, in cases of alleged libel, by punishing not the man who exposes vice and holds it up to deserved infamy; but the man whose vicious conduct is exposed, and who to his crimes has added the farther crime of braving the disgrace, and committing violence upon the person who may justly and meritoriously have exposed him."—i. 136.

The reader may be curious to learn for what purpose this ludicrous fiction was invented. The purpose was, to render libel a penal offence, instead of being merely a civil injury. Had it been classed among private offences, under the head of injuries to reputation, it would have been necessary to prove, in the first place, that an injury had really been sustained; and then the damages awarded would not have exceeded a fair compensation for the actual injury which had been proved. To make it a public offence, it was erected into a sort of virtual breach of the peace, which, again, by another equally contemptible fiction, is the king's peace; and thus, a libel against an individual became an offence against the king. Englishmen, who have been accustomed to hear, and to believe, that the law is the perfection of human reason, will be astonished to learn, that there is scarcely one, even of its good principles, which has any thing better than such fictions as the above for its basis. *In fictione juris semper æquitas*, say the lawyers. It is an assertion which they would not venture to put forth, were not the apathy of the public a sufficient security for its being believed without inquiry. Yet here is, at any rate, one instance, (and every one who has examined the law without a resolution to find every thing as it should be, can supply many more), in which such fictions have been devised for the most mischievous of all purposes.

This technical definition answered to admiration, so long as there were no libels but against individuals, all the rest being heresy or treason; but when times altered, and it was no longer practicable to hang, draw, and quarter men for libel, judges were put to their shifts for a definition which should give them power really unlimited, without the appearance. The late lord Ellenborough, who, from his greater boldness of character, was in the habit of giving utterance to the pernicious doctrine with less of restraint and disguise than is usual, once said from the bench, that a libel was *any thing which hurts the feelings of any body.* This was acknowledging more than was quite safe. It was admitting, that, according to English law, as administered by English judges, it is a crime to impute either error or criminality to public functionaries or to individuals; since to impute even error to any one, if it does not in all cases actually hurt his feelings, has, at least, always a tendency to do so.

The words of an indictment for public libel, which, in the absence of a definition, are, it must be presumed, intended to give some indication of the meaning and import of the charge, are "tending to bring our Lord the King and his administration," or "the constitution and government of these realms," or "the two Houses of Parliament," or "the administration of justice, the trial by jury," &c. "into *great and public hatred and contempt.*"

Lord Ellenborough's *dictum* itself is not better adapted to bear out the judge in the most mischievous exertion of power, than this. It is criminal to bring rulers into "hatred and contempt." But hatred is the legitimate consequence of guilt; contempt the legitimate consequence of folly. To impute either guilt or folly, either intentional or unintentional error, to rulers, is, therefore, by English law, a crime.

The attempts at definition, bad as they are, have only been exceptions: the general rule has been, to maintain, that libel, though it ought to be punished, cannot, and ought not to be defined. The conspiracy, in truth, have a good reason for leaving the offence of libel undefined: for they would not dare to include in a definition all that the support of the conspiracy requires to be included. They would not dare to assume, by a specific law, all the power which they hope to enjoy by usurpation. Were they to make a definition which included all that they wish to be included, common feeling would be shocked; neither they nor other men would bear to look at it. Nothing, however, can be more gross than the inconsistency into which this necessarily drives them. They insist that libel cannot be defined, yet they say that twelve unlettered men are to judge what is libel and what is not. How can any man know what is included in a general rule, if he knows not what that rule is?

On the subject of libels against the constitution, the following is the language of Mr. Holt:

If the law protects the subject in his rights, and punishes every invasion of them, much more does it protect that system from which all these rights proceed, and by which alone they can be maintained. The government and constitution being the common inheritance, every attack made upon them, which affects their permanence and security, is in a degree an attack upon every individual in the state, and concerns the rights of all. If it be the highest crime known to our laws, to subvert by force that constitution and polity which the wisdom and valour of our ancestors have erected and confirmed, it is certainly a crime, though of inferior magnitude, yet of great enormity, to endeavour to despoil it of its best support, the veneration, esteem, and affection of the people. It is, therefore, a maxim of the law of England, flowing by natural consequence and easy deduction from the great principle of self-defence, to consider as libels and misdemeanours every species of attack by speaking or writing, the object of which is *wantonly to defame,* or *indecorously to calumniate,* that economy, order, and constitution of things, which make up the general system of the law and government of the country.—p. 74.

Considering the parade of logic, which characterizes Mr. Holt's book, it is not a little remarkable that, on the most important point of all, he should be detected in using language so utterly destitute of any definite or precise meaning. Such vagueness can have but one object; namely, to hide the absolute power which the words that he uses are intended to confer upon the judge.

In the first place, he is pleased to represent the constitution as a person, and talks of *defaming* the constitution, *cal-*

umniating the constitution, as if an abstract term could be defamed or calumniated. Then it is *wantonly* to defame, and *indecorously* to calumniate. Whether any thing be added to, or taken from the sense by these epithets, we profess ourselves unable to understand.

What is the constitution? merely the aggregate of the securities for good government, which are provided by the existing law, whatever those securities may be, more or less complete. This must be the meaning of the word, constitution, if it has any: and if by a sort of metaphor we speak of the constitution as being calumniated, we can only mean, that these securities are represented as insufficient for the prevention of mis-government; that the constitution is represented as not attaining its end.

Consider what is implied, when it is said, that the securities for good government which, being taken collectively, we call the constitution, are inadequate to their end. It is implied, that, to a certain extent at least, if not altogether, we are as if we had no constitution; and that rulers have the power to tyrannize over us with impunity. If this be true, it will not be openly asserted that, to make it known would not be highly meritorious. The supposition, therefore, must be, that it is not true. This cannot be proved, without suffering those who deny it to be heard. It is, therefore, taken for granted without proof.

It being, therefore, according to this doctrine, allowable for English rulers to take for granted, without proof, that their own form of government is the best possible, it must be equally allowable for all other rulers to make the same assumption in favour of theirs. It will not, however, be contended, that all forms of government are the best. The doctrine, therefore, of the law of England, as expounded by Mr. Holt, is, that any rulers, in any country, may justly assume that the most detestable of all governments is the best, and upon that assumption may with perfect propriety inflict punishment to any extent upon all who presume to call in question its excellence.

Higher authorities than Mr. Holt have propounded the

same doctrine. Lord Camden says [Entick *v.* Carrington, 2 Wils. 275, apud Holt, p. 75],

"All governments must set their faces against libels, and whenever they come before a court and a jury, they will set their faces against them. And if juries do not prevent them, they may prove fatal to liberty, destroy government, and introduce anarchy; but tyranny is better than anarchy, and the worst government better than none at all."

It is here pretty distinctly intimated, that the worst government is justified in punishing all who hold it up to that detestation which it deserves; and the premises are equally edifying with the conclusion: if a tyrannical government be subverted, it is possible that anarchy may ensue; and anarchy, in the opinion of Lord Camden and of Mr. Holt, is a greater evil than the worst possible government. Adam Smith, indeed, thought differently; in the opinion of that great philosopher and practical judge of human nature, despotism is "more destructive of leisure and security, than anarchy itself." His lordship is welcome, however, as far as we are concerned, to whatever advantage he can derive from this assumption. But we submit that, if the worst possible government may be succeeded by anarchy, it may also be succeeded by a good government; and how must his mind be constituted who, if it were necessary, would fear to risk a few years, even of anarchy, for such a possibility!

In this investigation we have purposely avoided making the supposition, that the British constitution really is not the best possible. It is obvious, however, how much, if it be not, the strength of the argument is increased.

If we were as firmly convinced that the British constitution is, as we are convinced that it is not, the best possible government, we should be willing to expose even such a government to a very considerable degree of risk, rather than support it by means, which if they may be used for the preservation of the best government, may be equally used to perpetuate all the atrocities of the worst. But if the constitution be really imperfect—and who shall say that it is otherwise, if gainsayers are not suffered to be heard? then how greatly is the atrocity aggravated! and what are we to think of those who wickedly endeavour to prop up a bad cause, by means which even the best ought to reject with horror!

Mr. Holt seems to have been in some degree aware, that the mischievous purpose of the law would shew itself even through the vague and evasive language in which he has clothed it. After telling us that the judges have the power to punish every thing which they may pronounce intended to "despoil the constitution of its best support, the veneration, esteem, and affection of the people," he has thought it expedient to say something with a view to make it appear that they *have not* this power.

The constitution of this country, which is nothing but perfect reason, acknowledges in every man a right to set forth a general or individual hardship, and to suggest error, even in the highest branch of the magistracy. The constitution, indeed, is too wise not to acknowledge that the best interest of the state, as of human society at large, is truth. It opens, therefore, a ready ear to honest and useful truth of all kinds; and as it receives this truth from human beings, and therefore can only expect it as mingled up and adulterated with human passions, it will often pardon and overlook a natural warmth, for the sake of the truth which it produces. This is the character of the constitution with respect to public libels in good times. But every right has its limits. The right is given by the constitution, in so far as it is necessary and salutary, for the purposes of reminding kings of their duty, and parliaments of their trusts; the right stops at that point where its exercise would endanger the permanence and due weight of government; that is, where it serves no other purpose than to revive the original anarchy and to spread disaffection and tumult through the state.—p. 76.

It is not easy to enumerate all the gratuitous assumptions, all the shifts and evasions, which this one passage contains.

In the first place, it is assumed, that to "endanger the permanence of government" (such are the words of Mr. Holt) can have no object but to "revive the original anarchy:" which is precisely the assumption by which all bad rulers, from time immemorial, have begged the question in favour of themselves.

In the next place, we are informed that the right of unfavourable representation is allowed, so far as is necessary to "remind kings of their duty, and parliaments of their trusts;" but not to such a degree as to "spread disaffection through the state." So said the Mogul emperor: his subjects might state their grievances for his information, and if he thought fit, he would redress them; with this reservation, however, that if he should happen to take offence at their representations, he might cut off their heads upon the spot.

But, thirdly, it seems, even this limited right of unfavourable representation is allowed only in good times; the question, what are and are not good times, being of course left to be decided by the government itself. It is not difficult to see what, by such a judge, would be pronounced to be good times. So long as the people were perfectly quiet, and any breath of censure which might be heard boded no danger to profitable abuses, that censure might be tolerated, simply because there would be no motive for its suppression. But as soon as a feeling began to be excited, that there was something wrong, something calling for reformation; as soon as there began to be a chance, that unfavourable representations, if they continued, might at length have the effect of forcing upon rulers some degree of amendment; then would be the time for declaring that the "permanence and due weight of government" were endangered: then would be the time for suspending the habeas corpus act, and extending, like Mr. Pitt, the strong arm of power, to crush every writer who presumed to insinuate, that all was not for the best.

One admission, however (we shall see how far it is sincere), is made in the above passage; that the constitution does permit censure, if not at all times, and on all subjects, yet at some times, and on some subjects. Now mark the language of Mr. Holt, a few pages afterwards:

If [a writer] forgetting the wholesome respect which is due to authority and to the maintenance of *every system*, proposes to reform the evils of the state by *lessening the reverence of the laws*; the law, under such circumstances, considers him as abusing to the purposes of anarchy, what it has given him for the purposes of defence.—p. 103.

It is not to the doctrine, that not only a good system, but every system ought to be maintained, that we would at present direct the attention of our readers. It is to the declaration, that nothing must be done tending to lessen the reverence for the laws: that to whatever degree a law may be bad, its badness shall not be suffered to be exposed, nor any representation to be made which shall convince the people of the necessity for its repeal. What, then, is to be said of the assertions that "the constitution acknowledges the best interest of the state to be truth"; that it "opens a ready ear to honest and useful truth of all kinds?" What, but that they are cant, disgusting from its hypocrisy, as mischievous as false, and put forth solely to deceive the people into a belief that the constitution and the law are much better than they really are?

From libels on the constitution, Mr. Holt passes to libels on the king and his government, and to this subject we shall follow him, promising to the reader, that, after all that we have already said, we shall not detain him long.

From Mr. Holt's general view of the law on this subject, one passage has been already extracted. We now give it entire.

Every Englishman has a clear right to discuss public affairs freely, inasmuch as, from the renewable nature of the popular part of our constitution, and the privilege of choosing his representatives, he has a particular, as well as a general interest in them. He has a right to point out error and abuse in the conduct of the affairs of state, and freely and temperately to canvass every question connected with the public policy of the country. But, if instead of the sober and honest discussion of a man prudent and attentive to his own interests, his purpose is, to misrepresent, and find a handle for faction; if, instead of the respectful language of complaint and decorous remonstrance, he assumes a tone and a deportment which can belong to no individual in civil society; if, forgetting the wholesome respect which is due to authority, and to the maintenance of every system, he proposes to reform the evils of the state by lessening the reverence

of the laws; if he indiscriminately assigns bad motives to imagined errors and abuses; if, in short, he uses the liberty of the
press to cloak a malicious intention, to the end of injuring
private feeling, and disturbing the peace, economy, and order of
the state; the law, under such circumstances, considers him as
abusing to the purposes of anarchy what it has given him for
the purposes of defence.—pp. 102, 103.

For the exposure of this doctrine, a few words are sufficient.

In the first place, the distinction between the censure
which is permitted, and the censure which is prohibited,
turns out to be, not any thing in the censure itself, but something in the intention. By what evidence is the intention to
be ascertained? By the greater severity of the censure? No:
for it surely does not follow, that a man must necessarily intend to misrepresent because he censures severely; unless it is
contended that governments can never act in such a manner
as to merit severe censure.

To obtain reform, you must point out defects. By pointing out defects, you bring discredit on the government. By
pointing out defects and seeking remedies, you shew your
malice. Yes; the same sort of malice which a man shews towards himself by going to a physician to know the defects of
his constitution, and how to remedy them.

Some parts of Mr. Holt's language, however, seem to insinuate, what he himself in other places denies, that censure
may be freely applied, provided it be without assigning bad
motives. "The law," says he, "in this respect, follows in the
line of our duty. Invective, and the assignment of bad motives, can evidently answer no good purpose. No man assuredly can justify such contumely, even towards a private individual, and society at least should have dignity enough to
communicate something of its sacredness to its officers."—
p. 103.

What is meant by the dignity of society, and communi-
cating sacredness to its officers, we do not pretend to understand. What Mr. Holt, or the judges, would consider as bad
motives, we do not know. Perhaps, by bad motives he means

criminality, as distinguished from innocent error; and, in that case, we utterly deny the assertion, that no good purpose is to be answered by exposing it. Is it of no importance that the public should know the character of those in whose hands the disposal of their whole happiness is placed? Apply this doctrine to the crimes of individuals: would Mr. Holt assert that it can answer no good purpose to distinguish between wilful murder and accidental homicide?

This part of the law of libel, as expounded by the judges, and by Mr. Holt, is, like all other parts of it, purposely left in such a state of vagueness, as to place every public writer absolutely at the mercy of the judge.

"Every thing," says Mr. Holt, "is a libel, the purpose of which is, to misrepresent and find a handle for faction." But what is faction? Every man opposing ministers. What is misrepresentation? Falsehood. Who is to judge what is falsehood? The government: and the government, therefore, is to judge in its own cause; the government is to decide upon the truth or falsehood of a charge of error or crime against itself, and if it pronounces the charge to be false, it is to have the power of inflicting punishment, to any extent, upon the accuser!

It may be thought, perhaps, that Mr. Holt has distorted the law. To prove that he has not, we shall next quote some of the *dicta* of judges; than which nothing can be more explicit, as to the illegality of all censure upon the government.

LORD HOLT. They say that nothing is a libel but what reflects on some particular person. But this is a very strange doctrine, to say that it is not a libel reflecting on the government; endeavouring to possess the people that the government is maladministered by corrupt persons that are employed in such stations, either in the navy or army. To say that corrupt officers are appointed to administer affairs is certainly a reflection on the government. If men should not be called to account for possessing the people with an ill opinion of the government, no government can subsist.—Holt's Rep. 424, and State Trials, v. 527, apud Holt, p. 108.

According to this judge, nothing is to be permitted which tends to possess the people with an ill opinion of the

government; that all censure has this for its object, it is unnecessary to remark. All censure, therefore, is prohibited.

LORD CHIEF JUSTICE RAYMOND. Even a private man's character is not to be scandalized, either directly or indirectly; because
there are remedies appointed by law, in case he has injured any
person, without maliciously scandalizing him in his character.
And much less is a magistrate, minister of state, or other public
person's character to be stained, either directly or indirectly.
And the law reckons it a greater offence when the libel is pointed
at persons in a public capacity, as it is a reproach to the government to have corrupt magistrates, &c. substituted by his majesty,
and tends to sow sedition, and disturb the peace of the kingdom.—State Trials, vol. ix., apud Holt, p. 111.

From this we learn two things: first, that nothing is permitted to be said which can be construed as either directly or
by implication a reproach upon the government. And secondly, that all persons whatever, public of private, are guaranteed by the law against all exposure of any misconduct,
however glaring, and however hurtful to the community.

SIR PHILIP YORKE (afterwards Lord Chancellor Hardwicke).
He (the printer) is not to publish any thing reflecting on the
character, and reputation, and *administration* of his majesty, or
his ministers.—*Ibid.*

This doctrine, which is honoured with the peculiar approbation of Mr. Holt [p.111], is in substance the same
with that which we last quoted; with this addition, that it
contains a prohibition of strictures, even upon particular
measures. The *"administration* of his majesty, or his ministers,"* is not to be reflected upon.

On the trial of Woolston for a deistical work, the Court
said, "that the Christian religion is established in this kingdom; and therefore they would not allow any books to be
written which should tend to alter that establishment."—
Holt, p. 55. Christianity is to be made an instrument of persecution because it is an *establishment;* no books are to be
written which tend to alter *establishments.* What sort of a
doctrine is this?

LORD ELLENBOROUGH. It is no new doctrine, that if a publication be calculated to alienate the affections of the people, by

bringing the government into disesteem, whether the expedient
be by ridicule or obloquy, the person so conducting himself is
exposed to the inflictions of the law. It is a crime, it has ever
been considered as a crime, whether wrapt in one form or another.—Case of the King v. Cobbett, apud Holt, p. 119.

Having commented at so much length upon similar
doctrines, we are under no inducement to spend time upon
this.

The two trials of Mr. Wooler, in the year 1817, for seditious libels, teem with similar *dicta,* both of the attorney-general who prosecuted, and the judge who presided. We quote
a report which was printed *verbatim* from the manuscript of
an eminent short-hand writer. On that occasion, the then
attorney-general, the present Master of the Rolls, and, if
report say true, the future Lord Chancellor, delivered himself in the following terms:

To impute to the ministers under any form of government,
whether monarchy or any other established form of government,
wicked and corrupt motives of a pecuniary nature, or of another
and a worse sort, viz. that corruption arising from a desire to destroy the liberties and the constitution of their country, and to
take away from the subjects of the state all the happiness intended to be given by the laws and constitution, is, I take leave
boldly to state, without hazard of contradiction from any lawyer
in the country, a libel against the administration of the government: against the ministers employed in that administration.—
Trials of Mr. Wooler, pp. 5, 6.

It would appear at first sight, to an incautious reader,
that the improved spirit of the times had produced some effect, even upon his majesty's attorney-general. The doctrine,
that all censure of ministers is a libel, was no longer dared to
be openly avowed. What was avowed, however, is, that when
ministers aim at subverting the constitution, at subverting
that, which, according to the attorney-general, is our only
security against every horror which mankind have, at any
period of history, endured from bad rulers; that when ministers aim at taking away this security, and plunging us into
these evils, no one shall be allowed to say so. That this is an
unfair interpretation we deny. Is it, or is it not, possible, that

ministers should wish to be absolute? If it be answered, that
such a design is possible, but that in this instance it was unjustly ascribed to them, we answer, that if despotism has
been the aim of some ministers, it may be the aim of the present, and we are not to believe that to be impossible which all
experience proves to be certain, merely because the attorney-
general thinks proper to deny it. This modest claim, however, he did not scruple to prefer.

They (the ministers) would not make their will the general
law, but it is not that they dare not, but, I take leave to state.
because they cannot and will not.—*Trials,* p. 14.

Here we are asked to believe that ministers are not men
of ordinary virtue, nor even men of extraordinary virtue, but
something infinitely superior to all men who ever did, or can
exist. Not so says the law of England. That law always presumes that men act according to their interest. So far is this
principle carried, that, if a man has a single shilling to gain
by perjury, the law presumes that he will perjure himself for
that shilling, and refuses to hear his evidence. And here we
are called upon to take it for granted, not only that the
strongest conceivable temptations are weaker than the virtue
of ministers, but that a man ought to be severely punished for
insinuating the contrary. And why? Because such is the *ipse
dixit* of his majesty's attorney-general.

The present Chief Justice Abbott, on the same occasion,
was pleased to deliver, as has been recently the usual practice, two contrary doctrines; both of which, of course, by his
pronouncing them, became equally the law of the land.

It is open to every subject of the country to discuss the measures of government, provided he do it reasonably, fairly, and
impartially; but if, instead of reasoning and discussing upon
measures general or particular, a person chooses to issue forth
to the world slander and calumny against the government, or
against the authors of those measures, he then becomes amenable
to the law; if I may so say, where reasoning ends and slander and
calumny begins, there is the line by which a judgment is to be
formed.—p. 80.

This is one doctrine. Shortly afterwards he, in a passage too long to quote, propounds, and praises Lord Holt for propounding, the other. This is, that it is libellous in any way to reflect upon, that is, to censure, the government, and to bring into discredit, that is again to censure, the two Houses of Parliament.

We will take the least bad doctrine of the two: that which asserts that reasoning is permitted, but slander and calumny prohibited.

What is the use of reasoning? To draw conclusions, we suppose. All reasoning is, we apprehend, for the sake of the conclusion. Reasoning, it seems, is fit and proper: is it proper to draw conclusions? If they are favourable, yes; if unfavourable, no; because in that case, they are slander and calumny.

We might quote many cases posterior to this, but we shall stop here, partly because we have already exhibited enough, partly because the more recent trials have not been published in an equally authoritative form. It is not because there is nothing to say on the trial of Mr. Harvey for a libel on a living king, or on that of Mr. John Hunt, for a libel on a dead one, that we refrain from particularly alluding to what was said by lawyers and judges on those memorable occasions. It is because it was not in our power to quote any better authority than newspaper reports; and it is not enough for us that our assertions are true; we would have them exempt even from the possibility of suspicion.

We notice the head "Libels against the two Houses of Parliament," only to say that, according to Mr. Holt, the one thing to which all the influence of public opinion over those assemblies is owing, the publication of their proceedings—is illegal.

Under the head, "Libels against Courts of Justice," Mr. Holt says,

It is, undoubtedly, within the natural compass of the liberty of the press, to discuss, in a peaceable and temperate manner, the decisions and judgments of a court of justice; to suggest even error, and, provided it be done in the language, and with the views, of fair criticism, to censure what is apparently wrong, but with this limitation, that no false or dishonest motives be assigned to any party.—p. 144.

"Any public reflection," he continues, "on the ministration of justice, is unquestionably libellous."

Here are two assertions: the one, that the law permits censure; the other that it does not. We shall now see which of them is borne out by the *dicta* of judges. And we shall content ourselves with quoting the first case, related under this branch of his subject, by Mr. Holt himself.

> JUSTICE BULLER. Nothing can be of greater importance to the welfare of the public, than to put a stop to the animadversions and censures which are so frequently made upon courts of justice in this country. They can be of no service, and may be attended with the most mischievous consequences. Cases may happen, in which the judge and jury may be mistaken; when they are, the *law has afforded a remedy,* and the party injured is entitled to pursue every method which the law allows to correct the mistake. But, when a person has recourse either by writing like the present, by publications in print, or by any other means, to calumniate the proceedings of a court of justice, the obvious tendency of it is, to weaken the administration of justice, and, in consequence, to sap the very foundation of the constitution itself.—*Holt,* p. 145.

The law has afforded a remedy! Yes; the injured party, if he can afford it, may move the very judge by whom he was condemned, for a new trial; and if by miracle he should obtain it, he may go again to be tried before the same, or a brother judge, subject to the same sinister interest, and a jury under the same influence. We may be permitted to doubt, however, whether his chance of obtaining redress in this way be so considerable, as to render all other means superfluous; or whether he would have any chance whatever of obtaining it, if he had not the means of influencing public opinion in his favour.

The doctrine inculcated in the above *dictum,* that it is criminal to censure the proceedings of a court of judicature, and that whoever presumes to do so, is an enemy to the administration of justice, became unhappily, by the artifices of judges and the influence of rulers, deeply rooted in the minds of Englishmen. It was long the prevailing cry, that the administration of justice must be preserved free from suspicion, that no reflections must be permitted on the administration of justice: as if any mischief could be done to good judges, and good judicature, by the exposure of bad; as if it were not the greatest possible injury to a good judge, to render it impossible for the public to distinguish him from a bad one.

So far is the conduct of judges from requiring no *surveillance*, that there is scarcely any set of public functionaries, whose conduct requires it so much. Receiving their appointments from government; having, of necessity, from the course they must have adopted to obtain those appointments, all their leanings on the side of power; having, most of them, sons and nephews at the bar, for whom they are in the habit of looking to advancement and patronage at the hands of government; vested with power, which, if thrown into the scale of government, goes so far to render it despotic, that no sacrifice, on the part of rulers, can be too great, by which their co-operation can be obtained; it is not easy for any set of persons to be exposed to stronger temptations: and that those temptations have invariably proved too strong for the virtue even of the best judges, we have only to look at the records of libel cases, to be convinced.

We are perpetually boasting, [says the writer of the pamphlet which stands, together with Mr. Mence's work, at the head of this article]. We are perpetually boasting of the integrity of the judges. The judges on the bench are always, for the time being, the best of judges, the wisest and most upright of men, men who will neither do nor suffer injustice, men who will drive from their presence all who seek to pervert the law, or who take advantage of its defects to do injury to any one. Woe to him who shall dare to impeach the conduct of a living judge!

Yet how few are the dead judges whose conduct has not been impeached, and that, too, on good grounds. Were the judges really and truly independent of the executive power, and were the people at liberty, as they ought to be, but as, with the consent of the judges, they never will be, were they at liberty to canvass the conduct of a living judge to the necessary extent, so

that no judge could commit acts of folly or of injustice with impunity, very few such acts would be committed. Had this security
been taken, and this freedom been enjoyed in time past, the
evils which have been accumulating for ages would have had no
existence, the law would have been precise, clear, and sufficient,
and its administration very different indeed from that which we
are compelled to witness.—pp. 5, 6.

We regard it, then, as one of the most favourable signs
of the times, that this indiscriminating reverence for all the
instruments of judicature is giving way; that the proceedings
of judges begin to obtain their due share of examination,
and their misconduct of reprobation. And we take this opportunity of declaring our conviction, that this great and
salutary change has been in a great degree owing to the in-
defatigable exertions of the Morning Chronicle; a journal,
in which we have now been long accustomed to look for excellence of all sorts, but which has displayed, more particularly, in its strictures on the language and conduct of judicial
functionaries, a degree of true courage, of ability, and of morality in its highest and least common shape, which it has
been but too rarely our lot to witness in the periodical press
of this country.

The two following conclusions may now, we think, be
regarded as fully established:

That the law of England, as delivered by its authorized
interpreters, the judges, however earnestly the same judges
may occasionally disavow this doctrine, prohibits all unfavourable representation with respect to institutions, and with
respect to the government and its acts:

And, consequently, that if any freedom of discussion
is permitted to exist, it is only because it cannot be repressed;
the reason why it cannot be repressed, being, the dread of
public opinion.

And now, having established these two propositions, we
have only further to recommend them to the most serious
consideration of our readers.

The importance of free discussion, though frequently
dwelt upon by public writers, is seldom fully appreciated by

those who, not being themselves exposed to the danger of becoming its martyrs, erroneously consider themselves little affected by its violations. It concerns in fact equally every member of the community. It is equal in value to good government, because without it good government cannot exist. Once remove it, and not only are all existing abuses perpetuated, but all which, in the course of successive ages, it has overthrown, revive in a moment, along with that ignorance and imbecility, against which it is the only safeguard. Conceive the horrors of an oriental despotism—from this and worse we are protected only by the press. Carry next the imagination, not to any living example of prosperity and good government, but to the furthest limit of happiness which is compatible with human nature; and behold that which may in time be attained, if the restrictions under which the press still groans, merely for the security of the holders of mischievous power, be removed. Such are the blessings of a free press: and again and again be it repeated, there cannot be a free press without freedom of censure.

8

On the Emancipation of Roman Catholics

1826

The emancipation of Catholics was the first great victory in the long struggle to reorganize English society on a non-sectarian or non-creedal basis. Debated almost continuously in the 1820's, the rights of Catholics in England and Ireland to vote, to sit in Parliament, and to hold most government posts were finally secured in 1829. All other social disabilities on Catholics remained, however, and the act of 1829 included many features, such as banning the Jesuits by name, that were intended to protect Anglican England against the alleged political power of the Pope and his subordinates. It is not surprising that both Mills interested themselves in the question. In 1826, John wrote a long review of Catholic affairs in the short-lived radical annual, *Parliamentary History and Review*.

Mill's full analysis dealt with the major questions of Irish policy during the session of 1825. The section given here touches an issue still very alive in certain circles—the possible dangers to society of granting freedom to a group whose creed and organization are, in many respects, in deep conflict with the beliefs of the majority of citizens. Mill, however, is arguing for Catholic political freedom in a society that is still using religious belief as a test for citizenship. Catholic emancipation, four years after Mill's essay, was a major break in the legal conception of England as an Anglican society.

The only ground on which disabilities for religious opinions are justified at all, Mill claims, is that they constitute an actual danger to society. Although Mill demolishes the arguments that

Catholics as full citizens would endanger England, he leaves many important questions unanswered. What would his position be if they did constitute a danger? What does "danger to society" mean? Does it signify a threat to society's beliefs, and, if so, who speaks for society? Or does Mill imply, as the liberal tradition seems to hold, that only illegal *actions* would be subject to prosecution? If it is actions only, are speech or publications actions?

After more than a century of speculation on how to govern a society without inquiry into beliefs, we have not finished debating the questions that first became important in Mill's time.

An Article from *Parliamentary History and Review* of 1826

It is now our duty, conformably with the plan of this work, to pass judgment upon that portion of the proceedings of Parliament, a report of which is contained under the general head of *Ireland.*

These proceedings divide themselves into two parts; the one consisting of acts, the other of discussions: the one comprising what was *done,* by one or other House, as a body; the other, what was *said,* by individual members.

In our examination of what was *done,* it will be necessary to state our own opinions on the great public questions which occupied the attention of Parliament; to assign the grounds of those opinions, without which neither our opinions, nor those of any one, are worth regarding; and, lastly, to examine how far what *was* done, did or did not accord with what, in our estimation, ought to have been done.

In our examination of what was *said,* it will be our duty to scrutinize rigidly the arguments advanced on both sides of every question; to expose the shifts and pretences of a bad cause, and rid a good one of those bad arguments by which its real merits are often so materially obscured.

When a ground shall thus have been laid for passing a deliberate judgment upon the conduct, both of the legislature as a whole, and of every member of it individually;

something more will be necessary, to give to this part of our work all the utility of which it is susceptible.

Though many proceedings in Parliament are very important in their effects, few of them are so important in their effects, as they are in their causes. When an event, in addition to whatever good or evil may result immediately from itself, gives indication of the existence of a cause, from which an indefinite number of events of like tendency may be expected to flow; an estimate of its importance would be very imperfect, in which this indication should not be included.

The actions of public, like those of private, men, are governed by their interests. Their interests result directly from the institutions under which they live: if these be good, public men have no interest that is not in unison with the interest of the community: under bad institutions, their interest is frequently different from, and even opposite to, that of the community. Accordingly, the working of good or bad institutions may always be traced in the conduct of public men. If the institutions be good, their conduct is directed towards the advantage of the community, which in that case is also their own. If the institutions be bad, they pursue either their individual interest, or that of the class, or party, to which they belong; and the interest of the community is sacrificed.

In our comments, therefore, upon the proceedings in Parliament, we shall endeavour, in each instance, to bring to view, not only the events themselves, but their causes; viz.—the interests, generated by political institutions, and variously modified by those numerous and diversified circumstances which compose what is termed the spirit of the age.

In all these points of view, few events will demand a greater share of our attention, than the proceedings of the last session in regard to the Catholics of Ireland. The range of these proceedings took in, not one only, but several great questions: the Catholic Association; the Catholic Claims; and the two measures, called the wings. On each of these, rooted prejudices exist: the merits, therefore, of the different questions must be entered into, at least sufficiently to place every conclusion upon evidence sufficient to support it. The multiplicity of arguments, or what passed under that name, which were brought forward by all parties, render a proportional number of words necessary for making a due estimate of their validity: and finally, discussions, in which almost every prominent person in both Houses took a part, bore unusually strong marks of that general character which is impressed upon British statesmen by British institutions, and by the particular stage of intellectual and moral improvement at which the British nation has arrived.

The main question—that of Catholic emancipation—is, in our opinion, by no means a difficult one: and that any person capable of reasoning should feel a moment's doubt upon the subject, would surprise us, if we did not know that the strongest reasoning powers desert their possessor, when he is frightened. With all opponents of the Catholic Claims, in whose instance private interest is out of the question, the contest is simply, as it seems to us, between the great principles of justice on the one hand, and vague apprehensions on the other.

The public mind, in this country, is now so far advanced, that we may affirm, without hazard of being openly contradicted, even by those who would contradict us if they dared, that to subject any person to temporal inconvenience in any shape, on the ground of his religious opinions, is, *prima facie,* injustice and oppression: that it cannot be justified on any such ground as that his religion is bad, or unacceptable in the sight of God: nor by any thing but the certainty, or at least a preponderant probability, that some great temporal calamity will befall the rest of the community, unless averted by imposing restraints, disabilities, or penalties, upon persons of some particular faith. It will also be allowed, that if there be a danger, and if security against that danger require the imposition of disabilities on account of religious opinions; at least no disability should exist which does not, in some way or another, conduce to the end in view; that end being, security. We might join issue on both points, and maintain, not only the non-existence of danger, but the existence of disabilities, which, with whatever view they were *imposed,* can under no conceivable supposition (except that of extreme mental imbecility) be now *maintained,* with any such view as that of guarding against danger. But as we have not space to argue both these questions, we will confine ourselves to the first and most important.

Before we can be called upon to say, what the danger is *not,* we are entitled to expect that the opponents of Catholic emancipation will declare what it *is.* This, however, the greater number of them would find an embarrassing question: accordingly few of them have ever attempted to answer it. So vague and indefinite are those fears, on the ground of which they are willing to degrade five or six millions of their countrymen to the condition of an inferior caste, that if they were asked *what* great calamity it is which they apprehend from the concession of the Catholic claims, we doubt whether one in ten of them could tell. What they have in their minds is an indistinct feeling that the Catholics are dangerous persons: and this being assumed, it never occurs to them to consider, whether the Catholics *not emancipated* are not fully as dangerous as the Catholic *emancipated* would be.

We will concede one point, about which there has been much unprofitable discussion: that no confidence is to be reposed in the professions of the Catholics; that, whatever they may *now* say, or think, they would not be satisfied with equality, if they could obtain superiority. We know of no body of men who would. We have no doubt—it would be absurd to doubt—that the Catholic clergy would willingly possess themselves of the temporalities of the Protestant Church; that the Catholic nobility and gentry, in destroying Protestant ascendancy, would willingly supply its place by the ascendancy of their own creed; and that the great body of the Catholics would gladly embrace any opportunity, and any means, of making their own religion the dominant religion of the state. We will even allow that they would aim at the suppression of all other religions, by persecution: for this is no more than *has* been done by Catholics; and not by Catholics only, but, in every age and country, by that sect of religionists who have been uppermost, as far as they have dared.

That the Catholic aristocracy and clergy should desire a monopoly of political power, and of the wealth which that power affords, is no more than natural. The propensity to pursue their own interests, is not peculiar to *Catholic* human beings. To persecute, indeed, is not the interest of any sect: and this the majority of every sect would see, if they were wise. But the majority of every sect has hitherto been un- wise: accordingly no sect (with at most but one or two ex- ceptions) which has had the power to persecute, has ever failed to make use of it. The Romish Church persecuted, and does persecute, wherever it is strong enough: so did the Church of England, as long as it was strong enough; so did the Greek Church; so did the Presbyterian.

Now, therefore, when we have made every concession against the Catholics which the most unreasonable opponent could demand, we require of our antagonists, in our turn, that they will find some better ground for imposing disabilities upon millions of human beings, than the mischief which it is feared they would do, if it were but in their power.

If the Catholic disabilities were upheld as a measure of hostility, it would be fit to consider whether the Catholics were proper objects of hostility. But as they are professedly measures, not of hostility, but of security; the question, and the only question, is, not what the Catholics would be will- ing, but what they would be able, to do.

It is hard to guess what precise evil the fears of most of the Anti-Catholic orators point to. Some of them talk of a *divided allegiance.* "The Protestant" says Lord Liverpool, "gives an entire allegiance to his sovereign; the Catholic, a divided one. The service of the first is complete, of the last only qualified."

Now, if by the sovereign be meant the king, we should be sorry to think that every, or any, Protestant gave to his sovereign an unqualified allegiance. If allegiance mean obedience, and what else it can mean we know not, an entire allegiance is suitable only to a despotic government. What there is of meaning in this accusation, must be, that the Catholics acknowledge a foreigner as the head of their church, to whose interests, it is imagined, they are disposed to sacrifice the interests of their country. That there is a party of persons, professing the Catholic faith, who are so disposed, is true: that this party is anything but a small minority, is not true: for, if it were, what must be the situation, we do not say of Protestant states in which Catholics lie under no disqualifications, but of countries in which a vast majority of the people are Catholics, as France, Austria, and Spain? If the authority of the Pope be *there* paramount to that of the temporal sovereign; if the Pope be there suffered to depose kings; the danger apprehended is real: if not, it is imaginary.

The few Anti-Catholics who can tell what they are afraid of, seem chiefly to fear that the Catholics would attempt to subvert the established church; and this is the only tangible ground which they have assigned for their alarm.

In the first place, then, we think we may lay it down as an indisputable axiom, that the re-establishment of Catholicism, as the dominant religion in this country, is an event quite beyond the range of human probability. That six millions of persons, not having the powers of government in their hands, should either convert or conquer twelve millions, does not seem a very probable contingency. If probable at all, however, it is more probable before emancipation than after: since the power, whether of converting or of conquering, is the same, and the motive incomparably greater. They are six millions now, they would be but six millions then: their clergy would hardly be more eager to convert, nor their laity more able to rebel.

But though they might not be able, in opposition to the whole body of Protestants, to make their own religion the religion of the state; they might still, it is perhaps supposed, in concert with the sectarians, and with those other Protestants who are hostile to a church establishment, bring about the downfall of the existing church, and make all religions equal in the eye of the law.

This is to suppose, that, persons of all persuasions being included, a decided majority of the population of the two islands either is, or is likely to become, hostile to the continuance of the present church establishment. For, under any other supposition, it is difficult to see what danger there could be in throwing an additional weight into a scale, which would continue, notwithstanding, to be the lighter. Now, if this be true; without giving any opinion on the question, how far good government, good order, or religion itself, would suffer, if all religions *were* made equal in the eye of the law; we may be permitted to doubt whether the minority should be allowed to establish *their* religion, against the will of the majority; and whether the few might not, with as much justice, tax the many to build palaces for them as churches, and to pay their physicians and their lawyers as their clergy. But we do not wish to argue the question on a ground which would provoke so much opposition.

If the church were to be subverted, it would be in one of two ways: by means of the legislature, or in opposition to it; that is, by rebellion. If, then, after emancipation, it would be in the power of the Catholics, aided or not by the dissenters, to effect, in either of these two ways, the subversion of the church; what hinders them from doing it at this moment? Is it to be done by physical force? But if they are not strong enough now, emancipation would not make them so. Is it to be done by commanding a majority in Parliament? A few Catholic peers would take their seats in the Upper House; but in the Lower, beyond those whom they command at present, they would not be able to command a single vote. There would not be one Catholic elector—the Catholic aristocracy would not possess one borough—more than at present. They would indeed be enabled to return Catholics to Parliament; and, if nobody could be found but Catholics to assail the church, the disabilities would be some security: but it would be affectation in the most zealous churchman to pretend to doubt that the number of Protestants who are hostile to the church, is at least sufficient to fill the few seats which are at the disposal of the Catholic party. How happens it then that the church is not destroyed? The question is absurd. With almost every liberal Protestant on their side, the Catholics cannot command votes enough to carry their own emancipation; and it is supposed that with the great body of the Protestants against them they could command enough to overthrow the Protestant church!— But their influence in Parliament may increase. The Catholic electors may grow more numerous; more Catholics may become borough proprietors.—They may: and so they may, while their disabilities continue, and to the full as easily.

For the above reasons, and many others which we have not room to mention, we dismiss the idea of danger from Catholic emancipation. On the other hand, we are inclined to abate much from the current estimate of its advantages. An importance has been attached to it, both in respect of good and of evil, for which we are at a loss to find any adequate ground. We do not think that of itself it would do much for Ireland; the evils by which that country is afflicted, are not to be so summarily cured: and though Catholic emancipation might be a useful preparative to other and more important ameliorations, we do not think that it is by any means a necessary one.

Catholic emancipation would do nothing for the body of the people. Eligibility to office would be to them but a nominal privilege: excluded in *fact* by their situation in life, it is scarcely an additional evil to be excluded in *law* too. If they really feel as strongly on the subject of emancipation, as the friends of that measure wish it to be believed, —a belief which we find it difficult to entertain,—they must expect much more from it than the removal of disabilities; they must expect something which cannot be realized: to them, therefore, the effect of emancipation would be disappointment; and disappointment is seldom followed by tranquility.

It is idle to expect tranquility in Ireland so long as its

inhabitants are the poorest and the most oppressed people in Europe. That they are the poorest, appears from the testimony of all who know them: that they are the most oppressed, no unprejudiced person can doubt, who will read the evidence taken before the Committees of the two Houses in the sessions of 1824 and 1825. He will there find, that whatever the end of government in Ireland may *be*, it at any rate is *not* the protection of the weak against the strong: that government and law exist in that country solely for the benefit of the strong: that, while the Negro slave is at least protected against the encroachments of all masters except his own, the Irish peasant is at the mercy, not only of a whole series of landlords, from the proprietor of the soil down to the lowest middleman, but moreover of the tithe-owner and the tithe-farmer or proctor, to say nothing of vestries and grand juries: that against undue demands on the part of all these persons he has no remedy: that there is no law, no administration of justice for *him;* the superior courts being at all times inaccessible to him, and those of the country magistrates who do not take bribes, being for the most part leagued together to deny him redress; which is in general the less difficult, as the defects of the law are such, that he who would oppress under color of the law must be exceedingly unskilful if he cannot accomplish his object without incurring the penalties of the law.

All these causes of misery, and of that discontent which does, and, we hope, ever will, accompany all remediable evils, are perfectly independent of the Catholic disabilities, and would in no respect be affected by their removal. And why should we deem it impossible to apply remedies to these evils, leaving the Catholic disabilities as they are? That "purer administration of justice," which even the bishop of Chester admits to be necessary, would of itself suffice, and without it nothing will suffice, to tranquillize Ireland. It is not the power of the Protestant over the Catholic, which has made Ireland what she is: it is the power of the rich over the poor.

A superficial observer might perhaps infer, from the

active demonstrations of hostility between the two sects, that it is the Catholics who are oppressed as Catholics, not the poor as poor, and that the body of the people, if they were not oppressed as Catholics, would not be oppressed at all. But if, in removing the Catholic disabilities, the power of landlords over tenants, of the tithe-owner over the tithe-payer, and of magistrates over the great body of the people, were left untouched, we cannot perceive that the condition of the Irish peasantry would be in any respect altered for the better. There is no evidence that a Catholic landlord treats his tenants better than a Protestant landlord. Catholic emancipation would not affect the mode of collecting tithes; and the few Catholic magistrates that there are, have now an interest in protecting the poor against their brother magistrates, which, in the event of emancipation, it is possible they might not retain.

That the Protestant aristocracy, who are now in possession of a monopoly of political power and of its attendant profit, should be averse to sharing that power and profit with the Catholic aristocracy, is quite natural. It is quite natural also that the Catholic aristocracy should feel uneasy under this forced exclusion: and as the aristocracy are much better able to make their complaints heard, than the people are, it is also natural that their grievances should be more thought of, than those of the people; but we are not therefore to suppose them of more importance.

There still remains another question to be answered, before we proceed with our comment upon the debates. If the Catholic disabilities be not in reality the grand evil of Ireland, how happens it that, in the two Houses of Parliament, they are so often spoken of as if they were?

Questions of this sort are what, in the sequel of this work, we shall very frequently have occasion to put.

In reviewing the proceedings of Parliament, it may in general be remarked, that the great abuses almost always escape its notice. The composition of the Parliament affords a key to this, as it does to so many of its other peculiarities.

The truth is, that there is scarcely an individual in either

House whose interest it is that the great abuses should be reformed. The members of both Houses belong, almost all of them, to those classes for the benefit of which all great abuses exist; and not being accountable to, nor in any other way under the influence of, that much larger class, who suffer by the abuses, they have abundant motives to uphold, and no sufficient motive to redress them.

This interest being common to both parties in the two Houses of Parliament, the great abuses are, in Parliamentary discussions, by a sort of tacit consent kept out of view. The Opposition party, however, must have something to attack; or they could shew no ground for finding fault with the party in power. Nothing, therefore, remains for them to do, except to fall might and main upon the small abuses, and do every thing in their power to cause them to be taken for great ones.

To apply these principles to the case now in hand. Here is a country, the most miserable, and at the same time the most turbulent, of all countries pretending to civilization; and that, under a set of institutions, which all—that is, all who derive either money or power from them—unite in designating as the best institutions that wisdom ever devised for the government of mankind. Here then is an anomaly to be explained; a cause must be found for it, and that too without imputing blame to these admirable institutions. The Catholic Question, appearing well adapted to the purpose, is eagerly laid hold of by the Whigs, and a part of the Tories, and exalted into a sovereign remedy for the ills of Ireland. It answers the purposes of the Whigs, by affording a handle for attacking the ministry, who, having such a *panacea* in their hands, neglect to apply it. It serves the purposes of both sections of the Tories, by diverting the public attention, from much more important grievances. All parties being thus interested in making as much noise about this question as possible, it is not wonderful that so much noise has been made.

9

On the Protection of Minorities

1828

In this newspaper article, Mill skillfully reverses a Tory attack on some tradesmen for obstructing a proposed public improvement in London.

The Tories claimed that the members of Parliament, even though they were nominated for the most part by a few hundred families and elected by a small minority of the population, did not represent particular interests, but deliberated with the well-being of all England in mind. All Englishmen were thus "virtually represented." In 1828, Mill believed, to the contrary, that the only way to protect everyone's interest was to give all interests a vote. Later, when "everyone" did receive the vote but a majority decided for "everyone," his argument would have to be viewed in a different light.

AN ARTICLE FROM *The British Traveler*
OF SEPTEMBER 29, 1828

The approaches to the New London Bridge are every day becoming the subject of increased discussion. Perhaps if in deciding upon this point, nothing were requisite to be taken into the account except public convenience, it would have been disposed of in a more summary manner. But it seems that in this, as in so many other projects of improvement, a consideration has intruded itself, which, under our national institutions, and with our national modes of thinking, is apt to be esteemed far more important than public convenience, and this is, the convenience of particular individuals.

Nobody, in this or in any other country, is so impudent as to say, that his individual interest ought to be attended to first, and the public interest afterwards. But instead of one man, put the case that there are two or three score, much more if there be two or three hundred, and what no one of them would have the face to claim for himself, every man among them will boldly demand for himself and company.

If nobody felt and acted in this manner, except the grocers and cheesemongers of Fish Street Hill, no doubt it would be very justly considered a flagrant enormity. If, however, these shopkeepers are only following the admired and applauded example of their betters, it might be expected that what is thought very proper and patriotic in those bet-ters, would hardly be stigmatized as unjust and selfish to *them*. We were therefore surprised to find an attempt made, in a recent number of a Tory paper, to hold up these respect-able persons to public disapprobation, because they, too, thought it proper to stand up for the interests of their "order."

But there is a distinction running through the whole frame of English society, which, when it is fully seized, explains no small quantity of what would otherwise appear altogether enigmatical in the workings of that society. Fielding describes Bridewell as "that house where the inferior sort of people may learn one good lesson, viz.—respect and deference to their superiors, since it must show them the wide distinction fortune intends between those persons who are to be corrected for their faults, and those who are not." The *New Times,* in its animadversions upon the Fish Street Hill shopkeepers, intends, no doubt, to read them a similar lesson; to put them in mind of the wide distinction which our institutions intend between those who are to have their interest preferred to the general interest, and those who are not.

There is no other country in the world, says the *New*

Times, in which the best avenues to such a structure as London Bridge would be rejected, for fear of affecting the paltry interests of a few shopkeepers. We hope not; and we hope, likewise, that there is no other country in the world in which the public would be taxed ten or twelve millions in the price of their bread, and exposed to incessant vicissitudes of glut and famine, for fear of affecting the paltry interests of a few landlords. We are sure that there is no other country in which a bill, such as the County Courts' Bill, for extending the benefits of an administration of justice to the largest portion of the people, to whom at present it may be said, with scarcely any exaggeration, to be altogether inaccessible, would be rejected year after year by the legislature on the avowed ground, that it would affect the paltry interests of Lord Ellenborough, and two or three other holders of law sinecures.

It was doubtless a great piece of presumption in the persons whom the *New Times* reprehends, to imagine that what might be proper and commendable in so exalted a personage as Lord Ellenborough, was allowable in persons who were no better than shopkeepers, and who lived in no other street than Fish Street Hill. If the proposed approaches had encroached upon a Nobleman's park, or had passed so much as within a quarter of a mile of his game preserves, it is probable that we should have heard another story about paltry interests. But it is a mistake, to suppose that cheesemongers can have vested rights. Cheesemongers are only virtually represented. Lords and Landlords not only are actually represented, but virtually represent the Cheesemongers themselves. They may, therefore, possess vested rights: if they possess any thing which they do not like to give up, it is a vested right: and having received this name, however little they may be entitled to it, or however imperatively the public interest may require the sacrifice of it, to demand it would be to infringe upon the sacred rights of property. All this, to the *New Times,* is gospel: but that journal is far too acute not to seize the distinction between

Fish Street Hill, and Grosvenor Square, and to perceive, that with lawgivers as well as other men, there is all the difference in the world between doing a dishonest thing for their own interest, and doing exactly the same thing for the interest of other people.

"Civilization—Signs of the Times"

1836

In the eight years that elapsed between the previous selection and the publication of this notable essay, Mill came increasingly under the influence of the Coleridgeans and the continental thinkers mentioned in the general introduction. Mrs. Taylor was taking greater interest in the problems of individualism and diversity, and Mill followed many of her suggestions. The French Revolution of 1830 and the Reform Bill of 1832 inspired much of Mill's writing, but the general range of his interests was greater than ever. In 1832 Mill published *On Genius,* in which he expressed his fears about future standards of intellectual excellence; his apprehensions were confirmed when he read *Democracy in America* in 1835.

Along with Tocqueville's great work, Mill's *Civilization—Signs of the Times* is one of the first successful modern attempts at a speculative sociology of democratic life. Unlike Plato and Aristotle, who drew influential and unflattering portraits of democracy, both Mill and Tocqueville believed that democratic life could be essentially benign—more humane, in fact, than any society and government the world had yet known. To help save democracy from degenerating into what Aristotle feared would be selfish rule by the impoverished majority or into what Plato thought would be rule by the lowest appetites in the mass of men, they relied on a force that liberal-democrats have often criticized—the materialism of modern democracy. This intense concentration on a high level of physical well-being, although the despair of those who would like to see a more spiritual, less crass society, acts as an efficient check on demagogues. The great wealth of modern democracies, if widely shared, can keep envy, the major democratic vice, from becoming too sharp and too programmatic. Democratic men are either too well off to rush to the barricades or not poor enough to risk what little they have on ideological adventures.

The material satisfactions of democratic industrial societies require cooperation and team work. Men must learn to get along with each other, to keep down prejudices and dislikes. In assessing equality of opportunity in America, Tocqueville had observed that in no other society did one find greater human possibilities and in no society greater frustration. Equal opportunity encourages the positive virtues of "live and let live" and blunts fanaticism. But democracy also arouses more appetites in more people than it can at first fulfill. Without the firmest alliance with technology and science, an egalitarian society would be either impossible to achieve or more aggressive in its vices than it usually is.

Throughout the nineteenth century, a persistent conservative attack on the masses was based on their ignorance and poverty. Conservatives often tended to look on democracy as the cry of the man who wanted to pick your pocket or cut your throat. Give the masses power, they feared, and rapacious appetite and unchained will would destroy all that the careful and cautious work of civilization had achieved. It was no mere chance that many conservatives were also believers in original sin. At the very beginnings of democratic culture, Mill foresaw the possibility of a different democratic fate. It is some refutation of the conservative or orthodox Christian's fears that, as Mill predicted, democratic man has settled so easily for so little.

If democracy's virtues are modest, so are its vices. Torpor, sloth, decreased energy and vigor, "let it ride," "don't rock the boat" are the usual democratic weaknesses. It is these that most concern Mill in *Civilization*.

Democracy's success in achieving equality of conditions could well be its undoing. It is not so much passion about favorite opinions that lies behind democratic arrogance, where it appears, as the smugness and unawareness of men content with their lot and constantly flattered by those who seek their favors or patronage. Such men can scarcely conceive of another kind of life being attractive or even possible. *Civilization* warns us less of the aroused and fully-armed, opinionated majority (he will come to this later in *On Liberty*) and more of the un-militant majority which saps vitality by enticing men to follow the mere shadows of the liberal virtues. Instead of real tolerance, decency, kindness, generosity, and open-mindedness, a debased "civilization" breeds the culture of mindless "togetherness," of the unaware "nice guy," of people who are "human" because they are not discriminating.

In the last section of *Civilization,* Mill indicates the role of education in preventing democratic society from dissipating the energy and inventiveness it was intended to release. Although many of his points have by now become familiar, his words still convey their freshness and pertinence. What is especially remarkable is that, unlike many later liberal critics of "mass society," Mill does not presume that every man can achieve intellectual autonomy. He asserts rather that those who can be independent should have the chance to become so, and that our national life, through their example and influence, should be capable of the heroic and difficult as well as the comfortable and easy.

AN ARTICLE FROM *The Westminster Review*
OF APRIL, 1836

The word "civilization," like many other terms of the philosophy of human nature, is a word of double meaning. It sometimes stands for *human improvement* in general, and sometimes for *certain kinds* of improvement in particular.

We are accustomed to call a country more civilized if we think it more improved; more eminent in the best characteristics of man and society; farther advanced in the road to perfection; happier, nobler, wiser. This is one sense of the word "civilization." But, in another sense, it stands for that kind of improvement only which distinguishes a wealthy and powerful nation from savages or barbarians. It is in this sense that we may speak of the vices or the miseries of civilization; and that the question has been seriously propounded, whether civilization is, on the whole, a good or an evil. Assuredly, we entertain no doubt on this point: we hold that civilization is a good; that it is the cause of much good, and not incompatible with any; but we think there is other good, much even of the highest good, which civilization in this sense does not provide for, and some which it has a tendency (though that tendency may be counteracted) to impede.

The inquiry into which these considerations would lead is calculated to throw light upon many of the characteristic features of our time. The present era is pre-eminently the era of civilization in the narrow sense,—whether we consider what has already been achieved, or the rapid advances making towards still greater achievements. We do not regard the age as either equally advanced or equally progressive in many of the other kinds of improvement. In some, it appears to us stationary; in some, even retrograde. Moreover, the irresistible consequences of a state of advancing civilization; the new position in which that advance has placed, and is every day more and more placing, mankind; the entire inapplicability of old rules to this new position; and the necessity, if we would either realize the benefits of the new state or preserve those of the old, that we should adopt many new rules, and new courses of action,—are topics which seem to require a more comprehensive examination than they have usually received.

We shall on the present occasion use the word "civilization" only in the restricted sense; not that in which it is synonymous with improvement, but that in which it is the direct converse or contrary of rudeness or barbarism. Whatever be the characteristics of what we call savage life, the contrary of these, or the qualities which society puts on as it throws off these, constitute civilization. Thus a savage tribe consists of a handful of individuals, wandering or thinly scattered over a vast tract of country: a dense population, therefore, dwelling in fixed habitations, and largely collected together in towns and villages, we term civilized. In savage life, there is no commerce, no manufactures, no agriculture, or next to none: a country rich in the fruits of agriculture, commerce, and manufactures, we call civilized. In savage communities, each person shifts for himself: except in war (and even then very imperfectly), we seldom see any joint operations carried on by the union of many; nor do savages, in general, find much pleasure in each other's society. Wherever, therefore, we find human beings acting together for common purposes in large bodies, and enjoying the pleasures of social intercourse, we term them civilized. In savage life, there is little or no law, or administration of justice; no systematic employment of the collective strength of society to protect individuals against injury from one another: every one trusts to his own strength or cunning; and, where that fails, he is generally without resource. We accordingly call a people civilized, where the arrangements of society for protecting the persons and property of its members are sufficiently perfect to maintain peace among them; i.e., to induce the bulk of the community to rely for their security mainly upon social arrangements, and renounce for the most part, and in ordinary circumstances, the vindication of their interests (whether in the way of aggression or of defence) by their individual strength or courage.

These ingredients of civilization are various; but consideration will satisfy us that they are not improperly classed together. History, and their own nature, alike show that they begin together, always co-exist, and accompany each other in their growth. Wherever there has arisen sufficient knowledge of the arts of life, and sufficient security of property and person, to render the progressive increase of wealth and population possible, the community becomes and continues progressive in all the elements which we have just enumerated. These elements exist in modern Europe, and especially in Great Britain, in a more eminent degree, and in a state of more rapid progression, than at any other place or time. We propose to consider some of the consequences which that high and progressive state of civilization has already produced, and of the further ones which it is hastening to produce.

The most remarkable of those consequences of advancing civilization, which the state of the world is now forcing upon the attention of thinking minds, is this,—that power passes more and more from individuals, and small knots of individuals, to masses; that the importance of the masses becomes constantly greater, that of individuals less.

The causes, evidences, and consequences of this law of human affairs well deserve attention.

There are two elements of importance and influence among mankind: the one is property; the other, powers and acquirements of mind. Both of these, in an early stage of civilization, are confined to a few persons. In the beginnings of society, the power of the masses does not exist, because property and intelligence have no existence beyond a very small portion of the community; and, even if they had, those who possessed the smaller portions would be, from their incapacity of co-operation, unable to cope with those who possessed the larger.

In the more backward countries of the present time, and in all Europe at no distant date, we see property entirely concentrated in a small number of hands; the remainder of the people being, with few exceptions, either the military retainers and dependants of the possessors of property, or serfs, stripped and tortured at pleasure by one master, and pillaged by a hundred. At no period could it be said that there was literally no middle class, but that class was extremely feeble, both in numbers and in power; while the laboring people, absorbed in manual toil, with difficulty earned, by the utmost excess of exertion, a more or less scanty and always precarious subsistence. The character of this state of society was the utmost excess of poverty and impotence in the masses;

the most enormous importance and uncontrollable power of
a small number of individuals, each of whom, within his
own sphere, knew neither law nor superior.

We must leave to history to unfold the gradual rise of
the trading and manufacturing classes, the gradual emancipation of the agricultural, the tumults and *bouleversements*
which accompanied these changes in their course, and the
extraordinary alterations in institutions, opinions, habits,
and the whole of social life, which they brought in their
train. We need only ask the reader to form a conception of
all that is implied in the words "growth of a middle class,"
and then to reflect on the immense increase of the numbers
and property of that class throughout Great Britain, France,
Germany, and other countries, in every successive generation,
and the novelty of a laboring class receiving such wages as are
now commonly earned by nearly the whole of the manufacturing, that is, of the most numerous, portion of the operative
classes of this country,—and ask himself, whether, from
causes so unheard of, unheard-of effects ought not to be expected to flow. It must at least be evident, that if, as civilization advances, property and intelligence become thus widely
diffused among the millions, it must also be an effect of civilization, that the portion of either of these which can belong to
an individual must have a tendency to become less and less
influential, and all results must more and more be decided
by the movements of masses, provided that the power of
combination among the masses keeps pace with the progress of their resources. And that it does so, who can doubt?
There is not a more accurate test of the progress of civilization than the progress of the power of co-operation.

Consider the savage: he has bodily strength, he has
courage, enterprise, and is often not without intelligence.
What makes all savage communities poor and feeble? The
same cause which prevented the lions and tigers from long
ago extirpating the race of men,—incapacity of co-operation.
It is only civilized beings who can combine. All combination
is compromised: it is the sacrifice of some portion of individual will for a common purpose. The savage cannot bear

to sacrifice, for any purpose, the satisfaction of his individual will. His social cannot even temporarily prevail over his selfish feelings, nor his impulses bend to his calculations. Look again at the slave: he is used, indeed, to make his will give way, but to the commands of a master, not to a superior purpose of his own. He is wanting in intelligence to form such a purpose: above all, he cannot frame to himself the conception of a fixed rule; nor, if he could, has he the capacity to adhere to it. He is habituated to control, but not to self-control: when a driver is not standing over him with a whip, he is found more incapable of withstanding any temptation, or restraining any inclination, than the savage himself.

We have taken extreme cases, that the fact we seek to illustrate might stand out more conspicuously. But the remark itself applies universally. As any people approach to the condition of savages or of slaves, so are they incapable of acting in concert. Consider even war, the most serious business of a barbarous people: see what a figure rude nations, or semi-civilized and enslaved nations, have made against civilized ones, from Marathon downwards! Why? Because discipline is more powerful than numbers, and discipline —that is, perfect co-operation—is an attribute of civilization. To come to our own times, the whole history of the Peninsular War bears witness to the incapacity of an imperfectly civilized people for co-operation. Amidst all the enthusiasm of the Spanish nation struggling against Napoléon, no one leader, military or political, could act in concert with another; no one would sacrifice one iota of his consequence, his authority, or his opinion, to the most obvious demands of the common cause: neither generals nor soldiers could observe the simplest rules of the military art. If there be an interest which one might expect to act forcibly upon the minds even of savages, it is the desire of simultaneously crushing a formidable neighbor whom none of them are strong enough to resist single-handed; yet none but civilized nations have ever been capable of forming an alliance. The native states of India have been conquered by the English, one by one; Turkey made peace with Russia in the very moment of her invasion by France; the nations of the world never could form a confederacy against the Romans, but were swallowed up in succession, some of them being always ready to aid in the subjugation of the rest. Enterprises requiring the voluntary co-operation of many persons independent of one another, in the hands of all but highly civilized nations, have always failed.

It is not difficult to see why this incapacity of organized combination characterizes savages, and disappears with the growth of civilization. Co-operation, like other difficult things, can be learnt only by practice; and, to be capable of it in great things, a people must be gradually trained to it in small. Now, the whole course of advancing civilization is a series of such training. The laborer in a rude state of society works singly; or, if several are brought to work together by the will of a master, they work side by side, but not in concert: one man digs his piece of ground; another digs a similar piece of ground close by him. In the situation of an ignorant laborer, tilling even his own field with his own hands, and associating with no one except his wife and his children, what is there that can teach him to co-operate? The division of employments; the accomplishment, by the combined labor of several, of tasks which could not be achieved by any number of persons singly,—is the great school of co-operation. What a lesson, for instance, is navigation, as soon as it passes out of its first simple stage!—the safety of all constantly depending upon the vigilant performance, by each, of the part peculiarly allotted to him in the common task. Military operations, when not wholly undisciplined, are a similar school; so are all the operations of commerce and manufactures which require the employment of many hands upon the same thing at the same time. By these operations, mankind learn the value of combination; they see how much and with what ease it accomplishes, which never could be accomplished without it; they learn a practical lesson of submitting themselves to guidance, and subduing themselves to act as interdependent parts of a complex whole. A people thus progressively trained to combination by the business of their lives become capable of carrying the same habits into new things. For it holds universally, that the one only mode of learning to do any thing is actually doing something of the same kind under easier circumstances. Habits of discipline, once acquired, qualify human beings to accomplish all other things for which discipline is needed. No longer either spurning control, or incapable of seeing its advantages, whenever any object presents itself which can be attained by co-operation, and which they see or believe to be beneficial, they are ripe for attaining it.

The characters, then, of a state of high civilization being the diffusion of property and intelligence, and the power of co-operation, the next thing to observe is the unexampled development which all these elements have assumed of late years.

The rapidity with which property has accumulated and is accumulating in the principal countries of Europe, but especially in this island, is obvious to every one. The capital of the industrious classes overflows into foreign countries, and into all kinds of wild speculations. The amount of capital annually exported from Great Britain alone, surpasses, probably, the whole wealth of the most flourishing commercial republics of antiquity. But this capital, collectively so vast, is mainly composed of small portions; very generally so small, that the owners cannot, without other means of livelihood, subsist on the profits of them. While such is the growth of property in the hands of the mass, the circumstances of the higher classes have undergone nothing like a corresponding improvement. Many large fortunes have, it is true, been accumulated; but many others have been wholly or partially dissipated: for the inheritors of immense fortunes, as a class, always live at least up to their incomes when at the highest; and the unavoidable vicissitudes of those incomes are always sinking them deeper and deeper into debt. A large proportion of the English landlords, as they themselves are constantly telling us, are so overwhelmed with mortgages, that they have ceased to be the real owners of the bulk of their estates. In other countries, the large properties have very generally been broken down; in France, by revolution, and the revolutionary law of inheritance; in Prussia, by successive edicts of that substantially democratic though formally absolute government.

With respect to knowledge and intelligence, it is the truism of the age, that the masses, both of the middle and even of the working classes, are treading upon the heels of their superiors.

If we now consider the progress made by those same masses in the capacity and habit of co-operation, we find it equally surprising. At what period were the operations of productive industry carried on upon any thing like their present scale? Were so many hands ever before employed at the same time, upon the same work, as now in all the principal departments of manufactures and commerce? To how enormous an extent is business now carried on by joint-stock companies!—in other words, by many small capitals thrown together to form one great one. The country is covered with associations. There are societies for political, societies for religious, societies for philanthropic purposes. But the greatest novelty of all is the spirit of combination which has grown up among the working classes. The present age has seen the commencement of benefit societies; and they now, as well as the more questionable Trades Unions, overspread the whole country. A more powerful, though not so ostensible, instrument of combination than any of these, has but lately become universally accessible,—the newspaper. The newspaper carries home the voice of the many to every individual among them: by the newspaper, each learns that others are feeling as he feels; and that, if he is ready, he will find them also prepared to act upon what they feel. The newspaper is the telegraph which carries the signal throughout the country, and the flag round which it rallies. Hundreds of newspapers speaking in the same voice at once, and the rapidity of communication afforded by improved means of locomotion, were what enabled the whole country to combine in that simultaneous energetic demonstration of determined will which carried the Reform Act. Both these facilities are on the increase, every one may see how rapidly; and they will enable the people on all decisive occasions to form a collective will, and render that collective will irresistible.

To meet this wonderful development of physical and mental power on the part of the masses, can it be said that there has been any corresponding quantity of intellectual power or moral energy unfolded among those individuals or classes who have enjoyed superior advantages? No one, we think, will affirm it. There is a great increase of humanity, a decline of bigotry, as well as of arrogance and the conceit of caste, among our conspicuous classes; but there is, to say the least, no increase of shining ability, and a very marked decrease of vigor and energy. With all the advantages of this age, its facilities for mental cultivation, the incitements and the rewards which it holds out to exalted talents, there can scarcely be pointed out in the European annals any stirring times which have brought so little that is distinguished, either morally or intellectually, to the surface.

That this, too, is no more than was to be expected from the tendencies of civilization, when no attempt is made to correct them, we shall have occasion to show presently. But, even if civilization did nothing to lower the eminences, it would produce an exactly similar effect by raising the plains. When the masses become powerful, an individual, or a small band of individuals, can accomplish nothing considerable except by influencing the masses; and to do this becomes daily more difficult, from the constantly increasing number of those who are vying with one another to attract the public attention. Our position, therefore, is established, that, by the natural growth of civilization, power passes from individuals to masses, and the weight and importance of an individual, as compared with the mass, sink into greater and greater insignificance.

The change which is thus in progress, and to a great extent consummated, is the greatest ever recorded in social affairs; the most complete, the most fruitful in consequences, and the most irrevocable. Whoever can meditate on it, and not see that so great a revolution vitiates all existing rules of government and policy, and renders all practice and all predictions grounded only on prior experience worthless, is wanting in the very first and most elementary principle of statesmanship in these times.

"Il faut," as M. de Tocqueville has said, "une science politique nouvelle à un monde tout nouveau." The whole face of society is reversed; all the natural elements of power have definitively changed places; and there are people who talk of standing up for ancient institutions, and the duty of sticking to the British Constitution settled in 1688! What is still more extraordinary, these are the people who accuse others of disregarding variety of circumstances, and imposing their abstract theories upon all states of society without discrimination.

We put it to those who call themselves conservatives, whether, when the chief power in society is passing into the hands of the masses, they really think it possible to prevent the masses from making that power predominant as well in the government as elsewhere. The triumph of democracy, or, in other words, of the government of public opinion, does not depend upon the opinion of any individual, or set of individuals, that it ought to triumph, but upon the natural laws of the progress of wealth, upon the diffusion of reading, and the increase of the facilities of human intercourse. If Lord Kenyon or the Duke of Newcastle could stop these, they might accomplish something. There is no danger of the prevalence of democracy in Syria or Timbuctoo. But he must be a poor politician who does not know, that whatever is the growing power in society will force its way into the government by fair means or foul. The distribution of constitutional power cannot long continue very different from that of real power, without a convulsion; nor, if the institutions which impede the progress of democracy could be by any miracle preserved, could even they do more than render that progress a little slower. Were the constitution of Great Britain to remain henceforth unaltered, we are not the less under the dominion, becoming every day more irresistible, of public opinion.

With regard to the advance of democracy, there are two different positions which it is possible for a rational person to take up, according as he thinks the masses prepared or unprepared to exercise the control which they are acquiring over their destiny, in a manner which would be an improvement upon what now exists. If he thinks them prepared, he will aid the democratic movement; or, if he deem it to be proceeding fast enough without him, he will at all events refrain from resisting it. If, on the contrary, he thinks the masses unprepared for complete control over their government,—seeing at the same time, that, prepared or not, they cannot long be prevented from acquiring it,—he will exert his utmost efforts in contributing to prepare them: using all means, on the one hand, for making the masses themselves wiser and better; on the other, for so rousing the slumbering energy of the opulent and lettered classes, so storing the youth of those classes with the profoundest and most valuable knowledge, so calling forth whatever of individual greatness exists or can be raised up in the country, as to create a power which might partially rival the mere power of the masses, and might exercise the most salutary influence over them for their own good. When engaged earnestly in works like these, one can understand how a rational person might think, that, in order to give more time for the performance of them, it were well if the current of democracy, which can in no sort be stayed, could be prevailed upon, for a time, to flow less impetuously. With conservatives of this sort, all democrats of corresponding enlargement of aims could fraternize as frankly and cordially as with most of their own friends; and we speak from an extensive knowledge of the wisest and most high-minded of that body, when we take upon ourselves to answer for them, that they would never push forward their own political projects in a spirit or with a violence which could tend to frustrate any rational endeavors towards the object nearest their hearts,—the instruction of the understandings, and the elevation of the characters, of all classes of their countrymen.

But who is there, among the political party calling themselves conservatives, that professes to have any such object in view? Do they seek to employ the interval of respite, which they might hope to gain by withstanding democracy, in qualifying the people to wield the democracy more wisely when it comes? Would they not far rather resist any such endeavor, on the principle that knowledge is power, and that its further diffusion would make the dreaded evil come sooner? Do the leading conservatives in either house of Parliament feel that the character of the higher classes needs renovating, to qualify them for a more arduous task and a keener strife than has yet fallen to their lot? Is not the character of a Tory lord or country gentleman, or a Church-of-England parson, perfectly satisfactory to them? Is not the existing constitution of the two universities,—those bodies whose especial duty it was to counteract the debilitating influence of the circumstances of the age upon individual character, and to send forth into society a succession of minds, not the creatures of their age, but capable of being its improvers and regenerators,—the universities, by whom this, their especial duty, has been basely neglected, until, as is usual with all neglected duties, the very consciousness of it as a duty has faded from their remembrance,—is not, we say, the existing constitution, and the whole existing system of these universities, down to the smallest of their abuses,—the exclusion of Dissenters,—a thing for which every Tory, though he may not, as he pretends, die in the last ditch, will at least vote in the last division? The Church, professedly the other great instrument of national culture, long since perverted (we speak of rules, not exceptions) into a grand instrument for discouraging all culture inconsistent with blind obedience to established maxims and constituted authorities,—what Tory has a scheme in view for any changes in this body, but such as may pacify assailants, and make the institution wear a less disgusting appearance to the eye? What political Tory will not resist to the very last moment any alteration in that Church, which would prevent is livings from being the provision for a family, its dignities the reward of political or of private services? The Tories, those at least connected with Parliament or office, do not aim at having good institutions, or even at preserving the present ones: their object is to profit by them while they exist.

We scruple not to express our belief, that a truer spirit of conservation, as to every thing good in the principles and professed objects of our old institutions, lives in many who are determined enemies of those institutions in their present state, than in most of those who call themselves conservatives. But there are many well-meaning people who always confound attachment to an end with pertinacious adherence to any set of means by which it either is, or is pretended to be, already pursued; and have yet to learn, that bodies of men who live in honor and importance upon the pretence of fulfilling ends which they never honestly seek are the great hinderance to the attainment of those ends, and that whoever has the attainment really at heart must expect a war of extermination with all such confederacies.

Thus far as to the political effects of civilization. Its moral effects, which as yet we have only glanced at, demand further elucidation. They may be considered under two heads,—the direct influence of civilization itself upon individual character, and the moral effects produced by the insignificance into which the individual falls in comparison with the masses.

One of the effects of a high state of civilization upon character is a relaxation of individual energy, or rather the concentration of it within the narrow sphere of the individual's money-getting pursuits. As civilization advances, every person becomes dependent for more and more of what most nearly concerns him, not upon his own exertions, but upon the general arrangements of society. In a rude state, each man's personal security, the protection of his family, his property, his liberty itself, depend greatly upon his bodily strength and his mental energy or cunning: in a civilized state, all this is secured to him by causes extrinsic to himself. The growing mildness of manners is a protection to him against much that he was before exposed to; while, for the remainder, he may rely with constantly increasing assurance upon the soldier, the policeman, and the judge, and (where the efficiency or purity of those instruments, as is usually the case, lags behind the general march of civilization) upon the advancing strength of public opinion. There remain, as inducements to call forth energy of character, the desire of wealth or of personal aggrandizement, the passion of philanthropy, and the love of active virtue. But the objects to which these various feelings point are matters of choice, not of necessity; nor do the feelings act with any thing like equal force upon all minds. The only one of them which can be considered as any thing like universal is the desire of wealth; and wealth being, in the case of the majority, the most accessible means of gratifying all their other desires, nearly the whole of the energy of character which exists in highly civilized societies concentrates itself on the pursuit of that object. In the case, however, of the most influential classes,—those whose energies, if they had them, might be exercised on the greatest scale and with the most considerable result,—the desire of wealth is already sufficiently satisfied to render them averse to suffer pain or incur much voluntary labor for the sake of any further increase. The same classes also enjoy, from their station alone, a high degree of personal consideration. Except the high offices of the state, there is hardly any thing to tempt the ambition of men in their circumstances. Those offices, when a great nobleman could have them for asking for, and keep them with less trouble than he could manage his private estate, were, no doubt, desirable enough possessions for such persons; but when they become posts of labor, vexation, and anxiety, and, besides, cannot be had without paying the price of some previous toil, experience shows, that, among men unaccustomed to sacrifice their amusements and their ease, the number upon whom these high offices operate as incentives to activity, or in whom they call forth any vigor of character, is extremely limited. Thus it happens, that in highly civilized countries, and particularly among ourselves, the energies of the middle classes are almost confined to money-getting, and those of the higher classes are nearly extinct.

There is another circumstance to which we may trace much both of the good and of the bad qualities which distinguish our civilization from the rudeness of former times. One of the effects of civilization (not to say one of the ingredients in it) is, that the spectacle, and even the very idea, of pain, is kept more and more out of the sight of those classes who enjoy in their fulness the benefits of civilization. The state of perpetual personal conflict, rendered necessary by the circumstances of former times, and from which it was hardly possible for any person, in whatever rank of society, to be exempt, necessarily habituated every one to the spectacle of harshness, rudeness, and violence, to the struggle of one indomitable will against another, and to the alternate suffering and infliction of pain. These things, consequently, were not as revolting even to the best and most actively benevolent men of former days as they are to our own; and we find the recorded conduct of those men frequently such as would be universally considered very unfeeling in a person of our own day. They, however, thought less of the infliction of pain, because they thought less of pain altogether. When we read of actions of the Greeks and Romans, or of our own ancestors, denoting callousness to human suffering, we must not think that those who committed these actions were as cruel as we must become before we could do the like. The pain which they inflicted they were in the habit of voluntarily undergoing from slight causes: it did not appear to them as great an evil as it appears, and as it really is, to us; nor did it in any way degrade their minds. In our own time, the necessity of personal collision between one person and another is, comparatively speaking, almost at an end. All those necessary portions of the business of society which oblige any person to be the immediate agent or ocular witness of the infliction of pain are delegated by common consent to peculiar and narrow classes,—to the judge, the soldier, the surgeon, the butcher, and the executioner. To most people in easy circumstances, any pain, except that inflicted upon the body by accident or disease, and upon the mind by the inevitable sorrows of life, is rather a thing known of than actually experienced. This is much more emphatically true in the more refined classes, and as refinement advances; for it is in avoiding the presence, not only of actual pain, but of whatever suggests offensive or disagreeable ideas, that a great part of refinement consists. We may remark, too, that this is possible only by a perfection of mechanical arrangements impracticable in any but a high state of civilization. Now, most kinds of pain and annoyance appear much more unendurable to those who have little experience of them than to those who have much. The consequence is, that, compared with former times, there is in the more opulent classes of modern civilized communities much more of the amiable and humane, and much less of the heroic. The heroic essentially consists in being ready, for a worthy object, to do and to suffer, but especially to do, what is painful or disagreeable; and whoever does not early learn to be capable of this will never be a great character. There has crept over the refined classes, over the whole class of gentlemen in England, a moral effeminacy, an inaptitude for every kind of struggle. They shrink from all effort, from every thing which is troublesome and disagreeable. The same causes which render them sluggish and unenterprising, make them, it is true, for the most part, stoical under inevitable evils. But heroism is an active, not a passive quality; and when it is necessary not to bear pain, but to seek it, little needs be expected from the men of the present day. They cannot undergo labor, they cannot brook ridicule, they cannot brave evil tongues: they have not hardihood to say an unpleasant thing to any one whom they are in the habit of seeing, or to face, even with a nation at their back, the coldness of some little coterie which surrounds them. This torpidity and cowardice, as a general characteristic, is new in the world; but (modified by the different temperaments of different nations) it is a natural consequence of the progress of civilization, and will continue until met by a system of cultivation adapted to counteract it.

If the source of great virtues thus dries up, great vices are placed, no doubt, under considerable restraint. The *régime* of public opinion is adverse to at least the indecorous vices; and as that restraining power gains strength, and certain classes or individuals cease to possess a virtual exemption from it, the change is highly favorable to the outward decencies of life. Nor can it be denied, that the diffusion of even such knowledge as civilization naturally brings has no slight tendency to rectify, though it be but partially, the standard of public opinion; to undermine many of those prejudices and superstitions which made mankind hate each other for things not really odious; to make them take a juster measure of the tendencies of actions, and weigh more correctly the evidence on which they condemn or applaud their fellow-creatures; to make, in short, their approbation direct itself more correctly to good actions, and their disapprobation to bad. What are the limits to this natural improvement in public opinion, when there is no other sort of cultivation going on than that which is the accompaniment of civilization, we need not at present inquire. It is enough that within those limits there is an extensive range; that as much improvement in the general understanding, softening of the feelings, and decay of pernicious errors, as naturally attends the progress of wealth and the spread of reading, suffices to render the judgment of the public upon actions and persons, so far as evidence is before them, much more discriminating and correct.

But here presents itself another ramification of the effects of civilization, which it has often surprised us to find so little attended to. The individual becomes so lost in the crowd, that, though he depends more and more upon opinion, he is apt to depend less and less upon well-grounded opinion,—upon the opinion of those who know him. An established character becomes at once more difficult to gain, and more easily to be dispensed with.

It is in a small society, where everybody knows every-

body, that public opinion, so far as well directed, exercises
its most salutary influence. Take the case of a tradesman in
a small country town. To every one of his customers he is
long and accurately known: their opinion of him has been
formed after repeated trials: if he could deceive them once,
he cannot hope to go on deceiving them, in the quality of his
goods: he has no other customers to look for if he loses
these; while, if his goods are really what they profess to be,
he may hope, among so few competitors, that this also will
be known and recognized, and that he will acquire the character, individually and professionally, which his conduct
entitles him to. Far different is the case of a man setting
up in business in the crowded streets of a great city. If he
trust solely to the quality of his goods, to the honesty and
faithfulness with which he performs what he undertakes, he
may remain ten years without a customer: be he ever so
honest, he is driven to cry out on the housetops that his wares
are the best of wares, past, present, and to come; while if he
proclaim this, however false, with sufficient loudness to excite the curiosity of passers-by, and can give his commodities
"a gloss, a salable look," not easily to be seen through at a
superficial glance, he may drive a thriving trade, though no
customer ever enter his shop twice. There has been much
complaint of late years of growth, both in the world of trade
and in that of intellect, of quackery, and especially of puffing:
but nobody seems to have remarked that these are the inevitable fruits of immense competition; of a state of society,
where any voice, not pitched in an exaggerated key, is lost
in the hubbub. Success, in so crowded a field, depends, not
upon what a person is, but upon what he seems: mere market-
able qualities become the object instead of substantial ones,
and a man's labor and capital are expended less in doing any
thing than in persuading other people that he has done it.
Our own age has seen this evil brought to its consummation.
Quackery there always was; but it once was a test of the absence of sterling qualities: there was a proverb, that good
wine needed no bush. It is our own age which has seen the
honest dealer driven to quackery by hard necessity, and the

certainty of being undersold by the dishonest. For the first time, arts for attracting public attention form a necessary part of the qualifications even of the deserving; and skill in these goes farther than any other quality towards insuring success. The same intensity of competition drives the trading public more and more to play high for success; to throw for all or nothing; and this, together with the difficulty of sure calculations in a field of commerce so widely extended, renders bankruptcy no longer disgraceful, because no longer an almost certain presumption either of dishonesty or imprudence: the discredit which it still incurs belongs to it, alas! mainly as an indication of poverty. Thus public opinion loses another of those simple criteria of desert, which, and which alone, it is capable of correctly applying; and the very cause, which has rendered it omnipotent in the gross, weakens the precision and force with which its judgment is brought home to individuals.

It is not solely on the private virtues that this growing insignificance of the individual in the mass is productive of mischief. It corrupts the very fountain of the improvement of public opinion itself; it corrupts public teaching; it weakens the influence of the more cultivated few over the many. Literature has suffered more than any other human production by the common disease. When there were few books, and when few read at all save those who had been accustomed to read the best authors, books were written with the well-grounded expectation that they would be read carefully, and, if they deserved it, would be read often. A book of sterling merit, when it came out, was sure to be heard of, and might hope to be read, by the whole reading class: it might succeed by its real excellences, though not got up to strike at once; and, even if so got up, unless it had the support of genuine merit, it fell into oblivion. The rewards were then for him who wrote *well*, not *much;* for the laborious and learned, not the crude and ill-informed writer. But now the case is reversed. "This is a reading age; and, precisely because it is so reading an age, any book which is the result of profound meditation is perhaps less likely to be duly and

profitably read than at a former period. The world reads
too much and too quickly to read well. When books were
few, to get through one was a work of time and labor: what
was written with thought was read with thought, and with
a desire to extract from it as much of the materials of knowledge as possible. But when almost every person who can
spell, can and will write, what is to be done? It is difficult to
know what to read, except by reading every thing; and so
much of the world's business is now transacted through the
press, that it is necessary to know what is printed, if we desire
to know what is going on. Opinion weighs with so vast a
weight in the balance of events, that ideas of no value in themselves are of importance from the mere circumstance that
they *are* ideas, and have a *bonâ-fide* existence as such anywhere out of Bedlam. (The world, in consequence, gorges
itself with intellectual food; and, in order to swallow the
more, *bolts* it.) Nothing is now read slowly, or twice over.
Books are run through with no less rapidity, and scarcely
leave a more durable impression, than a newspaper-article. It
is from this, among other causes, that so few books are produced of any value. The lioness in the fable boasted, that,
though she produced only one at a birth, that one was a lion;
but if each lion only counted for one, and each leveret for
one, the advantage would all be on the side of the hare.
When every unit is individually weak, it is only multitude
that tells. What wonder that the newspapers should carry
all before them? A book produces hardly a greater effect
than an article, and there can be three hundred and sixty-
five of these in one year. He, therefore, who should and
would write a book, and write it in the proper manner of
writing a book, now dashes down his first hasty thoughts, or
what he mistakes for thoughts, in a periodical. And the public is in the predicament of an indolent man, who cannot
bring himself to apply his mind vigorously to his own affairs,
and over whom, therefore, not he who speaks most wisely,
but he who speaks most frequently, obtains the influence." *

Hence we see that literature is becoming more and more

* From a paper by the author.

ephemeral: books, of any solidity, are almost gone by; even reviews are not now considered sufficiently light: the attention cannot sustain itself on any serious subject, even for the space of a review-article. In the more attractive kinds of literature, novels and magazines, though the demand has so greatly increased, the supply has so outstripped it, that even a novel is seldom a lucrative speculation. It is only under circumstances of rare attraction that a bookseller will now give any thing to an author for copyright. As the difficulties of success thus progressively increase, all other ends are more and more sacrificed for the attainment of it: literature becomes more and more a mere reflection of the current sentiments, and has almost entirely abandoned its mission as an enlightener and improver of them.

There are now in this country, we may say, but two modes left in which an individual mind can hope to produce much direct effect upon the minds and destinies of his countrymen generally,—as a member of Parliament, or an editor of a London newspaper. In both these capacities, much may still be done by an individual; because, while the power of the collective body is very great, the number of participants in it does not admit of much increase. One of these monopolies will be opened to competition when the newspaper stamp is taken off; whereby the importance of the newspaper-press in the aggregate, considered as the voice of public opinion, will be increased, and the influence of any one writer in helping to form that opinion necessarily diminished. This we might regret, did we not remember to what ends that influence is now used, and is sure to be so while newspapers are a mere investment of capital for the sake of mercantile profit.

Is there, then, no remedy? Are the decay of individual energy, the weakening of the influence of superior minds over the multitude, the growth of charlatanerie, and the diminished efficacy of public opinion as a restraining power, —are these the price we necessarily pay for the benefits of civilization? and can they only be avoided by checking the diffusion of knowledge, discouraging the spirit of combination, prohibiting improvements in the arts of life, and repressing the further increase of wealth and of production? Assuredly not. Those advantages which civilization cannot give—which in its uncorrected influence it has even a tendency to destroy—may yet co-exist with civilization; and it is only when joined to civilization that they can produce their fairest fruits. All that we are in danger of losing we may preserve, all that we have lost we may regain, and bring to a perfection hitherto unknown; but not by slumbering, and leaving things to themselves, no more than by ridiculously trying our strength against their irresistible tendencies: only by establishing counter-tendencies, which may combine with those tendencies, and modify them.

The evils are, that the individual is lost and becomes impotent in the crowd, and that individual character itself becomes relaxed and enervated. For the first evil, the remedy is, greater and more perfect combination among individuals; for the second, national institutions of education, and forms of polity calculated to invigorate the individual character.

The former of these desiderata, as its attainment depends upon a change in the habits of society itself, can only be realized by degrees, as the necessity becomes felt; but circumstances are even now, to a certain extent, forcing it on. In Great Britain especially (which so far surpasses the rest of the Old World in the extent and rapidity of the accumulation of wealth), the fall of profits, consequent upon the vast increase of population and capital, is rapidly extinguishing the class of small dealers and small producers, from the impossibility of living on their diminished profits; and is throwing business of all kinds more and more into the hands of large capitalists, whether these be rich individuals, or joint-stock companies formed by the aggregation of many small capitals. We are not among those who believe that this progress is tending to the complete extinction of competition, or that the entire productive resources of the country will, within any assignable number of ages, if ever, be administered by, and for the benefit of, a general association of the whole community. But we believe that the multiplication of competitors in all branches of business and in all professions—which renders it more and more difficult to obtain success by merit alone, more and more easy to obtain it by plausible pretence —will find a limiting principle in the progress of the spirit of co-operation; that, in every over-crowded department, there will arise a tendency among individuals so to unite their labor or their capital, that the purchaser or employer will have to choose, not among innumerable individuals, but among a few groups. Competition will be as active as ever; but the number of competitors will be brought within manageable bounds.

Such a spirit of co-operation is most of all wanted among the intellectual classes and professions. The amount of human labor, and labor of the most precious kind, now wasted, and wasted, too, in the cruelest manner, for want of combination, is incalculable. What a spectacle, for instance, does the medical profession present! One successful practitioner burthened with more work than mortal man can perform, and which he performs so summarily, that it were often better let alone: in the surrounding streets, twenty unhappy men, each of whom has been as laboriously and expensively trained as he has to do the very same thing, and is possibly as well qualified, wasting their capabilities, and starving for want of work. Under better arrangements, these twenty would form a corps of subalterns, marshalled under their more successful leader; who (granting him to be really the ablest physician of the set, and not merely the most successful impostor) is wasting time in physicking people for headaches and heartburns, which he might with better economy of mankind's resources turn over to his subordinates, while he employed his maturer powers and greater experience in studying and treating those more obscure and difficult cases upon which science has not yet thrown sufficient light, and to which ordinary knowledge and abilities would not be adequate. By such means, every person's capacities would be turned to account; and, the highest minds being kept for the highest things, these would make progress, while ordinary occasions would be no losers.

But it is in literature, above all, that a change of this sort is of most pressing urgency. There the system of individual competition has fairly worked itself out, and things can hardly continue much longer as they are. Literature is a province of exertion, upon which more, of the first value to human nature, depends, than upon any other; a province in which the highest and most valuable order of works—those which most contribute to form the opinions and shape the characters of subsequent ages—are, more than in any other class of productions, placed beyond the possibility of appreciation by those who form the bulk of the purchasers in the book-market; insomuch that, even in ages when these were a far less numerous and more select class than now, it was an admitted point, that the only success which writers of the first order could look to was the verdict of posterity. That verdict could, in those times, be confidently expected by whoever was worthy of it: for the good judges, though few in number, were sure to read every work of merit which appeared; and, as the recollection of one book was not in those days immediately obliterated by a hundred others, they remembered it, and kept alive the knowledge of it to subsequent ages. But in our day, from the immense multitude of writers (which is now not less remarkable than the multitude of readers), and from the manner in which the people of this age are obliged to read, it is difficult, for what does not strike during its novelty, to strike at all: a book either misses fire altogether, or is so read as to make no permanent impression; and the good equally with the worthless are forgotten by the next day.

For this there is no remedy, while the public have no guidance beyond booksellers' advertisements, and the ill-considered and hasty criticisms of newspapers and small periodicals, to direct them in distinguishing what is not worth reading from what is. The resource must in time be some organized co-operation among the leading intellects of the age, whereby works of first-rate merit, of whatever class, and of whatever tendency in point of opinion, might come forth, with the stamp on them, from the first, of the approval of those whose names would carry authority. There are many causes why we must wait long for such a combination; but (with enormous defects both in plan and in execution) the Society for the Diffusion of Useful Knowledge was as considerable a step towards it as could be expected in the present state of men's minds, and in a first attempt. Literature has had in this country two ages: it must now have a third. The age of patronage, as Johnson a century ago proclaimed, is gone. The age of booksellers, it has been proclaimed by Mr. Carlyle, has well nigh died out. In the first, there was nothing intrinsically base; nor, in the second, any thing inherently independent and liberal. Each has done great things: both have had their day. The time is perhaps coming, when authors, as a collective guild, will be their own patrons and their own booksellers.

These things must bide their time. But the other of the two great desiderata, the regeneration of individual character among our lettered and opulent classes, by the adaptation to that purpose of our institutions, and, above all, of our educational institutions, is an object of more urgency, and for which more might be immediately accomplished, if the will and the understanding were not alike wanting.

This, unfortunately, is a subject on which, for the inculcation of rational views, every thing is yet to be done; for all that we would inculcate, all that we deem of vital importance, all upon which we conceive the salvation of the next and all future ages to rest, has the misfortune to be almost equally opposed to the most popular doctrines of our own time, and to the prejudices of those who cherish the empty husk of what has descended from ancient times. We are at issue equally with the admirers of Oxford and Cambridge, Eton and Westminster, and with the generality of their professed reformers. We regard the system of those institutions, as administered for two centuries past, with sentiments little short of utter abhorrence. But we do not conceive that their vices would be cured by bringing their studies into a closer connection with what it is the fashion to term "the business of the world;" by dismissing the logic and classics which are still professedly taught, to substitute modern languages and experimental physics. We would have classics and logic taught far more really and deeply than at present; and we would add to them other studies more alien than any which yet exist to the "business of the world," but more germane to the great business of every rational being,—the strengthening and enlarging of his own intellect and character. The empirical knowledge which the world demands, which is the stock in trade of money-getting life, we would leave the world to provide for itself; content with infusing into the youth of our country a spirit, and training them to habits, which would insure their acquiring such knowledge easily, and using it well. These, we know, are not the sentiments of the vulgar: but we believe them to be those of the best and wisest of all parties; and we are glad to corroborate our opinion by a quotation from a work written by a friend to the universities, and by one whose tendencies are rather conservative than liberal; a book which, though really, and not in form merely, one of fiction, contains much subtle and ingenious thought, and the results of much psychological experience, combined, we are compelled to say, with much caricature, and very provoking (though we are convinced unintentional) distortion and misinterpretation of the opinions of some of those with whose philosophy that of the author does not agree.

"You believe" a clergyman *loquitur* "that the university is to prepare youths for a successful career in society: I believe the sole object is to give them that manly character which will enable them to resist the influences of society. I do not care to prove that I am right, and that any university which does not stand upon this basis will be rickety in its childhood, and useless or mischievous in its manhood: I care only to assert that this was the notion of those who founded Oxford and Cambridge. I fear that their successors are gradually losing sight of this principle; are gradually beginning to think that it is their business to turn out clever lawyers and serviceable treasury-clerks; are pleased when the world compliments them upon the goodness of the article with which they have furnished it; and that this low vanity is absorbing all their will and their power to create great men, whom the age will scorn, and who will save it from the scorn of the times to come."

"One or two such men" said the liberal "in a generation may be very useful; but the university gives us two or three thousand youths every year. I suppose you are content that a portion shall do week-day services."

"I wish to have a far more hard-working and active race than we have at present," said the clergyman; "men more persevering in toil, and less impatient of reward: but all experience —a thing which the schools are not privileged to despise, though the world is—all experience is against the notion, that the means to procure a supply of good ordinary men is to attempt nothing higher. I know that nine-tenths of those whom the university sends out must be hewers of wood, and drawers of water; but, if I train the ten-tenths to be so, depend upon it the wood will be badly cut, the water will be spilt. Aim at something noble: make your system such that a great man may be formed by it, and there will be a manhood in your little men, of which you do not dream. But when some skilful rhetorician, or lucky rat, stands at the top of the ladder; when the university, instead of disclaiming the creature, instead of pleading, as an excuse for themselves, that the healthiest mother may, by accident, produce a shapeless abortion, stands shouting, that the world may know what great things they can do, 'We taught the boy!' when the hatred which worldly men will bear to religion always, and to learning whenever it teaches us to soar, and not to grovel, is met, not with a frank defiance, but rather with a deceitful argument, to show that trade is the better for them,—is it wonderful that a puny, beggarly feeling should pervade the mass of our young men; that they should scorn all noble achievements; should have no higher standard of action than the world's opinion; and should conceive of no higher reward than to sit down amidst loud cheering, which continues for several moments?" *

Nothing can be more just or more forcible than the description here given of the objects which university education should aim at: we are at issue with the writer, only on the proposition that these objects ever were attained, or

* From the novel of *Eustace Conway*, attributed to Mr. Maurice.

ever could be so, consistently with the principle which has always been the foundation of the English universities; a principle, unfortunately, by no means confined to them. The difficulty which continues to oppose either such reform of our old academical institutions, or the establishment of such new ones, as shall give us an education capable of forming great minds, is, that, in order to do so, it is necessary to begin by eradicating the idea which nearly all the upholders and nearly all the impugners of the universities rootedly entertain as to the objects, not merely of academical education, but of education itself. What is this idea? That the object of education is, not to qualify the pupil for judging what is true or what is right, but to provide that he shall think true what we think true, and right what we think right; that to teach, means to inculcate our own opinions; and that our business is, not to make thinkers or inquirers, but disciples. This is the deep-seated error, the inveterate prejudice, which the real reformer of English education has to struggle against. Is it astonishing that great minds are not produced in a country where the test of a great mind is, agreeing in the opinions of the small minds? where every institution for spiritual culture which the country has—the Church, the universities, and almost every dissenting community—are constituted on the following as their avowed principle?—that the object is, *not* that the individual should go forth determined and qualified to seek truth ardently, vigorously, and disinterestedly; *not* that he be furnished at setting out with the needful aids and facilities, the needful materials and instruments, for that search, and then left to the unshackled use of them; *not* that, by a free communion with the thoughts and deeds of the great minds which preceded him, he be inspired at once with the courage to dare all which truth and conscience require, and the modesty to weigh well the grounds of what others think, before adopting contrary opinions of his own: *not* this,—no; but that the triumph of the system, the merit, the excellence in the sight of God which it possesses, or which it can impart to its pupil, is, that his speculations shall terminate in the adoption, in words, of a particu-

lar set of opinions;—that, provided he adhere to these opinions, it matters little whether he receive them from authority
or from examination; and, worse, that it matters little by
what temptations of interest or vanity, by what voluntary or
involuntary sophistication with his intellect, and deadening
of his noblest feelings, that result is arrived at; that it even
matters comparatively little whether to his mind the words
are mere words, or the representatives of realities,—in what
sense he receives the favored set of propositions, or whether
he attaches to them any sense at all. Were ever great minds
thus formed? Never. The few great minds which this country has produced have been formed in spite of nearly every
thing which could be done to stifle their growth. And all
thinkers much above the common order, who have grown up
in the Church of England or in any other church, have been
produced in latitudinarian epochs, or while the impulse
of intellectual emancipation, which gave existence to the
Church, had not quite spent itself. The flood of burning
metal which issued from the furnace flowed on a few paces
before it congealed.

That the English universities have, throughout, proceeded on the principle, that the intellectual association of
mankind must be founded upon articles,—i.e., upon a promise of belief in certain opinions; that the scope of all they do
is to prevail upon their pupils, by fair means or foul, to acqui-
esce in the opinions which are set down for them; that the
abuse of the human faculties, so forcibly denounced by
Locke under the name of *"principling"* their pupils, is their
sole method in religion, politics, morality, or philosophy,—
is vicious indeed: but the vice is equally prevalent without
and within their pale, and is no farther disgraceful to them
than inasmuch as a better doctrine has been taught for a century past by the superior spirits, with whom, in point of intelligence, it was their duty to maintain themselves on a
level. But that, when this object was attained, they cared for
no other; that, if they could make church-men, they cared
not to make religious men; that, if they could make Tories,
whether they made patriots was indifferent to them; that, if

they could prevent heresy, they cared not if the price paid were stupidity,—this constitutes the peculiar baseness of those bodies. Look at them. While their sectarian character, while the exclusion of all who will not sign away their freedom of thought, is contended for, as if life depended upon it, there is hardly a trace in the system of the universities that any other object whatever is seriously cared for. Nearly all the professorships have degenerated into sinecures. Few of the professors ever deliver a lecture. One of the few great scholars who have issued from either university for a century (and he was such before he went thither), the Rev. Connop Thirlwall, has published to the world, that, in his university at least, even theology—even Church-of-England theology—is not taught; and his dismissal, for this piece of honesty, from the tutorship of his college, is one among the daily proofs how much safer it is for twenty men to neglect their duty, than for one man to impeach them of the neglect. The only studies really encouraged are classics and mathematics; neither of them a useless study, though the last, as an exclusive instrument for fashioning the mental powers, greatly overrated: but Mr. Whewell, a high authority against his own university, has published a pamphlet, chiefly to prove that the kind of mathematical attainment by which Cambridge honors are gained (expertness in the use of the calculus) is not that kind which has any tendency to produce superiority of intellect.* The mere shell and husk of the syllogistic logic at the one university, the wretchedest smattering of Locke and Paley at the other, are all of moral

* The erudite and able writer in the Edinburgh Review (Sir William Hamilton), who has expended an almost superfluous weight of argument and authority in combating the position incidentally maintained in Mr. Whewell's pamphlet, of the great value of mathematics as an exercise of the mind, was, we think, bound to have noticed the fact, that the far more direct object of the pamphlet was one which partially coincided with that of its reviewer. We do not think that Mr. Whewell has done well what he undertook: he is vague, and is always attempting to be a profounder metaphysician than he can be; but the main proposition of his pamphlet is true and important; and he is entitled to no little credit for having discerned that important truth, and expressed it so strongly.

or psychological science that is taught at either.† As a means of educating the many, the universities are absolutely null. The youth of England are not educated. The attainments of any kind required for taking all the degrees conferred by these bodies, are, at Cambridge, utterly contemptible; at Oxford, we believe, of late years, somewhat higher, but still very low. Honors, indeed, are not gained but by a severe struggle; and, if even the candidates for honors were mentally benefited, the system would not be worthless. But what have the senior wranglers done, even in mathematics? Has Cambridge produced, since Newton, one great mathematical genius?—we do not say an Euler, a Laplace, or a Lagrange, but such as France has produced a score of during the same period. How many books which have thrown light upon the history, antiquities, philosophy, art, or literature of the ancients, have the two universities sent forth since the Reformation? Compare them, not merely with Germany, but even with Italy or France. When a man is pronounced by them to have excelled in their studies, what do the universities do? They give him an income, not for continuing to learn, but for having learnt; not for doing any thing, but for what he has already done; on condition solely of living like a monk, and putting on the livery of the Church at the end of seven years. They bribe men by high rewards to get their arms ready, but do not require them to fight.

Are these the places of education which are to send forth minds capable of maintaining a victorious struggle with the debilitating influences of the age, and strengthening the weak side of civilization by the support of a higher cultivation? This, however, is what we require from these institutions; or, in their default, from others which should take their place. And the very first step towards their reform should be to unsectarianize them wholly, not by the paltry

† We should except, at Oxford, the Ethics, Politics, and Rhetoric of Aristotle. These are part of the course of classical instruction; and are so far an exception to the rule, otherwise pretty faithfully observed at both universities, of cultivating only the least useful parts of ancient literature.

measure of allowing Dissenters to come and be taught orthodox sectarianism, but by putting an end to sectarian teaching altogether. The principle itself of dogmatic religion,
dogmatic morality, dogmatic philosophy, is what requires to
be rooted out, not any particular manifestation of that principle.

The very corner-stone of an education intended to form
great minds must be the recognition of the principle, that
the object is to call forth the greatest possible quantity of intellectual *power,* and to inspire the intensest *love of truth;*
and this without a particle of regard to the results to which
the exercise of that power may lead, even though it should
conduct the pupil to opinions diametrically opposite to those
of his teachers. We say this, not because we think opinions
unimportant, but because of the immense importance which
we attach to them: for in proportion to the degree of intellectual power, and love of truth, which we succeed in creating, is the certainty, that (whatever may happen in any one
particular instance), in the aggregate of instances, true opinions will be the result; and intellectual power and practical
love of truth are alike impossible where the reasoner is
shown his conclusions, and informed beforehand that he is
expected to arrive at them.

We are not so absurd as to propose that the teacher
should not set forth his own opinions as the true ones, and
exert his utmost powers to exhibit their truth in the strongest light. To abstain from this would be to nourish the worst
intellectual habit of all,—that of not finding, and not looking for, certainty in any thing. But the teacher himself
should not be held to any creed; nor should the question be,
whether his own opinions are the true ones, but whether he
is well instructed in those of other people, and, in enforcing
his own, states the arguments for all conflicting opinions
fairly. In this spirit it is that all the great subjects are taught
from the chairs of the German and French universities. As
a general rule, the most distinguished teacher is selected,
whatever be his particular views; and he consequently

teaches in the spirit of free inquiry, not of dogmatic imposition.

Such is the principle of all academical instruction which aims at forming great minds. The details cannot be too various and comprehensive. Ancient literature would fill a large place in such a course of instruction, because it brings before us the thoughts and actions of many great minds,— minds of many various orders of greatness, and these related and exhibited in a manner tenfold more impressive, tenfold more calculated to call forth high aspirations, than in any modern literature. Imperfectly as these impressions are made by the current modes of classical teaching, it is incalculable what we owe to this, the sole ennobling feature in the slavish, mechanical thing which the moderns call education. Nor is it to be forgotten among the benefits of familiarity with the monuments of antiquity, and especially those of Greece, that we are taught by it to appreciate and to admire intrinsic greatness, amidst opinions, habits, and institutions most remote from ours; and are thus trained to that large and catholic toleration which is founded on understanding, not on indifference, and to a habit of free, open sympathy with powers of mind, and nobleness of character, howsoever exemplified. Were but the languages and literature of antiquity so taught that the glorious images they present might stand before the student's eyes as living and glowing realities; that instead of lying a *caput mortuum* at the bottom of his mind, like some foreign substance in no way influencing the current of his thoughts or the tone of his feelings, they might circulate through it, and become assimilated, and be part and parcel of himself!—then should we see how little these studies have yet done for us, compared with what they have yet to do.

An important place in the system of education which we contemplate would be occupied by history, because it is the record of all great things which have been achieved by mankind, and because, when philosophically studied, it gives a certain largeness of conception to the student, and familiar-

izes him with the action of great causes. In no other way can
he so completely realize in his own mind (howsoever he may
be satisfied with the proof of them as abstract propositions)
the great principles by which the progress of man and the
condition of society are governed. Nowhere else will the
infinite varieties of human nature be so vividly brought home
to him, and any thing cramped or one-sided in his own standard of it so effectually corrected; and nowhere else will he
behold so strongly exemplified the astonishing pliability of
our nature, and the vast effects which may under good guidance be produced upon it by honest endeavor. The literature of our own and other modern nations should be studied
along with the history, or rather as part of the history.

In the department of pure intellect, the highest place
will belong to logic and the philosophy of mind: the one,
the instrument for the cultivation of all sciences; the other,
the root from which they all grow. It scarcely needs be said
that the former ought not to be taught as a mere system of
technical rules, nor the latter as a set of concatenated abstract
propositions. The tendency, so strong everywhere, is strongest of all here, to receive opinions into the mind without any
real understanding of them, merely because they seem to
follow from certain admitted premises, and to let them lie
there as forms of words, lifeless, and void of meaning. The
pupil must be led to interrogate his own consciousness, to
observe and experiment upon himself: of the mind, by any
other process, little will he ever know.

With these should be joined all those sciences in which
great and certain results are arrived at by mental processes
of some length or nicety: not that all persons should study
all these sciences, but that some should study all, and all
some. These may be divided into sciences of mere ratiocination, as mathematics; and sciences partly of ratiocination, and
partly of what is far more difficult,—comprehensive observation and analysis. Such are, in their *rationale*, even the
sciences to which mathematical processes are applicable; and
such are all those which relate to human nature. The philosophy of morals, of government, of law, of political econ-

omy, of poetry and art, should form subjects of systematic instruction, under the most eminent professors who could be found; these being chosen, not for the particular doctrines they might happen to profess, but as being those who were most likely to send forth pupils qualified in point of disposition and attainments to choose doctrines for themselves. And why should not religion be taught in the same manner? Not until then will one step be made towards the healing of religious differences; not until then will the spirit of English religion become catholic instead of sectarian, favorable instead of hostile to freedom of thought and the progress of the human mind.

With regard to the changes, in forms of polity and social arrangements, which, in addition to reforms in education, we conceive to be required for regenerating the character of the higher classes,—to express them even summarily would require a long discourse. But the general idea from which they all emanate may be stated briefly. Civilization has brought about a degree of security and fixity in the possession of all advantages once acquired, which has rendered it possible for a rich man to lead the life of a Sybarite, and nevertheless enjoy throughout life a degree of power and consideration which could formerly be earned or retained only by personal activity. We cannot undo what civilization has done, and again stimulate the energy of the higher classes by insecurity of property, or danger of life or limb. The only adventitious motive it is in the power of society to hold out is reputation and consequence; and of this as much use as possible should be made for the encouragement of desert. The main thing which social changes can do for the improvement of the higher classes—and it is what the progress of democracy is insensibly but certainly accomplishing—is gradually to put an end to every kind of unearned distinction, and let the only road open to honor and ascendency be that of personal qualities.

On the Oxford Movement

1842

John Stuart Mill never met John Henry Newman. No two men in nineteenth century England were farther apart intellectually and, at the same time, so close temperamentally. Newman was perhaps the greatest English authoritarian critic of the century. He ended his life as Cardinal Newman, the foremost priest of the Roman Catholic Church in England. When Mill's *Logic* was published, the Newmanites greeted it by asserting that if Mill's "principles be adopted as a full statement of the truth, the whole fabric of Christian Theology must totter and fall." Yet, despite their ultimate differences in outlook, Newman and Mill were both antagonistic to a doctrinaire secular liberalism. Mill resisted it because he detested all authoritarianism: Newman, because it opposed dogmatic Christian faith. There are many other curious ways in which Mill and Newman resemble each other. Newman believed, for example, that in the development of Christian doctrine, heresy served to refine the understanding of God's word and that truth emerged in history through intellectual controversy.

The Oxford Movement arose in reaction to the attempts of liberal Christians, at Oxford and elsewhere, to reinvigorate English faith. Rationalist and historical in their theology, broad in their conception of the church, and deferential to state control over the forms of worship, creed, and church property, the Oxford liberals sought to make Christianity speak in the language of the day. Instead, the conservatives charged, they merely made the language of the day sound like Christianity. The Church, claimed the orthodox, was given by God, and thereby had transcendent guarantees for its theology, worship, and property. If liberalism was successful, the church might be treated with no more deference than the post-office.

The first leader of the conservative attempt to refresh and redefine the dogmatic basis of Anglicanism was John Keble. Newman succeeded him and, in the 1830's, helped publish numerous tracts on the chief issues in the growing theological debate. As the tone of these tracts became more intransigent and more anti-liberal, and as the brilliance and intellect of the "Tractarians" gathered followers, the movement spread beyond Oxford. In 1841, Newman went too far toward orthodoxy for the liberals. They drove him from Oxford, and his unofficial leadership passed to Edward Pusey, who was to remain the leading High (or orthodox) Churchman in England for the next two generations.

Mill's wonderful letters on the sincerity and competence of the Puseyites demonstrate his genuine desire that all public debates enlist the best possible opponents. He was so eager to refute all arguments for state control over creeds, that he failed to realize that many of the Puseyites, although demanding freedom to teach and preach what they believed, would have welcomed the subordination of the English state to the church.

———————

A LETTER FROM *The Morning Chronicle*
OF JANUARY 1, 1842

SIR,

I address you as one of, I believe, many who although most remote from any connection, either personal, or through their opinions, with Puseyism, have seen with pleasure the letters of "Philo Puseyite," in the first place, because we agree with that writer in a large portion of his sentiments, but also, and still more, because we approve of the tone of mind, which is less eager to hold up to obloquy the errors of an adversary, than conscientiously to examine what portion of truth exists in those errors, and gives them their plausibility. We not only esteem it a more healthful exercise of the

mind to employ itself in learning from an enemy, than in in-
veighing against him; but, we believe, that the extirpation
of what is erroneous in any system of belief is in no way so
much promoted as by extricating from it, and incorporating
into our own systems, whatever in it is true. If your correspondent, "Miso-Jesuit," had taken heed of these things, he
would probably have spared you his ill-tempered and un-
courteous second letter—a document which would prove, if
such proof were required, that there is nothing which a zealot,
Christian or infidel, dissenter or churchman, can so little pardon, or on which he is so incapable of putting a candid interpretation as the offence of not going with him to the full
length of his narrow-minded antipathies.

It was scarcely needful for your correspondent to remind "Philo-Puseyite" that the Oxford theologians would
not thank him for such advocacy as his, and that whoever
stands up for toleration or charity in their behalf claims for
the Puseyites what the Puseyites would not be willing to bestow. The leaders of this sect, for a sect it is, are, as it is evident that "Miso-Jesuit" himself is, conscientious bigots: like
him, however, they are not bigots to error, but to one-half of
the truth; and are, in the present writer's estimation, entitled to the approbation and goodwill which he cannot but
feel towards all such persons, provided that the portion of
truth they contend for is one which the age specially needs,
and provided (he must add) they have not the power of burning him for heresy, a fate which, to say truth, if their doctrines
ever obtained the ascendancy in this country, he does not
well see how he could hope to escape. It is not, therefore,
out of any special partiality to them that he undertakes their
apology. But not to our friends alone is justice due from us
and to the Puseyites; permit me to say, it is more particularly
due from your paper, inasmuch as you have repeatedly in
your leading articles done them cruel injustice, of the kind
likely to be most severely felt by conscientious men, and most
likely also to prejudice impartial bystanders against your
good cause, by your perpetual denunciations of them as hypocrites and mammon-servers, because, holding doctrines which

you (not they) deem inconsistent with the articles of the church, they yet do not secede from it.

Can you be serious, sir, in addressing this particular reproach to men of whom it is the distinctive feature, among all other religious parties, to maintain that no difference of opinion whatever is capable of justifying the sin of schism? That the first command of Christ is adherence to the standard which he has erected upon earth, and for the recognition of which he has appointed certain criteria, of which the profession of a particular set of theological tenets is *not* one; that even if the whole human race, one person excepted, should desert that standard and set up another, by proclaiming a church of man's ordinance, not God's, it is they who apostatize, and he, that one person, be his opinions what they may, is the Christian church upon earth; or if, instead of themselves seceding from the communion, they forcibly exclude him from it (as the Roman church did Luther), he refusing and protesting, they, by so doing, constitute their church a schismatic body, while he remains a member of the church as before! In common candour, sir, ask yourself whether persons of whose belief this is a correct expression, are sacrificing their principles to lucre because they do not take upon their consciences what they esteem a deadly sin.

And since we are on the subject of interested motives, give me leave to ask you, as a man acquainted with the world, and aware of the ordinary course of affairs in political life, whether you do or can think other of these men than that by professing their opinions they are abandoning all hope of further advancement in worldly advantages? If the extraordinary acquirements and powers, for example, of Mr. Newman had been employed in any of the modes in which able men in the church of England usually seek to distinguish themselves—in the paths, for instance, by which Dr. Blomfield or Dr. Philpotts rose to eminence, is there any dignity in the Establishment to which he might not have aspired? And do you believe that either the present government, or any other ministry that could be formed, would dare to raise an avowed and active Puseyite to episcopal, or any other high

ecclesiastical honors? Let me answer for you, sir. You know
the contrary: you are not ignorant of the sort of feelings with
which practical politicians of every class invariably regard
the speculative men who formulize either into philosophic
theories or religious dogmas the extreme doctrines of their
own party. You know that those whose business is concilia-
tion and compromise, the smoothing of difficulties and the
allaying of apprehensions, do not hold their most determined adversaries in so much dread as they do those who
display to public view all the vulnerable points in their system of opinions, in the manner most fertile of misgiving to
friends, and irritation to opponents, and proclaim as sacred
principles, to be acted upon, without qualification or reserve,
all which *they* in their practice not only sedulously guard by
countless modifications and restrictions, but are so often
forced, even honestly, to surrender altogether, in points of
detail at least, on the summons of declared opponents. If *we*
know this, think you that Mr. Newman knows it not? Think
you that a man so deeply read in history, and who has ana-
lysed in so one-sided, but yet so profound a manner, the
course of the stream of human affairs from age to age, is ignorant of what every school-boy knows, that the philosophers
of a creed are seldom its successful politicians?

It would do you credit, sir, to desist from these incessant attacks upon the disinterestedness of the Oxford theologians, or to reserve them until you find the Puseyites
violating the doctrines of their own creed, by disobeying the
authority, canonically exercised, of their ecclesiastical superiors. Such imputations of insincerity are applied with a very
bad grace to a party from whom, whatever may be said
against the unreasonableness or the real Christianity of many
of their doctrines, this acknowledgment cannot be withheld,
that instead of being insincere members of the church, they
are the only party in it who attempt, or even pretend to attempt, to be perfectly sincere. I assert this without qualification as one of the greatest, or rather as the very greatest of
the peculiarities which, in my opinion, entitle this school to
be warmly welcomed among us. They are the first persons in

the Church of England who for more than a century past have conscientiously and rigidly endeavoured to live up to what they nominally profess—to obey the regulations of that church of which they call themselves members. Even Philo-Puseyite speaks of their "predilection for ceremonies, and vestments, and fastings, and vigils, and saint's days," as something "revolting." But is it forgotten that these things are actual ordinances of the church of England, and that the Puseyites are simply acting out the written code of their religion? If these things are absurdities, with whom lies the fault? They were not placed in the Rubric by the Puseyites. The charge of insincerity brought against this party for remaining in the church without assenting, or while assenting only in a latitudinarian sense, to the articles, may be much more fairly retorted upon those who, without considering, as the Puseyites do, adherence to the church to be the paramount duty of a Christian, nevertheless remain in it with a tacit reservation that they are to conform to just as many of its rules and authoritative precepts as to them appear reasonable. Let the opposite party, then, bestir themselves to cause such as the ceremonies and such of the religious exercises prescribed by the church as they disapprove of, to be abrogated in the lawful manner, by canonical authority. But until this is done, I confess I honour far more those who act up to what is professed by all, than those who take one part of it and leave another, as suits themselves.

It is not, Sir, by continuing to profess opinions and silently forbearing to act upon them, that either religious or any other prevailing doctrines are to be freed from whatever of irrational or pernicious they may contain. It is too true that this is the ordinary course of changes of opinion. It is a disgusting, but sometimes inevitable era of transition between the pristine vigour and final downfall of creeds or doctrines, originally too deeply rooted in the soil to admit of being eradicated unless they have first reached an advanced stage of corruption and decomposition. In religion, and also in politics, the whole eighteenth century was a period of this kind. But that is a happy day for renovated humanity, when first a sincere man, indignant at the more and more complete severance of profession from practice, stands up as a fulfiller, in his own person, and a vindicator to the world, of the solemn duty of *doing* the whole of that which he daily professes that he ought to do. By carrying out this principle, and even because he carries it out to its last and absurdest consequences, he challenges and compels inquiry into the grounds of the belief itself and the degree in which it is or is not still adopted to be the rule of conduct for humanity in its altered state; and by the very vigour with which he asserts the false parts of his creed, he, by a reaction as certain as it is salutary, calls forth into corresponding activity and energy those opposite truths, in the minds of other people, which are the suitable means of expelling the false opinions without prejudice to the just views with which they are always, but not inseparably interwoven: thus giving to the world over again that without which its whole scheme would be an abortion and a failure—notions of duty made to be executed, not to be locked up as too good for use, or worn for outside show.

I must not, sir, encroach further on your space; but if you should deem this letter worthy of insertion, I may perhaps return to the subject, and lay before you in a more particular manner the grounds on which I contend that Puseyism is one of the most important and interesting phenomena which has appeared above the horizon of English speculation for many years past.

HISTORICUS

A LETTER FROM The Morning Chronicle
OF JANUARY 13, 1842

SIR,

Let me begin by thanking you for your prompt insertion of my former communication, and not less sincerely for the comments in a subsequent editorial article which in temper and candour were all that could be desired, and in substantials quite as favourable as I had reason to expect. I never did so much injustice to the writer of the denunciations of Puseyism which have so often appeared in your paper, as to imagine that he would have thus written with opinions of the subject so weak as to be shaken by the first breath of controversy. You have said what there is to be said for your view of the question, and it is satisfactory to find that there is so little. I cannot say that I perceive in it anything new, or which, as you seem to surmise, I had previously overlooked. The topics are such as no one could overlook, who attempted to anticipate what you would say. How, for example, after charging with hypocrisy, for not seceding from the church, men who hold that to recede from her would be to renounce their baptism, could you possibly defend yourself without drawing the distinction, and making as much of it as you could, between remaining in the communion of the church and partaking of its emoluments? The point could not be missed: a *nisi prius* advocate of the lowest grade could not have failed to take advantage of it.

I wish, sir, that it were as easy to exculpate the Pusey-ites, or Newmanites (as I admit that they may be more properly called) from every other of the accusations brought against them, as it is from this, of dishonestly retaining a state fee of which they violate the conditions. You would scarcely continue to bring this charge if you had sufficiently considered what it implies, or how widely the theory of the relation between spiritual teachers and temporal governors, which you seem to hold, differs both from that of the New-manites themselves, and from the doctrines of the most enlightened friends of liberty in the present and in past ages.

It would be a sufficient vindication of this party against the imputation of dishonesty, to show that their conduct is strictly consistent with their own principles; especially when those principles are not theirs peculiarly, but common to them with the great body of churchmen, or at least with the principal defenders of the Church of England as a political establishment. By what right do you require the Newman-ites to make themselves martyrs for opinions which are not theirs; to acknowledge as a truth, by recognizing as obliga-

tory upon them in practice, the doctrine that the endowments of the Church of England are a state fee given as a
consideration for teaching certain religious tenets? Do they
hold this doctrine? Is there any party in the church worth
mentioning which holds it? Will they not answer, and will
not the whole Conservative body answer with them, that the
endowments, the far greater part of them at least, did not
come from the state, never belonged to the state at all, but to
private individuals who voluntarily gave them to the church,
for purposes and under expectations, which it is the very
crime charged against the Puseyites, that they far more
nearly fulfil than the party of the Protestants *par excellence*
think it right to do? Some kings did, it is true, give lands
from their hereditary domain, and the state, as a state, did
render compulsory the payment of tithes, not however until
the majority of landed proprietors throughout Christian
Europe had, from religious motives, consented to take the
payment upon themselves; and, at all events, when once
given, it was, according to the doctrine of all Conservative,
and of many liberal writers, given irrevocably; it became as
the land itself became in the hands of its feudal holders, not
a salary, but a property.

The Puseyites do not, and, consistently with their religious doctrines, cannot acknowledge that the state made the
church of England, or gave it the property it holds, or did or
could annex to that property any new conditions imposed by
itself. Its power, in their view, like that of any judicial tribunal, extends only to enforcing the conditions on which the
property is really held, which, according to them, are simply
and solely those of being in communion with the Church
Catholic, and having received ordination from a bishop to
whom the power of conferring it has descended by uninter-
rupted succession from the Apostles. They do not, indeed,
deny that the state, in the person of the tyrant Henry VIII.,
did assert another sort of power over these endowments, and
did nefariously abuse that power by seizing a full half of the
church property for the use of the monarch himself and of his
favourites. But is any one bound to resign what is his own,

because somebody who is stronger chooses to assert a claim to it which he does not and cannot substantiate, and to pretend that it is only held on sufferance from him? If the church of England has ever admitted that it is a national church by virtue of the King's appointment, that the Crown made it, or had anything to do with the matter but to recognize it as the portion of the church of Christ existing in this nation, there would be something to be said against the Newmanites. But this they deny. The mere acknowledgment of the King as head of the church, that is, as what the Pope, according to the best Catholic tradition, was before, the mere executive (the supreme authority being in the body itself), does not, in their view, nor in the view of many persons besides them, constitute such an admission.

I am not stating these as my own arguments. I do not concur in them. They are deduced from the principles of a religious and political creed which is not mine. But it is the creed of the Puseyites. They stand upon their *right* to the endowments. On their own premises they are justified in making this stand. And when men are accused of insincerity, it is by their own premises that they are entitled to be tried. I confess, however, that I should not feel the same interest in their cause if there were nothing concerned in it but their own honesty and consistency; if it did not appear to me to involve a great principle, which it is not necessary to be a Newmanite, or even a churchman to acknowledge, and which it more especially becomes those who call themselves Liberals to take every occasion of asserting and vindicating.

The endowments, which the Puseyites say are not derived from the state, I say are derived from it. I deny the inviolability of foundations, and not only claim it as a right, but affirm it as a duty, of the Legislature to alter the appropriation of all such as, after due deliberation, with due precaution against its own fallibility, it deems to be no longer beneficially employed. I therefore hold that the state can rightfully take away the endowments of the church of England, as many good and wise men have held that it ought to do; that it has a right to determine whether it will endow with this property, any body of religious teachers whatever, and if it does, has a right to select the body which it judges best qualified for that high function. Its power, therefore, of giving the endowments for the purpose of spiritual teaching, is absolute; but that it has a right to give them conditionally, the condition being that of teaching certain doctrines, and those only, I deny. It must bestow them for teaching what the teachers believe, not what itself believes. It is not to chuse doctrines, but instructors. If there is to be an endowed church at all, there must be a power in the legislature to judge what is the body which *shall* be recognised in that character. But this is the same thing with determining the doctrines that shall be taught. Is that work for a King's ministers and two Houses of Parliament? Are they the theologians from whom those who listen to the publicly accredited religious instructors are to take their religion? Have we rejected popes and councils to receive our doctrines from a pope in St. James', or a council in St. Stephen's? The state has a different duty to perform. It is to judge, not what is taught, but the title to teach. The Newmanites say that they, or rather the church to which they adhere, are the teachers, divinely commissioned, and have credentials from the Almighty, pointing them out as such: if so, let the state look to the credentials, and judge of them. If nobody can make out a title by appointment from above, those are entitled who can give best proof of having qualified themselves by the fitting studies and the fitting moral discipline. It is for the state to decide this. It is for the state to determine what communion or what body of persons is most fitted, in point of general competency, to put a right interpretation upon Christianity, and to bring its practical principles home to the national mind. But when we are told that the state has ordained certain religious tenets to be taught, and a certain interpretation to be put upon Christianity, under the penalty of not teaching under state authority at all, I can only answer that whether by the state are to be understood a dead Henry VIII., or a living Peel or Melbourne, they have no credentials for this trust, can show no qualifications for it. Their duty is to find who are, or ought to be, the national church; it is the church's duty to determine what the church ought to teach.

I am tempted, sir, as one who has for many years considered himself a Liberal, to ask what is become of several doctrines which were once considered the distinguishing principles of the extreme Liberal party. Among the rest we used, I remember, in former days, to profess much disapprobation of what was called a connection between church and state. Perhaps some of those who reproach the Puseyites for objecting to state interference with the church, could refresh my memory as to what we meant by this. I wonder if it was merely the acres, or the pound sterling, which we wanted to rescue from the church, and convert to our own uses; or whether we thought that there was nothing so certain to corrupt religious teaching, as the interference with it of temporal governors; that such persons when they meddle with prescribing religious doctrines, seldom do it for any good, and that the sole effect of making the church dependent on the state, is to make religion an instrument for upholding temporal despotism, and an ally of every abuse which the indolence of rulers suffers, or by which their cupidity profits. And has not such been, in fact, the history of every church which has held its commission from the state, or been dependent upon it? Of the Greek church, both at Constantinople and at Petersburgh? Of the church of England, and most Protestant churches, from their very commencement? And even the church of Rome, to which, corrupt and *effete* as it now is, humanity owes a debt never to be sufficiently appreciated, is not it chargeable with the same sin, from the time when that glorious struggle for which a Hildebrand lived and a Becket died—heroes who will eternally survive by the side of Martin Luther and John Knox—was shamefully wound up by the memorable blow inflicted upon Boniface the Eighth, at Anagni, by the emissary of Philippe le Bel— which established for all the centuries which have since elapsed the supremacy of the sceptre over the crosier, and of

which it was but a natural consequence that a few years after,
the pontiff of the Christian world sat at Avignon, for the
first time in history, as the degraded tool of a temporal oppressor, sanctioning the butchery of the Templars and every
other enormity of that rapacious despot?

Against this idea of a church establishment, the Newmanites protest, and I protest with them. If an established
church is not to be independent of state control, no established church ought to exist. A church bound to teach only
what the state commands! Why, it is the business of a church
to be a schoolmaster to the state, and a bridle or a spur to it
—the one or the other, or both, according as it needs them.
It is the business of a church to fill the minds of the people
with ideas and feelings of duty by which the temporal rulers
shall be restrained, and of which they shall stand in awe. If
these rulers, to be a check upon whom is one of the chief
uses of an organised body of religious teachers, are to prescribe to that body what it shall teach, can we expect anything but what has generally existed in the church of England, a tacit understanding that the peace is to be kept on all
points which would really stir up people's minds, and on all
matters of religion or morality which concern the higher
classes of society in their duties as governors; that so much of
Christianity shall alone be insisted upon as is good for the
lower orders, and that the church shall exist, in the words of
a clever and eloquent writer, only for the purpose of

. . . "Discreetly teaching all to choose,
The path their betters fain would have them use?" *

Most heartily is it to be rejoiced at, that a party has
arisen which asserts a higher position than this for the religious teachers of a nation, and with whose convictions it is
consistent, while claiming this higher character for the
church, to remain in the church—to assert these as *her* principles, not those of her enemies; and to revive the remembrance of the claims which the Christian church once made
to a more exalted destination, and of the services which she

---

* *The Election,* a poem recently published.

rendered in the fulfilment of it. I care not in what manner they reconcile this to their consciences, so that they do reconcile it. The principles by which they do so are those which they profess in common with almost every defender of the establishment; but were it otherwise—were it true that they silence their scruples by the most flimsy sophistry—it is not for us, who hold the same conclusions on firmer grounds, to meet them with reproach or discouragement.

The remaining part, sir, of your reply to my letter is chiefly employed in contending that the motives of these men are not so pure from mere worldly ambition, as, taking a rational view of their situation and prospects, I had concluded them to be. Your proofs of this are, that they are eager to propagate their opinions, to get newspapers, and reviews, and the younger clergy on their side, which you seem to think a very unpardonable stretch of priestly assumption; and that they have been, as you represent, very successful in these objects, although judging from present appearances their success even in their stronghold, Oxford, does not amount to any very substantial ascendancy. If the clergy and even the monkery of their own university will not consent, and it seems far from likely that they will, to raise one of this body to the dignity of a Poetry Professor and a salary of £100 a year, one would not give much for their chance of deaneries or mitres from the practical statesmen of the Conservative party, for whom, in fact, and for whose principles of action, instead of practising any sycophancy, they scarcely disguise their contempt. But suppose them to have been ten times more successful, what argument is this against them, any more than against Luther, or Wesley, or any other leader of a great religious movement? Grant them any degree of possible success, and they gain only a dim and distant prospect of what they would have been sure of by very ordinary exertion in the common road of preferment. You talk of the movement as having originated in a meeting held at the house of the Archbishop of Canterbury's chaplain, to consult about what should be done to protect the church against the encroachments of the Whig ministry. I am surprised that you should attach any importance to such an old nurse's tale. Is a profound and connected system of thought, embracing not only a complete body of theology and philosophy, but a consistent theory of universal history, a thing which can be got up suddenly in a year, or two years, for a momentary political exigency? That there may be persons in high places, both in and out of the clerical body, who have joined or countenanced this movement from such motives as you allege, is likely enough; every cause has its share of this sort of proselytes; and there very probably was such a meeting as you state: but that the set of doctrines called Puseyism originated from thence, it would take no ordinary portion of credulity to make any person believe. The circumstances of the times may have awakened serious thoughts in minds which otherwise would have slumbered; the dangers which menaced the institutions they most valued may have helped to lead even such men as Mr. Newman and Dr. Pusey to reflect more deeply than they otherwise would have done upon the spirit and original purposes of those institutions. But this dependence of our deepest and most conscientious thoughts upon the suggestions of our outward circumstances, is incident to the infirmity of our speculative faculties, and is no imputation upon the sincerity of any one, nor, to any great extent, even upon the strength of his judgment. If it be a reproach, it is one to which all mankind are liable.

But I must not encroach farther, and really I do not know what I could add, or in what way the vindication of any set of men could be more complete. On their doctrines, as distinguished from the characters of the men themselves, and on the position which they seem to me to hold in English speculation, I could say much on a future occasion, if you continue to do me the honour of inserting my letters.

HISTORICUS

On the Justice of a Court-martial

and

On Religion and Guardianship

1846

The smallest private cases of injustice, as well as the largest, could elicit Mill's support. The issues dealt with in these articles are the effects of class privilege on an unpopular enlisted man in the British army and the consequences of established religion for the rights of parents to educate their children in another faith.

————————

AN ARTICLE FROM *The Morning Chronicle*
OF OCTOBER 6, 1846

We think it very desirable that the Government and the public should keep their attention fixed on the case of Private Thomas Matthewson, who was tried by court-martial at Hounslow, on Tuesday last, for abusive language to a non-commissioned officer. Whether he was found guilty by the court has not yet transpired, as the publication of the sentence does not take place until it has been confirmed by the Commander-in-Chief; but there is far more than enough apparent on the proceedings to require that the result should be watched.

This man, Matthewson, it may be remembered, was one of the witnesses in the case of death from flogging, which contributed so much to bring about the partial abolition of that punishment. His evidence was of a nature to be peculiarly disagreeable to his commanding officer, being one of those which imputed to him, in the most direct manner, neglect and want of feeling with regard to the sufferer. Matthewson, also, was the witness to whom menaces were said to have been indirectly held out as to the probable consequences to himself of the evidence he gave; and although this was not thought to have been substantiated, it was not denied that Colonel Whyte publicly addressed him on parade, saying that he was as near as— (what type of nearness the colonel employed we do not think it necessary to repeat) —to having perjured himself. This gentle apostrophe, however merited it may in the colonel's opinion have been, neither betokened in the present, nor augured for the future, any amicable feelings on the part of the commanding officer towards Private Matthewson. We are far from implying that because an officer has received what he thinks provocation from a private, he must necessarily become his unscrupulous enemy. But Private Matthewson must have had far more than ordinary confidence in the magnanimity of his commanding officer, if he did not feel certain that, in some way or other, he would be made to smart severely for his evidence; that if a charge were not actually got up against him, an opportunity would be watched of exaggerating some trifling peccadillo into a grave offence; that, in short, he would be a marked man, and if not to the colonel himself, to some of those miserable waiters upon power, who, we may be sure, are not wanting in a regiment any more than in a court, and who might think that the ruin of one who had made himself obnoxious would be a satisfaction to those whom they wished to please, even if it were only the satisfaction derived from the fulfilment of a prophecy. If this surmise is not already verified by what has just taken place, there is a coincidence most unfortunate for all those upon whom any share of the suspicion can possibly fall.

We will suppose that Matthewson, after giving the evidence which reflected discredit upon Colonel Whyte, was really guilty of a serious military offence. We should have expected that, considering what had happened, and the prejudice likely to exist against him, not only in his own regiment, but among any officers composing a court-martial (for the great majority of officers are supporters of corporal punishment, and it is no secret that the sympathies of officers are almost always with the officer against the soldier) —we should have expected, we say, that scrupulous care would have been taken to make it impossible for even the prisoner himself to deny that the most generous justice was done him. We should have expected that the testimony against him would have been sifted with the most jealous vigilance; that rather a greater amount of evidence than is deemed sufficient in ordinary cases would have been insisted on; and that the most studious and ostentatious attention would have been paid to giving him every facility, and to showing that every facility had been given, for the production of any evidence which he might think available to weaken, though it were only in a slight degree, the strength of the case against him.

Instead of this, what do we see? By a most unfortunate accident, if it be an accident, the trial takes place after Matthewson's own regiment has left the neighbourhood, and along with it the witnesses whom he could have called, either to points of the case itself, or to his general character. This obstacle, probably, was not insuperable; he might have "applied to the commanding officer" (Colonel Whyte himself) to have the witnesses detained; and if he had done so, we will hope that the request would have been complied with. We, therefore, do not insist further on this point, which may be worse in appearance than in reality. But there is another feature in the case, which would be fatal to the prosecution —whether with a military tribunal we know not—but with any civil tribunal of decent impartiality. The man's alleged offence is the use of insulting words, and there is absolutely no evidence to the words he used, or to his having used insulting words at all, except that of Sergeant O'Donnell, the very man alleged to have been insulted. There is no circum-

stantial evidence, and no corroborative testimony but that of
Corporal Routh, who "was not sufficiently near to hear
what took place," and could only affirm that "by" his manner the prisoner appeared to be speaking "disrespectfully to
the sergeant." But it was not for disrespectfulness of *manner*
that he was brought before the court. In the circumstances
alleged there was nothing to explain or render probable the
abusive expressions said to have been used, which are such
as were only likely to be employed in the heat of passion, or
as the consequence of a previous altercation. When police-
men are declared to be in the habit of giving false evidence
against innocent persons, is it too much to suspect an af-
fronted sergeant of some exaggeration? Especially when the
prisoner declares him to have been drunk at the time, and
against the assertion of one of the two parties to a dispute
it is not unfair to oppose the denial of the other.

We have argued the matter on the footing of simple justice, and the treatment due to every human being. If it were
to be looked at on grounds of chivalrous or gentlemanly
feeling, it would be much more concisely disposed of. Supposing such feelings to have had any voice in the matter, the
commanding officer, one may presume, would rather have
given up his commission than that Private Matthewson,
while under his command, should be in a position in which
it would be felt that the one was inflicting, and the other
undergoing vengeance for unacceptable evidence in a court
of justice. There are means enough for ridding a regiment
of a troublesome character, when his presence is no longer
supportable. If Matthewson was such a character, the consequences of giving him his discharge would have been (in the
peculiar circumstances of this case) less prejudicial to discipline than the moral impression of his being made a victim
—which, truly or not, he will be thought to be, if found
guilty and sentenced on this inadequately supported charge.

The part of prosecutor was worthily filled by a Viscount
St. Lawrence, who came armed with all the means which the
books of the regiment and his own testimony could supply
for crushing the already crushed man.

AN ARTICLE FROM *The Morning Chronicle*
OF DECEMBER 29, 1846

The case of the North family, heard last week before
Vice Chancellor Knight Bruce, and on which that judge has
pronounced at least a temporary decision, suggests some
queries on the state of the law respecting maternal rights, to
which this judgment, if it represents the law correctly, gives
anything but a satisfactory answer.

The parties to the cause are the widow of Lieut. Dudley
North on the one side, and his mother and sister on the other,
and the contest is for the guardianship of the four children.
The facts of the case are these:—The parents, originally
members of the Church of England, had for some time before the father's death been in the habit of attending, along
with two of their children, a Roman Catholic chapel, but
had not publicly professed the Catholic religion. The father
died from the effects of a coach accident, and on his death-
bed refused to receive the Protestant clergyman who had
been brought to the house by one of his relations. The widow
soon after became an avowed Roman Catholic, as she asserts
on oath that, according to her belief, her husband, but for
his untimely decease, would have done. The husband's relations got possession of the children by a stratagem, and
refused to restore them to their mother, placing them under
the care of a maiden aunt. The mother sought legal redress;
and the result is, that the Vice-Chancellor directs a reference
to a Master, to appoint a guardian or guardians, and decides
that in the meantime the children shall remain in the custody
of their paternal relations, the mother "to have access to them
for two hours daily," but only in the presence of one or more
of the said relations.

We have attempted to discover, from the reported
judgment, on what distinct principle this startling decision
is founded. Vice-Chancellor Knight Bruce does not positively affirm any principle, but makes indistinct reference to

two. He is very positive on one thing—that it is the duty
of the court to have the children brought up in the religion
of the Church of England. Sometimes it seems as if his reason was, that the father must be presumed to have intended
it. But there are other sayings on which it is difficult to put
any interpretation but that, even if the father had intended
otherwise, the court would not the less have thought it its
duty to see the children brought up in the religious belief
which this Vice-Chancellor sanctions by his approval.

It is a duty to society that a decision should be given by
the highest authority on this question of law: Is, or is not, a
widowed mother, in case of intestacy, the legal guardian of
her children? The counsel for the widow asserts that she is.
The judge, if we understand his meaning, decides that she is
not; that there is no legal guardian; that it rests with the
court to appoint one; that it is entirely at the court's discretion to appoint anybody, the mother, or any one else. If this
is correct; if the mother, even when she is the sole parent, is
in the eye of the law a stranger to her own children; if even
when the father is silent the mother has no rights over the
children, more than anybody has who chooses to claim them,
and *can* have no rights unless the court thinks fit to confer
them on her, as it is equally at liberty to do on any one else
—if this is the law, it ought to be made universally known,
in order that the common sense and sense of justice of the
community may speedily put an end to so iniquitous an outrage on the most universally recognised and strongest tie of
nature. Society is rigid in enforcing this tie *against* the
mother; there are no bounds to its aversion and contempt
for a mother who deserts her offspring: is it then entitled to
arrogate to itself the power to deprive her of them for no
presumed or alleged fault—nay, while saying, as in this case,
that the mother's conduct is unimpeachable? The idea is
monstrous, and repugnant to all feelings of justice. Again,
if the widowed mother is not the legal guardian of the children, with what justice can she be bound to maintain them
by her labour? In the case of mothers in the lower ranks,
can the law, which acknowledges between them and their

children no relationship, treat the mother as a parent for the sole purpose of forcing her to work for their maintenance?

But if the mother *is* the legal guardian of the children, unless the court for reasons assigned should appoint otherwise, what reasons appear in the Vice-Chancellor's statement which justify his setting aside her guardianship in this particular case? And here we cannot but express an opinion that the two reasons between which, as we before observed, the Vice-Chancellor halts, are each of them so bad, that we do not think he could have ventured to rest his decision upon the unassisted strength of either of them. He appears to intend to eke them out, one by another, under the idea that two bad reasons added together amount to a good one. In the first place, he argues at some length that the father, having never professed himself a Catholic, must be held to have died a Protestant, and to have intended therefore that the children should be brought up as Protestants. Now, if the mother has no rights, the father by his intestacy having abdicated his, it seems quite frivolous to discuss hypotheses about what the father may be presumed to have intended. The court, on this supposition, is the sole guardian, and ought to decide the matter on its own merits. But if the mother has rights, what can be more irrational than to supersede them on a presumption (not to say on a doubtful one) that the father desired something different? If he had desired anything different, he could have so provided by will; and his not doing so must be taken as complete evidence of his acquiescence in what, he had every reason to believe, would be the consequence of his intestacy—that the children would remain in the society and guardianship of their mother. Would the court have treated the question in this manner if it had been a question of property? A man dies possessed of an estate, which he could have bequeathed to whom he pleased; but he dies intestate, and it passes to the heir-at-law. Would the court receive evidence to prove that he disliked the heir-at-law, and would have preferred leaving the estate to some one else? The proposition is absurd, and would be so regarded. The deceased not having declared his intentions by will, the law would take its course, and the estate devolve on the person whom it had designated.

While, however, Vice-Chancellor Bruce is willing to make all the use he can, in favour of his conclusion, of the imaginary intentions of the father, he intimates the right of the court to direct the children's religion, let the father's purpose be what it may:—"That it should view the religion of the children as a matter of indifference is of course out of the question. That no one can do. *That the religion of the children should depend on the mere will and pleasure of the person or persons who may happen to be guardian or guardians,* especially *when there is no testamentary guardian*— appears to me to be equally out of the case. As it is the duty of the court to superintend the education of infants in all cases where its powers are not excluded, so especially and most importantly it is the duty of the court to superintend that course of religious education in which the children ought, until they are of years of discretion, and able and think fit to choose for themselves, to be educated." Not only therefore when there is not, but when there is, a lawful guardian, the court will not permit the religion of the children to depend on the guardian's decision, but will make it depend on the court's pleasure. Nor is the maxim limited to cases in which there is no testamentary guardian. If Mr. North had made a will appointing Mrs. North guardian, or any one else guardian, and the person appointed had been supposed to intend to make the children Roman Catholics, the court would have set aside the will.

Hear this all parents who think that you have the power of confiding your children after your death to the relatives or friends on whose integrity, judgment, and affection you most rely. If the friend or relative be a Roman Catholic, he may be your choice, but some other person, perhaps one you have the greatest reason to despise and dislike, will be Sir J. K. Bruce's. Nay, it is not certain that his interference will wait for your death. It is his duty, he says, to regulate the religious education of the children in all cases from which his powers are not "excluded;" and that they are not excluded from the case of children whose father is alive, Shelley's case and several other cases bear witness. For aught that appears, the children might have been taken out of the control of Mr. North himself, if he had lived to declare himself a Roman Catholic, and the Protestant maiden lady who has them in custody might have been *in loco* of both their parents, as she now is of their widowed mother. If we could smile on so serious a subject, we should be moved to do so by the doctrine that a maiden aunt is as nearly related to children as their mother!

The case has two stages yet to go through. The Master has to report; and his report, when made, must receive the sanction of the court; from which, if the present temporary decision is made a permanent one, we sincerely hope the case will be carried by appeal to the Lord Chancellor, and will not pass by without calling the attention of the public and of Parliament to the principles which it involves. It is they who should decide whether a mother is her child's nearest relation or no, and whether Sir J. K. Bruce, under cover of his court's powers as protector of infants, shall be permitted to commence, in the year 1846, a new form of religious persecution.

14

On French Restrictions on the Press

1848

Mill was one of the best students of French politics in his day. There was probably no Englishman who wrote more about French affairs; his newspaper articles about France would make a volume by themselves. During the French revolution of 1830, he had been a great enthusiast of the liberal cause. English Tory resistance to parliamentary reform then seemed impenetrable, and he was sufficiently inspired by the French resistance to Charles X to believe, for a time, that revolution would also be needed in England to bring about reform.

Throughout the 1840's, Mill's trips to France and his extensive correspondence with many Frenchmen, including Tocqueville, had kept him informed that King Louis-Phillipe was losing the enthusiasm and loyalty aroused by his accession to the throne in 1830. During the French revolution of 1848, Mill took extra pains to defend the Republican cause against English critics.

Mill was understandably chagrined when, in August 1848, the new French government he had defended passed its own laws against a free press. In effect, the French were converting republican rule and democratic procedures into dogma. Despite his own enthusiasm for the rights the French were trying to protect, Mill did not keep silent. He knew that one could not be liberal without opposing all authoritarianism, whether of kings or of democrats.

His attack has familiar themes: the danger the repressive law poses to discussion of great and vital questions, and the vagueness of its criteria. For the first time, however, Mill openly recognizes an actual authoritarianism of "the left."

The "panic" in England "within these few months," to which the article refers, is the last and greatest of the Chartist demonstrations, which took place in London in the spring of 1848 and failed. Chartism was a manysided democratic movement that flared up several times between 1831 and 1848; its essential demand was "one man, one vote."

An Article from *The Spectator* of August 19, 1848

The decree against the press, just passed almost with unanimity by the National Assembly of France, is one of the most monstrous outrages on the idea of freedom of discussion ever committed by the legislature of a country pretending to be free. It is the very law of Louis Philippe—the September law, once so indignantly denounced—with scarcely any alteration but the substitution of the word "Republic" for "Monarchy."

This precious specimen of Liberal legislation declares punishable by fine and imprisonment all attacks on "the rights and authority of the National Assembly—on the rights and authority which the members of the Executive derive from the decrees of the Assembly—on the Republican institutions and the Constitution—on the principle of the sovereignty of the people and of universal suffrage—on the liberty of worship, the principle of property, and the rights of family"; besides which, it ordains similar punishments for "exciting hatred and contempt towards the Government of the Republic," and for "public outrage committed (in their public character) against one or more members of the National Assembly, or against a Minister of any religion paid by the State."

This list of subjects on which discussion is prohibited, or permitted only on one side, includes all the great political and social questions of the age. If only one set of opinions is to be permitted on any matter which involves the right of property, the rights or obligations of family, the question of Republicanism, of universal suffrage, even the particular constitution which the Assembly may hereafter adopt, or the rightfulness of abolishing that constitution—what are the subjects, worth discussing, on which freedom of political discussion is to exist? "The acts of the Executive," says the decree. "The present provision is not to affect the right of discussion and censure on the acts of the Executive and of the Ministers." A most liberal concession, truly! The law is worse, with only this reservation in favour of freedom, than if there were no reservation at all; for the most tyrannical court of justice which could now exist in civilized Europe would reserve more than this. It is not declared that even the *actions* of the Legislature may be censured, but only those of the Executive; and with regard to laws or institutions, no liberty of censure is reserved at all. There was a wretched pretence by one or two of the speakers, that no restraint was intended on the "freedom of philosophical discussion"—that nothing was to be forbidden but incitements to hatred and contempt. But the decree says nothing of the kind. The decree prohibits "any attack." The distinction is good for nothing, even if it were made. To say that attacks are permitted, but not incitements to hatred and contempt, would be to say that discussion shall be lawful on condition that it be cold, dry, and unimpressive; that the dull and the indifferent shall be allowed to express opinions, but that persons of genius and feeling must hold their peace. Under such laws, it has been truly said in one of the French journals, Rousseau's discourse on Inequality never could have been published. Nor could any great writings of great reformers, religious or political, have seen the light if such laws had existed and had been obeyed.

How long shall we continue to see the regard for freedom of opinion, which all parties profess while they are on the oppressed side, thrown off by them all as soon as they are in the majority? How much longer must we wait for an example, anywhere in Europe, of a ruler or a ruling party who really desire fair play for any opinions contrary to their own? Is it not shameful that no sooner has a reforming party accomplished as much change in the institutions of the country as itself deems desirable, than it proceeds to decree that every person shall be fined or imprisoned, who proposes either to go a single step further or a step back? We are aware of the allowances to be made for men lately engaged in a desperate and at one time a doubtful contest against a determined attempt at insurrection; and we know too that this decree is avowedly a temporary measure, to be hereafter superseded by more deliberate legislation. But we lament to say, that in the tone assumed, and the doctrines professed by the speakers, we see no ground of assurance that the permanent measure will be at all different, in spirit and principle, from the transitional one.

It is not, however, for English Conservatives, either Whig or Tory, to indulge any self-complacent triumph over French Republicans. The new act of the French Assembly does not make the laws of France on the freedom of the press worse than those of England have always been. The freedom of the press, in England, is entirely an affair of opinion and custom, not of law. It exists because the laws are not enforced. The law of political libel, as laid down in all the books, is as inconsistent with free discussion as the laws of Russia. There is no censure of any established institution or constituted authority which is not an offence by law. And within these few months it has been seen how eagerly the English Parliament, under the influence of a far less degree of panic, have rushed to make the laws against what was deemed seditious speaking or writing more stringent than before.

A government cannot be blamed for defending itself against insurrection. But it deserves the severest blame if to prevent insurrection it prevents the promulgation of opinion. If it does so, it actually justifies insurrection in those to whom it denies the use of peaceful means to make their opinions prevail. Hitherto the French Government has been altogether in the right against all attempts to overthrow it. But by what right can the Assembly now reprobate any future attempt, either by Monarchists or Socialists, to rise in arms against the Government? It denies them free discussion. It says they shall not be suffered to bring their opinions to the touchstone of the public reason and conscience. It refuses them the chance which every sincere opinion can justly claim, of triumphing in a fair field. It fights them with weapons which can as easily be used to put down the most valuable truth as the most pernicious error. It tells them that they must prevail by violence before they shall be allowed to contend by argument. Who can blame persons who are deeply convinced of the truth and importance of their opinions, for asserting them by force, when that is the only means left them of obtaining even a hearing? When their mouths are *gagged,* can they be reproached for using their arms?

15

On Religious Qualifications for Parliament

1849

The removal of political restrictions on dissenting Protestants and Roman Catholics in the early nineteenth century helped change England from an Anglican to a Christian society. Although this broadened the creedal basis of citizenship, a religious oath still excluded Jews and atheists, among others, from Parliament. An early struggle, in the 1840's and 1850's, turned around the Jewish financier, Lionel Rothschild, head of the London branch of the great banking family. He was first elected an M.P. in 1847 but, although he was repeatedly reelected, he could not take his seat until 1858. By the 1880's the long campaign against oaths reached an end when Charles Bradlaugh, the freethinker, after constant reelection, was finally permitted to take his seat with a simple affirmation that he would do his duty.

The reluctance of the liberal Lord John Russell to admit sceptics and infidels other than Jews to Parliament is difficult to explain. As Mill indicates, Russell's sentiments as a humane and rational man were not strong enough to overcome his deeper beliefs that England was still primarily a Christian society. Exceptions might be made for Jews, but he could not bring himself to abolish completely doctrinal tests for office-holding.

In this article, Mill tries first to reduce Russell's argument to absurdity. He points out (as he has before) that two famous sceptics—David Hume, the great eighteenth-century Scottish philosopher, and Edward Gibbon, author of the *Decline and Fall of the Roman Empire*—would have been ineligible for Parliament under Russell's criteria. What Englishman today,

Mill asks, would accept their exclusion? He then restates his classic formula: that action, rather than opinion, is the safest test of character.

An Article from *The Daily News* of March 26, 1849

The bill of Lord John Russell for the admission of Jews into Parliament, affords by the mode it adopts of effecting that purpose, an example of the rooted aversion of our practical politicians to anything like a principle. If there *is* a principle which is supposed to be sacred in the eye of a Russell, it is religious freedom. If there is a maxim in politics which Whigs are understood to cherish, it is that no one should be subjected to civil disabilities on the ground of any opinions which he may entertain in matters of religion. Yet a Whig and a Russell, finding the Jews excluded from Parliament by the imposition of certain words interpreted as expressing a belief in Christianity purposes to dispense with the words, but to dispense with them for Jews only. For all who do not declare themselves to be Jews, he not only leaves the words as he found them, but actually re-enacts them. He is proposing to abolish the old oaths and to establish new, and in the oaths which he establishes he introduces *de novo* these very words, granting to Jews a special exemption from their use. He opens the door of Parliament just wide enough to allow one particular class of dissenters from Christianity to slip in, and closes it, as far as depends upon him, against all others.

Why is this? If we take his own account of the matter, it is because he does not think it right to announce that sceptics and infidels ought to be admitted into Parliament; therefore he declares ineligible, not only sceptics and infidels, but Hindoos, Buddhists, and Mahomedans, none of whom are commonly counted among infidels, and who compose nearly three-fourths of the population of the British dominions. But we will discuss the question as if it concerned only those whom Lord John would have it believed that he actually cares about rendering ineligible.

First, what sort of sceptics and infidels does he really suppose that his oaths will keep out of Parliament? Those who take his side of the question usually profess the charitable belief that infidels are persons whom oaths will not bind. It is certain at least that an infidel who can be excluded by such words as those used, "on the true faith of a Christian," words which rather insinuate than profess a belief in Christianity—equivocating, jesuitical words, which seem chosen on purpose to afford a loophole to the conscience—must be a person more than ordinarily under the influence of honour and moral obligation, and, therefore, more than ordinarily fit to be a member of an assembly where honest men are required; and more than usually undeserving to have any discreditable mark put upon him.

But (it will be said by Lord John Russell, or by somebody for him) the measure will not really keep anybody out. It is not meant to do so. It is only meant as a declaration that certain persons *ought* to be kept out. It is an admission under protest. It is a national testimony that nobody who disbelieves in Christianity can be a fit person to sit in Parliament.

If it be so, it is a testimony to something which every one who has any knowledge of life knows to be not true. We say nothing about Jews, whom this very measure is intended to let in. Were Hume and Gibbon improper persons to sit in Parliament? Conservatives, at least, will hardly be of that opinion; for they were both Tories; and the sons and daughters of Tories to this day got their first notions of English politics from a History written by one of them, and very false notions they are. Liberals, again, would deem them valuable members of Parliament for different reasons. It is not possible to imagine an assembly where great questions are to be discussed and important public business transacted, in which no good use could be made of such powers of mind as these men possessed.

It is unnecessary, however, to go back to a past age. The present times are sufficient. We should like to put a question to Lord John Russell. Let him mentally reckon up (if they are not too numerous to be reckoned), among persons now in Parliament or in office, or who have been so since he entered into public life, all those whom he either positively knows, or has good ground for believing, to be disbelievers in revelation—many of them in more than revelation. We put it to him as a man of the world. Many good Christians, in their innocence and inexperience, would be astonished and shocked at the supposition we are making, but Lord John must know enough of his time, and of the men of his time, to be more or less a competent judge. We wish that after revolving in his mind the various members of the present or any former House of Commons, whom he has known or believed to be what are usually termed infidels, he would ask himself whether, among all the members composing it, these, taken collectively, were the persons whom, in his sincere opinion, the House of Commons could have best spared? We do not mean that many, or perhaps any, of these persons are Humes and Gibbons, or have ever made any public attack on religion, or are at all likely to avow unbelief; if they did, they would emperil, among many other things, all their chances of re-election. The truth is, that there is generally nothing in their conduct by which they could, as a class, be distinguished from the great majority of believers. This ought not to be: a great difference in the conscientious convictions of human beings ought to make a visible difference of some kind or other in their conduct, but in point of fact it seldom does. Certain it is that neither Lord John Russell, nor any other man of the world, would trust the unbelievers less in any relation of life, or would consider them less eligible for the great majority of public functions, than the average of Christians. On this point we should not fear to take the opinion of any man who has been minister of England in the last thirty years, could we be sure that he would speak his real sentiments.

If Lord John Russell really believed that the words he

proposes would exclude from Parliament all the sincere un-believers who are now or may hereafter become members of it, we are convinced that he never would have proposed them. Why, then, has he done so? Because he believes that the ex-clusion will not exclude, but will be a mere *brutum fulmen*; and, with the usual indifference of our statesmen to a bad principle, when they do not expect that it will be followed by specific bad consequences, he thinks he may as well make this sacrifice at the shrine of bigotry, if it will gain him an addi-tional vote for letting in Mr. Rothschild. He has yet to learn that a legislature which either introduces or confirms a bad principle does more harm than is compensated by twenty good practical measures involving no principle: for it is by the principles contained in them that institutions educate the national mind, thus producing more effect for good or evil than "laws or kings" by their direct influence can either "cause or cure." As long as the laws keep up nominal per-secution on account of opinion, whether practically operative or not, the seal of bigotry will be upon us; and no letting in of one set of excluded persons after another by the backdoor of the constitution will avail much to make us otherwise.

16

On Liberty

1859

Considering the relative brevity of Mill's most famous work, its compression of argument and range of issues are extraordinary. The resulting complexity of *On Liberty* is not usually suggested by those who take the work as the classic liberal defense of diversity and toleration. As a lawyer's brief, *On Liberty* could not stand up well in a court; had Harriet Taylor lived, Mill might have polished the essay further. Some general reasons for the confused and ambiguous qualities in the essay as it stands, as well as for its major strengths, are suggested in the general Introduction.

On Liberty is an attack, not on government coercion and intolerant public policies, but largely on what Mill considers the oppressiveness of democratic public opinion. Against democratic conceits and arrogance, Mill has three major interests to defend: "the march of mind" toward progress, the development of a responsible and humane individualism, and the growth of social diversity necessary for both of these. At the beginning of the essay, he promises us a principle by which progress, individualism, and diversity can all be protected.

In trying to define that principle, Mill examines more fully than before the political implications of his theory of emergent truth. He had been developing his ideas about the "search for truth" for nearly forty years and had best expressed them previously in *A System of Logic*. Because progress, happiness, and the humane life all depend on the discovery of truth, suppressing opinions might deny mankind precisely the ideas it needs.

On the surface it would appear that, by the time he published *On Liberty,* Mill had lost any certainty about what was true or false in moral and religious life. He no longer repeated, for example, his early assertion that Christianity was the true faith. Mill did not doubt the value of decency, honor, and truthtelling; but he did fear that democracy would define its ideals too narrowly. He also thought that, however fine these ideals might be, individuals ought not to be treated like children. Short of violent extremes, such as selling himself into slavery, an individual should be free to make errors and suffer for them—free even to damn himself. Freedom, in other words, would not be complete unless men had the power to make their own mistakes.

In this light, it is a parody of Mill and of liberalism to suggest that Mill believed that "all values were relative," in the sense that civilized standards of behavior have no general claims. He believed in the superiority of the civilizing opinions, and, fearing what democratic enthusiasm might do to them, he sought to safeguard them by proving that freedom for all opinions is necessary if the best opinions are to do their work.

Mill did not, however, permit his insistence upon freedom for all opinions to obscure his own moral discriminations. In his early plea for Catholic emancipation, he could claim that religious freedom for the Irish, although just, was no panacea, and that his wish for toleration for Catholics did not exclude his belief that Roman Catholicism was a bad religion. Similarly, in *On Liberty,* he grants the moral interests of society or authority their due; he recognizes the genuine claims institutions have on men, and he acknowledges society's stake in decency and moral responsibility.

Mill most disliked frenzy for any political system, whatever its form, because he feared it would deny his greatest wish—to live in a society in which he could debate antagonists as good as Coleridge, the Tory, and Newman, the orthodox Christian, so that his liberal ideas would have to account for themselves against the best possible opposition. In our time, such qualities of mind seem increasingly rare. Everywhere, liberal institutions are on the defensive against totalitarians who claim for themselves the final victories of progress, reason, and control over man and nature. It thus seems, at times, a memory of a lost cause to recall that a man so close to public life and partisan strife as Mill was, could be willing, even eager, to understand and argue the best case for the other side. We come closest to Mill if, whatever our cause and whatever the future, we are willing to do the same.

On Liberty

The grand, leading principle, towards which every argument unfolded in these pages directly converges, is the
absolute and essential importance of human development
in its richest diversity.—Wilhelm von Humboldt: *Sphere
and Duties of Government.*

To the beloved and deplored memory of her who was the inspirer, and in part the author, of all that is best in my writings—the friend and wife whose exalted sense of truth and right was my strongest incitement, and whose approbation was my chief reward—I dedicate this volume. Like all that I have written for many years, it belongs as much to her as to me; but the work as it stands has had, in a very insufficient degree, the inestimable advantage of her revision; some of the most important portions having been reserved for a more careful re-examination, which they are now never destined to receive. Were I but capable of interpreting to the world one half the great thoughts and noble feelings which are buried in her grave, I should be the medium of a greater benefit to it, than is ever likely to arise from anything that I can write, unprompted and unassisted by her all but unrivaled wisdom.

On Liberty

I   INTRODUCTORY

The subject of this essay is not the so-called "liberty of the will," so unfortunately opposed to the misnamed doctrine of philosophical necessity; but civil, or social liberty: the nature and limits of the power which can be legitimately exercised by society over the individual. A question seldom stated, and hardly ever discussed in general terms, but which profoundly influences the practical controversies of the age by its latent presence, and is likely soon to make itself recognized as the vital question of the future. It is so far from being new that, in a certain sense, it has divided mankind almost from the remotest ages; but in the stage of progress into which the more civilized portions of the species have now entered, it presents itself under new conditions and requires a different and more fundamental treatment.

The struggle between liberty and authority is the most conspicuous feature in the portions of history with which we are earliest familiar, particularly in that of Greece, Rome, and England. But in old times this contest was between subjects, or some classes of subjects, and the government. By liberty was meant protection against the tyranny of the political rulers. The rulers were conceived (except in some of the popular governments of Greece) as in a necessarily antagonistic position to the people whom they ruled. They consisted of a governing One, or a governing tribe or caste, who derived their authority from inheritance or conquest, who, at all events, did not hold it at the pleasure of the governed, and whose supremacy men did not venture, perhaps did not desire, to contest, whatever precautions might be taken against its oppressive exercise. Their power was regarded as necessary, but also as highly dangerous; as a weapon which they would attempt to use against their subjects, no less than against external enemies. To prevent the weaker members of the community from being preyed upon by innumerable vultures, it was needful that there should be an animal of prey stronger than the rest, commissioned to keep them down. But as the king of the vultures would be no less bent upon preying on the flock than any of the minor harpies, it was indispensable to be in a perpetual attitude of defense against his beak and claws. The aim, therefore, of patriots was to set limits to the power which the ruler should be suffered to exercise over the community; and this limitation was what they meant by liberty. It was attempted in two ways. First, by obtaining a recognition of certain immunities, called political liberties or rights, which it was to be regarded as a breach of duty in the ruler to infringe, and which if he did infringe, specific resistance or general rebellion was held to be justifiable. A second, and generally a later, expedient was the establishment of constitutional checks by which the consent of the community, or of a body of some sort, supposed to represent its interests, was made a necessary condition to some of the more important acts of the governing power. To the first of these modes of limitation, the ruling power, in most European countries, was compelled, more or less, to submit. It was not so with the second; and, to attain this, or, when already in some degree possessed, to attain it more completely, became everywhere the principal object of the lovers of liberty. And so long as mankind were content to combat one enemy by another, and to be ruled by a master on condition of being guaranteed more or less efficaciously against his tyranny, they did not carry their aspirations beyond this point.

A time, however, came, in the progress of human affairs, when men ceased to think it a necessity of nature that their governors should be an independent power opposed in interest to themselves. It appeared to them much better that the various magistrates of the state should be their tenants or delegates, revocable at their pleasure. In that way alone, it seemed, could they have complete security that the powers of government would never be abused to their disadvantage. By degrees this new demand for elective and temporary rulers became the prominent object of the exertions of the popular party wherever any such party existed, and superseded, to a considerable extent, the previous efforts to limit the power of rulers. As the struggle proceeded for making the ruling power emanate from the periodical choice of the ruled, some persons began to think that too much importance had been attached to the limitation of the power itself. *That* (it might seem) was a resource against rulers whose interests were habitually opposed to those of the people. What was now wanted was that the rulers should be identified with the people, that their interest and will should be the interest and will of the nation. The nation did not need to be protected against its own will. There was no fear of its tyrannizing over itself. Let the rulers be effectually responsible to it, promptly removable by it, and it could afford to trust them with power of which it could itself dictate the use to be made. Their power was but the nation's own power, concentrated and in a form convenient for exercise. This mode of thought, or rather perhaps of feeling, was common among the last generation of European liberalism, in the Continental section of which it still apparently predominates. Those who admit any limit to what a government may do, except in the case of such governments as they think ought not to exist, stand out as brilliant exceptions among the political thinkers of the Continent. A similar tone of sentiment might by this time have been prevalent in our own country if the circumstances which for a time encouraged it had continued unaltered.

But, in political and philosophical theories as well as in persons, success discloses faults and infirmities which failure might have concealed from observation. The notion that the people have no need to limit their power over themselves might seem axiomatic, when popular government was a thing only dreamed about, or read of as having existed at some distant period of the past. Neither was that notion necessarily disturbed by such temporary aberrations as those of the French Revolution, the worst of which were the work of a usurping few, and which, in any case, belonged, not to the permanent working of popular institutions, but to a sudden and convulsive outbreak against monarchical and aristocratic despotism. In time, however, a democratic republic came to occupy a large portion of the earth's surface and made itself felt as one of the most powerful members of the community of nations; and elective and responsible government became subject to the observations and criticisms which wait upon a great existing fact. It was now perceived that such phrases as "self-government," and "the power of the people over themselves," do not express the true state of the case. The "people" who exercise the power are not always the same people with those over whom it is exercised; and the "self-government" spoken of is not the government of each by himself, but of each by all the rest. The will of the people, moreover, practically means the will of the most numerous or the most active *part* of the people —the majority, or those who succeed in making themselves accepted as the majority; the people, consequently, *may* desire to oppress a part of their number, and precautions are as much needed against this as against any other abuse of power. The limitation, therefore, of the power of government over individuals loses none of its importance when the holders of power are regularly accountable to the community, that is, to the strongest party therein. This view of things, recommending itself equally to the intelligence of thinkers and to the inclination of those important classes in European society to whose real or supposed interests democracy is adverse, has had no difficulty in establishing itself; and in political speculations "the tyranny of the majority" is now generally included among the evils against which society requires to be on its guard.

Like other tyrannies, the tyranny of the majority was at first, and is still vulgarly, held in dread, chiefly as operating through the acts of the public authorities. But reflecting persons perceived that when society is itself the tyrant—

society collectively over the separate individuals who compose it—its means of tyrannizing are not restricted to the acts which it may do by the hands of its political functionaries. (Society can and does execute its own mandates; and if it issues wrong mandates instead of right, or any mandates at all in things with which it ought not to meddle, it practices a social tyranny more formidable than many kinds of political oppression, since, though not usually upheld by such extreme penalties, it leaves fewer means of escape, penetrating much more deeply into the details of life, and enslaving the soul itself.) Protection, therefore, against the tyranny of the magistrate is not enough; there needs protection also against the tyranny of the prevailing opinion and feeling, against the tendency of society to impose, by other means than civil penalties, its own ideas and practices as rules of conduct on those who dissent from them; to fetter the development and, if possible, prevent the formation of any individuality not in harmony with its ways, and compel all characters to fashion themselves upon the model of its own. There is a limit to the legitimate interference of collective opinion with individual independence; and to find that limit, and maintain it against encroachment, is as indispensable to a good condition of human affairs as protection against political despotism.

But though this proposition is not likely to be contested in general terms, the practical question where to place the limit—how to make the fitting adjustment between individual independence and social control—is a subject on which nearly everything remains to be done. All that makes existence valuable to anyone depends on the enforcement of restraints upon the actions of other people. Some rules of conduct, therefore, must be imposed—by law in the first place, and by opinion on many things which are not fit subjects for the operation of law. What these rules should be is the principal question in human affairs; but if we except a few of the most obvious cases, it is one of those which least progress has been made in resolving. No two ages, and scarcely any two countries, have decided it alike; and the

decision of one age or country is a wonder to another. Yet
the people of any given age and country no more suspect any
difficulty in it than if it were a subject on which mankind had
always been agreed. The rules which obtain among themselves appear to them self-evident and self-justifying. This
all but universal illusion is one of the examples of the magi-
cal influence of custom, which is not only, as the proverb says,
a second nature but is continually mistaken for the first. The
effect of custom, in preventing any misgiving respecting the
rules of conduct which mankind impose on one another, is
all the more complete because the subject is one on which it
is not generally considered necessary that reasons should be
given, either by one person to others or by each to himself.
People are accustomed to believe, and have been encouraged
in the belief by some who aspire to the character of philosophers, that their feelings on subjects of this nature are better
than reasons and render reasons unnecessary. The practical
principle which guides them to their opinions on the regulation of human conduct is the feeling in each person's mind
that everybody should be required to act as he, and those
with whom he sympathizes, would like them to act. No one,
indeed, acknowledges to himself that his standard of judgment is his own liking; but an opinion on a point of conduct,
not supported by reasons, can only count as one person's
preference; and if the reasons, when given, are a mere appeal to a similar preference felt by other people, it is still
only many people's liking instead of one. To an ordinary
man, however, his own preference, thus supported, is not
only a perfectly satisfactory reason but the only one he generally has for any of his notions of morality, taste, or propriety, which are not expressly written in his religious creed,
and his chief guide in the interpretation even of that. Men's
opinions, accordingly, on what is laudable or blamable are
affected by all the multifarious causes which influence their
wishes in regard to the conduct of others, and which are as
numerous as those which determine their wishes on any other
subject. Sometimes their reason; at other times their
prejudices or superstitions; often their social affections, not

seldom their antisocial ones, their envy or jealousy, their
arrogance or contemptuousness; but most commonly their
desires or fears for themselves—their legitimate or illegitimate self-interest. Wherever there is an ascendant class, a
large portion of the morality of the country emanates from
its class interests and its feelings of class superiority. The
morality between Spartans and Helots, between planters
and Negroes, between princes and subjects, between nobles
and roturiers, between men and women has been for the
most part the creation of these class interests and feelings;
and the sentiments thus generated react in turn upon the
moral feelings of the members of the ascendant class, in their
relations among themselves. Where, on the other hand, a
class, formerly ascendant, has lost its ascendancy, or where its
ascendancy is unpopular, the prevailing moral sentiments
frequently bear the impress of an impatient dislike of superiority. Another grand determining principle of the
rules of conduct, both in act and forbearance, which have
been enforced by law or opinion, has been the servility of
mankind toward the supposed preferences or aversions of
their temporal masters or of their gods. This servility,
though essentially selfish, is not hypocrisy; it gives rise to
perfectly genuine sentiments of abhorrence; it made men
burn magicians and heretics. Among so many baser influences, the general and obvious interests of society have, of
course, had a share, and a large one, in the direction of the
moral sentiments; less, however, as a matter of reason, and
on their own account, than as a consequence of the sympathies
and antipathies which grew out of them; and sympathies
and antipathies which had little or nothing to do with the
interests of society have made themselves felt in the establishment of moralities with quite as great force.

The likings and dislikings of society, or of some powerful portion of it, are thus the main thing which has practically determined the rules laid down for general observance,
under the penalites of law or opinion. And in general,
those who have been in advance of society in thought and
feeling have left this condition of things unassailed in prin-

ciple, however they may have come into conflict with it in
some of its details. They have occupied themselves rather
in inquiring what things society ought to like or dislike than
in questioning whether its likings or dislikings should be a
law to individuals. They preferred endeavoring to alter the
feelings of mankind on the particular points on which they
were themselves heretical rather than make common cause in
defense of freedom with heretics generally. The only case
in which the higher ground has been taken on principle and
maintained with consistency, by any but an individual here
and there, is that of religious belief: a case instructive in
many ways, and not least so as forming a most striking instance of the fallibility of what is called the moral sense;
for the *odium theologicum,* in a sincere bigot, is one of the
most unequivocal cases of moral feeling. Those who first
broke the yoke of what called itself the Universal Church
were in general as little willing to permit difference of religious opinion as that church itself. But when the heat of
the conflict was over, without giving a complete victory to
any party, and each church or sect was reduced to limit its
hopes to retaining possession of the ground it already occupied, minorities, seeing that they had no chance of becoming majorities, were under the necessity of pleading to
those whom they could not convert for permission to differ.
It is accordingly on this battlefield, almost solely, that the
rights of the individual against society have been asserted
on broad grounds of principle, and the claim of society to
exercise authority over dissentients openly controverted.
The great writers to whom the world owes what religious
liberty it possesses have mostly asserted freedom of conscience
as an indefeasible right, and denied absolutely that a human
being is accountable to others for his religious belief. Yet
so natural to mankind is intolerance in whatever they really
care about that religious freedom has hardly anywhere been
practically realized, except where religious indifference,
which dislikes to have its peace disturbed by theological
quarrels, has added its weight to the scale. In the minds of
almost all religious persons, even in the most tolerant coun-

tries, the duty of toleration is admitted with tacit reserves. One person will bear with dissent in matters of church government, but not of dogma; another can tolerate everybody, short of a Papist or a Unitarian; another, everyone who believes in revealed religion; a few extend their charity a little further, but stop at the belief in a God and in a future state. Wherever the sentiment of the majority is still genuine and intense, it is found to have abated little of its claim to be obeyed.

In England, from the peculiar circumstances of our political history, though the yoke of opinion is perhaps heavier, that of law is lighter than in most other countries of Europe; and there is considerable jealousy of direct interference by the legislative or the executive power with private conduct, not so much from any just regard for the independence of the individual as from the still subsisting habit of looking on the government as representing an opposite interest to the public. The majority have not yet learned to feel the power of the government their power, or its opinions their opinions. When they do so, individual liberty will probably be as much exposed to invasion from the government as it already is from public opinion. But, as yet, there is a considerable amount of feeling ready to be called forth against any attempt of the law to control individuals in things in which they have not hitherto been accustomed to be controlled by it; and this with very little discrimination as to whether the matter is, or is not, within the legitimate sphere of legal control; insomuch that the feeling, highly salutary on the whole, is perhaps quite as often misplaced as well grounded in the particular instances of its application. There is, in fact, no recognized principle by which the propriety or impropriety of government interference is customarily tested. People decide according to their personal preferences. Some, whenever they see any good to be done, or evil to be remedied, would willingly instigate the government to undertake the business, while others prefer to bear almost any amount of social evil rather than add one to the departments of human interests amenable to governmental control. And men range themselves on one or the other side in any particular case, according to this general direction of their sentiments, or according to the degree of interest which they feel in the particular thing which it is proposed that the government should do, or according to the belief they entertain that the government would, or would not, do it in the manner they prefer; but very rarely on account of any opinion to which they consistently adhere, as to what things are fit to be done by a government. And it seems to me that in consequence of this absence of rule or principle, one side is at present as often wrong as the other; the interference of government is, with about equal frequency, improperly invoked and improperly condemned.

The object of this essay is to assert one very simple principle, as entitled to govern absolutely the dealings of society with the individual in the way of compulsion and control, whether the means used be physical force in the form of legal penalties or the moral coercion of public opinion. That principle is that the sole end for which mankind are warranted, individually or collectively, in interfering with the liberty of action of any of their number is self-protection. That the only purpose for which power can be rightfully exercised over any member of a civilized community, against his will, is to prevent harm to others. His own good, either physical or moral, is not a sufficient warrant. He cannot rightfully be compelled to do or forbear because it will be better for him to do so, because it will make him happier, because, in the opinions of others, to do so would be wise or even right. These are good reasons for remonstrating with him, or reasoning with him, or persuading him, or entreating him, but not for compelling him or visiting him with any evil in case he do otherwise. To justify that, the conduct from which it is desired to deter him must be calculated to produce evil to someone else. The only part of the conduct of anyone for which he is amenable to society is that which concerns others. In the part which merely concerns himself, his independence is, of right, absolute.

Over himself, over his own body and mind, the individual
is sovereign.

It is, perhaps, hardly necessary to say that this doctrine
is meant to apply only to human beings in the maturity of
their faculties. We are not speaking of children or of young
persons below the age which the law may fix as that of manhood or womanhood. Those who are still in a state to require being taken care of by others must be protected against
their own actions as well as against external injury. For the
same reason we may leave out of consideration those backward states of society in which the race itself may be considered as in its nonage. The early difficulties in the way of
spontaneous progress are so great that there is seldom any
choice of means for overcoming them; and a ruler full of the
spirit of improvement is warranted in the use of any expedients that will attain an end perhaps otherwise unattainable. Despotism is a legitimate mode of government in dealing with barbarians, provided the end be their improvement and the means justified by actually effecting that end.
Liberty, as a principle, has no application to any state of
things anterior to the time when mankind have become capable of being improved by free and equal discussion. Until
then, there is nothing for them but implicit obedience to
an Akbar or a Charlemagne, if they are so fortunate as to
find one. But as soon as mankind have attained the capacity
of being guided to their own improvement by conviction or
persuasion (a period long since reached in all nations with
whom we need here concern ourselves), compulsion, either
in the direct form or in that of pains and penalties for non-
compliance, is no longer admissible as a means to their own
good, and justifiable only for the security of others.

It is proper to state that I forego any advantage which
could be derived to my argument from the idea of abstract
right as a thing independent of utility. I regard utility as
the ultimate appeal on all ethical questions; but it must be
utility in the largest sense, grounded on the permanent
interests of man as a progressive being. Those interests,
I contend, authorize the subjection of individual spontaneity

to external control only in respect to those actions of each which concern the interest of other people. If anyone does an act hurtful to others, there is a *prima facie* case for punishing him by law or, where legal penalties are not safely applicable, by general disapprobation. There are also many positive acts for the benefit of others which he may rightfully be compelled to perform, such as to give evidence in a court of justice, to bear his fair share in the common defense or in any other joint work necessary to the interest of the society of which he enjoys the protection, and to perform certain acts of individual beneficence, such as saving a fellow creature's life or interposing to protect the defenseless against ill usage— things which whenever it is obviously a man's duty to do he may rightfully be made responsible to society for not doing. A person may cause evil to others not only by his actions but by his inaction, and in either case he is justly accountable to them for the injury. The latter case, it is true, requires a much more cautious exercise of compulsion than the former. To make anyone answerable for doing evil to others is the rule; to make him answerable for not preventing evil is, comparatively speaking, the exception. Yet there are many cases clear enough and grave enough to justify that exception. In all things which regard the external relations of the individual, he is *de jure* amenable to those whose interests are concerned, and, if need be, to society as their protector. There are often good reasons for not holding him to the responsibility; but these reasons must arise from the special expediencies of the case: either because it is a kind of case in which he is on the whole likely to act better when left to his own discretion than when controlled in any way in which society have it in their power to control him; or because the attempt to exercise control would produce other evils, greater than those which it would prevent. When such reasons as these preclude the enforcement of responsibility, the conscience of the agent himself should step into the vacant judgment seat and protect those interests of others which have no external protection; judging himself all the more rigidly,

because the case does not admit of his being made accountable to the judgment of his fellow creatures.

But there is a sphere of action in which society, as distinguished from the individual, has, if any, only an indirect
interest: comprehending all that portion of a person's life
and conduct which affects only himself or, if it also affects
others, only with their free, voluntary, and undeceived consent and participation. When I say only himself, I mean
directly and in the first instance; for whatever affects himself may affect others through himself; and the objection
which may be grounded on this contingency will receive consideration in the sequel. This, then, is the appropriate region
of human liberty. It comprises, first, the inward domain of
consciousness, demanding liberty of conscience in the most
comprehensive sense, liberty of thought and feeling, absolute
freedom of opinion and sentiment on all subjects, practical
or speculative, scientific, moral, or theological. The liberty
of expressing and publishing opinions may seem to fall under
a different principle, since it belongs to that part of the
conduct of an individual which concerns other people, but,
being almost of as much importance as the liberty of thought
itself and resting in great part on the same reasons, is practically inseparable from it. Secondly, the principle requires
liberty of tastes and pursuits, of framing the plan of our life
to suit our own character, of doing as we like, subject to
such consequences as may follow, without impediment from
our fellow creatures, so long as what we do does not harm
them, even though they should think our conduct foolish,
perverse, or wrong. Thirdly, from this liberty of each individual follows the liberty, within the same limits, of combination among individuals; freedom to unite for any purpose not involving harm to others: the persons combining
being supposed to be of full age and not forced or deceived.

No society in which these liberties are not, on the whole,
respected is free, whatever may be its form of government;
and none is completely free in which they do not exist absolute and unqualified. The only freedom which deserves the

name is that of pursuing our own good in our own way, so long as we do not attempt to deprive others of theirs or impede their efforts to obtain it. Each is the proper guardian of his own health, whether bodily *or* mental and spiritual. Mankind are greater gainers by suffering each other to live as seems good to themselves than by compelling each to live as seems good to the rest.

Though this doctrine is anything but new and, to some persons, may have the air of a truism, there is no doctrine which stands more directly opposed to the general tendency of existing opinion and practice. Society has expended fully as much effort in the attempt (according to its lights) to compel people to conform to its notions of personal as of social excellence. The ancient commonwealths thought themselves entitled to practice, and the ancient philosophers countenanced, the regulation of every part of private conduct by public authority, on the ground that the State had a deep interest in the whole bodily and mental discipline of every one of its citizens—a mode of thinking which may have been admissible in small republics surrounded by powerful enemies, in constant peril of being subverted by foreign attack or internal commotion, and to which even a short interval of relaxed energy and self-command might so easily be fatal that they could not afford to wait for the salutary permanent effects of freedom. In the modern world, the greater size of political communities and, above all, the separation between spiritual and temporal authority (which placed the direction of men's consciences in other hands than those which controlled their worldly affairs) prevented so great an interference by law in the details of private life; but the engines of moral repression have been wielded more strenuously against divergence from the reigning opinion in self-regarding than even in social matters; religion, the most powerful of the elements which have entered into the formation of moral feeling, having almost always been governed either by the ambition of a hierarchy seeking control over every department of human conduct, or by the spirit of Puritanism. And some of those modern reformers who have placed themselves in strongest opposition to the religions of the past have been noway behind either churches or sects in their assertion of the right of spiritual domination: M. Comte, in particular, whose social system, as unfolded in his *Système de Politique Positive,* aims at establishing (though by moral more than by legal appliances) a despotism of society over the individual surpassing anything contemplated in the political ideal of the most rigid disciplinarian among the ancient philosophers.

Apart from the peculiar tenets of individual thinkers, there is also in the world at large an increasing inclination to stretch unduly the powers of society over the individual both by the force of opinion and even by that of legislation; and as the tendency of all the changes taking place in the world is to strengthen society and diminish the power of the individual, this encroachment is not one of the evils which tend spontaneously to disappear, but, on the contrary, to grow more and more formidable. The disposition of mankind, whether as rulers or as fellow citizens, to impose their own opinions and inclinations as a rule of conduct on others is so energetically supported by some of the best and by some of the worst feelings incident to human nature that it is hardly ever kept under restraint by anything but want of power; and as the power is not declining, but growing, unless a strong barrier of moral conviction can be raised against the mischief, we must expect, in the present circumstances of the world, to see it increase.

It will be convenient for the argument if, instead of at once entering upon the general thesis, we confine ourselves in the first instance to a single branch of it on which the principle here stated is, if not fully, yet to a certain point, recognized by the current opinions. This one branch is the Liberty of Thought, from which it is impossible to separate the cognate liberty of speaking and of writing. Although these liberties, to some considerable amount, form part of the political morality of all countries which profess religious toleration and free institutions, the grounds, both philosophical and practical, on which they rest are perhaps not so familiar to the general mind, nor so thoroughly appreciated by many, even of the leaders of opinion, as might have been expected. Those grounds, when rightly understood, are of much wider application than to only one division of the subject, and a thorough consideration of this part of the question will be found the best introduction to the remainder. Those to whom nothing which I am about to say will be new may therefore, I hope, excuse me if on a subject which for now three centuries has been so often discussed I venture on one discussion more.

II   OF THE LIBERTY OF THOUGHT AND DISCUSSION

The time, it is to be hoped, is gone by when any defense would be necessary of the "liberty of the press" as one of the securities against corrupt or tyrannical government. No argument, we may suppose, can now be needed against permitting a legislature or an executive, not identified in interest with the people, to prescribe opinions to them and determine what doctrines or what arguments they shall be allowed to hear. This aspect of the question, besides, has been so often and so triumphantly enforced by preceding writers that it needs not be specially insisted on in this place. Though the law of England, on the subject of the press, is as servile to this day as it was in the time of the Tudors, there is little danger of its being actually put in force against political discussion except during some temporary panic when fear of insurrection drives ministers and judges from their propriety;* and, speaking generally, it is not, in constitutional

* These words had scarcely been written when, as if to give them an emphatic contradiction, occurred the Government Press Prosecutions of 1858. That ill-judged interference with the liberty of public discussion has not, however, induced me to alter a single word in the text, nor has it at all weakened my conviction that, moments of panic excepted, the era of pains and penalties for political discussion has, in our own country, passed away. For, in the first place, the prosecutions were not persisted in; and, in the second, they were never, properly speaking, political prosecutions. The offense charged was not that of criticizing institutions or the acts or persons

countries, to be apprehended that the government, whether
completely responsible to the people or not, will often attempt to control the expression of opinion, except when in
doing so it makes itself the organ of the general intolerance
of the public. Let us suppose, therefore, that the government
is entirely at one with the people, and never thinks of exerting any power of coercion unless in agreement with what it
conceives to be their voice. But I deny the right of the people to exercise such coercion, either by themselves or by their
government. The power itself is illegitimate. The best
government has no more title to it than the worst. It is as
noxious, or more noxious, when exerted in accordance with
public opinion than when in opposition to it. If all mankind
minus one were of one opinion, mankind would be no more
justified in silencing that one person than he, if he had the
power, would be justified in silencing mankind. Were an
opinion a personal possession of no value except to the owner,
if to be obstructed in the enjoyment of it were simply a private injury, it would make some difference whether the injury
was inflicted only on a few persons or on many. But the peculiar evil of silencing the expression of an opinion is that it is
robbing the human race, posterity as well as the existing
generation—those who dissent from the opinion, still more

of rulers, but of circulating what was deemed an immoral doctrine, the law-
fulness of tyrannicide.

If the arguments of the present chapter are of any validity, there ought
to exist the fullest liberty of professing and discussing, as a matter of ethical
conviction, any doctrine, however immoral it may be considered. It would,
therefore, be irrelevant and out of place to examine here whether the doctrine
of tyrannicide deserves that title. I shall content myself with saying that the
subject has been at all times one of the open questions of morals; that the
act of a private citizen in striking down a criminal who, by raising himself
above the law, has placed himself beyond the reach of legal punishment or
control has been accounted by whole nations, and by some of the best and
wisest of men, not a crime by an act of exalted virtue; and that, right or
wrong, it is not of the nature of assassination, but of civil war. As such, I hold
that the instigation to it, in a specific case, may be a proper subject of
punishment, but only if an overt act has followed, and at least a probable
connection can be established between the act and the instigation. Even then
it is not a foreign government but the very government assailed which alone,
in the exercise of self-defense, can legitimately punish attacks directed against
its own existence.

than those who hold it. If the opinion is right, they are deprived of the opportunity of exchanging error for truth; if wrong, they lose, what is almost as great a benefit, the clearer perception and livelier impression of truth produced by its collision with error.

It is necessary to consider separately these two hypotheses, each of which has a distinct branch of the argument corresponding to it. We can never be sure that the opinion we are endeavoring to stifle is a false opinion; and if we were sure, stifling it would be an evil still.

First, the opinion which it is attempted to suppress by authority may possibly be true. Those who desire to suppress it, of course, deny its truth; but they are not infallible. They have no authority to decide the question for all mankind and exclude every other person from the means of judging. To refuse a hearing to an opinion because they are sure that it is false is to assume that *their* certainty is the same thing as *absolute* certainty. All silencing of discussion is an assumption of infallibility. Its condemnation may be allowed to rest on this common argument, not the worse for being common.

Unfortunately for the good sense of mankind, the fact of their fallibility is far from carrying the weight in their practical judgment which is always allowed to it in theory; for while everyone well knows himself to be fallible, few think it necessary to take any precautions against their own fallibility, or admit the supposition that any opinion of which they feel very certain may be one of the examples of the error to which they acknowledge themselves to be liable. Absolute princes, or others who are accustomed to unlimited deference, usually feel this complete confidence in their own opinions on nearly all subjects. People more happily situated, who sometimes hear their opinions disputed and are not wholly unused to be set right when they are wrong, place the same unbounded reliance only on such of their opinions as are shared by all who surround them, or to whom they habitually defer; for in proportion to a man's want of confidence in his own solitary judgment does he usually repose, with implicit trust, on the infallibility of "the world" in general. And the world, to each individual, means the part of it with which he comes in contact: his party, his sect, his church, his class of society; the man may be called, by comparison, almost liberal and large-minded to whom it means anything so comprehensive as his own country or his own age. Nor is his faith in this collective authority at all shaken by his being aware that other ages, countries, sects, churches, classes, and parties have thought, and even now think, the exact reverse. He devolves upon his own world the responsibility of being in the right against the dissentient worlds of other people; and it never troubles him that mere accident has decided which of these numerous worlds is the object of his reliance, and that the same causes which make him a churchman in London would have made him a Buddhist or a Confucian in Peking. Yet it is as evident in itself, as any amount of argument can make it, that ages are no more infallible than individuals—every age having held many opinions which subsequent ages have deemed not only false but absurd; and it is as certain that many opinions, now general, will be rejected by future ages, as it is that many, once general, are rejected by the present.

The objection likely to be made to this argument would probably take some such form as the following. There is no greater assumption of infallibility in forbidding the propagation of error than in any other thing which is done by public authority on its own judgment and responsibility. Judgment is given to men that they may use it. Because it may be used erroneously, are men to be told that they ought not to use it at all? To prohibit what they think pernicious is not claiming exemption from error, but fulfilling the duty incumbent on them, although fallible, of acting on their conscientious conviction. If we were never to act on our opinions, because those opinions may be wrong, we should leave all our interests uncared for, and all our duties unperformed. An objection which applies to all conduct can be no valid objection to any conduct in particular. It is the duty of governments, and of individuals, to form the true opinions they can; to form them carefully, and never impose them upon others unless they are quite sure of being right. But when they are sure (such reasoners may say), it is not conscientiousness but cowardice to shrink from acting on their opinions and allow doctrines which they honestly think dangerous to the welfare of mankind, either in this life or in another, to be scattered abroad without restraint, because other people, in less enlightened times, have persecuted opinions now believed to be true. Let us take care, it may be said, not to make the same mistake; but governments and nations have made mistakes in other things which are not denied to be fit subjects for the exercise of authority: they have laid on bad taxes, made unjust wars. Ought we therefore to lay on no taxes and, under whatever provocation, make no wars? Men and governments must act to the best of their ability. There is no such thing as absolute certainty, but there is assurance sufficient for the purposes of human life. We may, and must, assume our opinion to be true for the guidance of our own conduct; and it is assuming no more when we forbid bad men to pervert society by the propagation of opinions which we regard as false and pernicious.

I answer, that it is assuming very much more. There is the greatest difference between presuming an opinion to be true because, with every opportunity for contesting it, it has not been refuted, and assuming its truth for the purpose of not permitting its refutation. Complete liberty of contradicting and disproving our opinion is the very condition which justifies us in assuming its truth for purposes of action; and on no other terms can a being with human faculties have any rational assurance of being right.

When we consider either the history of opinion or the ordinary conduct of human life, to what is it to be ascribed that the one and the other are no worse than they are? Not certainly to the inherent force of the human understanding, for on any matter not self-evident there are ninety-nine persons totally incapable of judging of it for one who is capable; and the capacity of the hundredth person is only comparative, for the majority of the eminent men of every past generation held many opinions now known to be erroneous, and did or approved numerous things which no one will now justify. Why is it, then, that there is on the whole a preponderance among mankind of rational opinions and rational conduct? If there really is this preponderance—which there must be unless human affairs are, and have always been, in an almost desperate state—it is owing to a quality of the human mind, the source of everything respectable in man either as an intellectual or as a moral being, namely, that his errors are corrigible. He is capable of rectifying his mistakes by discussion and experience. Not by experience alone. There must be discussion to show how experience is to be interpreted. Wrong opinions and practices gradually yield to fact and argument; but facts and arguments, to produce any effect on the mind, must be brought before it. Very few facts are able to tell their own story, without comments to bring out their meaning. The whole strength and value, then, of human judgment depending on the one property, that it can be set right when it is wrong, reliance can be placed on it only when the means of setting it right are kept constantly at hand. In the case of any person whose judgment is really deserving of confidence, how has it become so? Because he has kept his mind open to criticism of his opinions and conduct. Because it has been his practice to listen to all that could be said against him; to profit by as much of it as was just, and to expound to himself, and upon occasion to others, the fallacy of what was fallacious. Because he has felt that the only way in which a human being can make some approach to knowing the whole of a subject is by hearing what can be said about it by persons of every variety of opinion, and studying all modes in which it can be looked at by every character of mind. No wise man ever acquired his wisdom in any mode but this; nor is it in the nature of human intellect to become wise in any other manner. The steady habit of correcting and completing his own opinion by collating it with those of others, so far from causing doubt and hesita-

tion in carrying it into practice, is the only stable foundation
for a just reliance on it; for, being cognizant of all that can, at
least obviously, be said against him, and having taken up his
position against all gainsayers—knowing that he has sought
for objections and difficulties instead of avoiding them, and
has shut out no light which can be thrown upon the subject
from any quarter—he has a right to think his judgment better than that of any person, or any multitude, who have not
gone through a similar process.

It is not too much to require that what the wisest of
mankind, those who are best entitled to trust their own judgment, find necessary to warrant their relying on it, should
be submitted to by that miscellaneous collection of a few wise
and many foolish individuals called the public. The most
intolerant of churches, the Roman Catholic Church, even at
the canonization of a saint admits, and listens patiently to, a
"devil's advocate." The holiest of men, it appears, cannot
be admitted to posthumous honors until all that the devil
could say against him is known and weighed. If even the Newtonian philosophy were not permitted to be questioned, mankind could not feel as complete assurance of its truth as they
now do. The beliefs which we have most warrant for have
no safeguard to rest on but a standing invitation to the
whole world to prove them unfounded. If the challenge is
not accepted, or is accepted and the attempt fails, we are far
enough from certainty still, but we have done the best that
the existing state of human reason admits of: we have
neglected nothing that could give the truth a chance of reaching us; if the lists are kept open, we may hope that, if there
be a better truth, it will be found when the human mind is
capable of receiving it; and in the meantime we may rely on
having attained such approach to truth as is possible in our
own day. This is the amount of certainty attainable by a
fallible being, and this the sole way of attaining it.

Strange it is that men should admit the validity of the
arguments for free discussion, but object to their being
"pushed to an extreme," not seeing that unless the reasons
are good for an extreme case, they are not good for any case.

Strange that they should imagine that they are not assuming infallibility when they acknowledge that there should be free discussion on all subjects which can possibly be *doubtful*, but think that some particular principle or doctrine should be forbidden to be questioned because it is so *certain*, that is, because *they are certain* that it is certain. To call any proposition certain, while there is anyone who would deny its certainty if permitted, but who is not permitted, is to assume that we ourselves, and those who agree with us, are the judges of certainty, and judges without hearing the other side.

In the present age—which has been described as "destitute of faith, but terrified at skepticism"—in which people feel sure, not so much that their opinions are true as that they should not know what to do without them—the claims of an opinion to be protected from public attack are rested not so much on its truth as on its importance to society. There are, it is alleged, certain beliefs so useful, not to say indispensable, to well-being that it is as much the duty of governments to uphold those beliefs as to protect any other of the interests of society. In a case of such necessity, and so directly in the line of their duty, something less than infallibility may, it is maintained, warrant, and even bind, governments to act on their own opinion confirmed by the general opinion of mankind. It is also often argued, and still oftener thought, that none but bad men would desire to weaken these salutary beliefs; and there can be nothing wrong, it is thought, in restraining bad men and prohibiting what only such men would wish to practice. This mode of thinking makes the justification of restraints on discussion not a question of the truth of doctrines but of their usefulness, and flatters itself by that means to escape the responsibility of claiming to be an infallible judge of opinions. But those who thus satisfy themselves do not perceive that the assumption of infallibility is merely shifted from one point to another. The usefulness of an opinion is itself matter of opinion—as disputable, as open to discussion, and requiring discussion as much as the opinion itself. There is the same need of an infallible judge of opinions to decide an opinion to be noxious as to decide it to be false, unless the opinion condemned has full opportunity of defending itself. And it will not do to say that the heretic may be allowed to maintain the utility or harmlessness of his opinion, though forbidden to maintain its truth. The truth of an opinion is part of its utility. If we would know whether or not it is desirable that a proposition should be believed, is it possible to exclude the consideration of whether or not it is true? In the opinion, not of bad men, but of the best men, no belief which is contrary to truth can be really useful; and can you prevent such men from urging that plea when they are charged with culpability for denying some doctrine which they are told is useful, but which they believe to be false? Those who are on the side of received opinions never fail to take all possible advantage of this plea; you do not find *them* handling the question of ability as if it could be completely abstracted from that of truth; on the contrary, it is, above all, because their doctrine is "the truth" that the knowledge or the belief of it is held to be so indispensable. There can be no fair discussion of the question of usefulness when an argument so vital may be employed on one side, but not on the other. And in point of fact, when law or public feeling do not permit the truth of an opinion to be disputed, they are just as little tolerant of a denial of its usefulness. The utmost they allow is an extenuation of its absolute necessity, or of the positive guilt of rejecting it.

In order more fully to illustrate the mischief of denying a hearing to opinions because we, in our own judgment, have condemned them, it will be desirable to fix down the discussion to a concrete case; and I choose, by preference, the cases which are least favorable to me—in which the argument against freedom of opinion, both on the score of truth and on that of utility, is considered the strongest. Let the opinions impugned be the belief in a God and in a future state, or any of the commonly received doctrines of morality. To fight the battle on such ground gives a great advantage to an unfair antagonist, since he will be sure to say (and many who have no desire to be unfair will say it internally), Are these the doctrines which you do not deem sufficiently certain to be taken under the protection of law? Is the belief in a God one of the opinions to feel sure of which you hold to be assuming infallibility? But I must be permitted to observe that it is not the feeling sure of a doctrine (be it what it may) which I call an assumption of infallibility. It is the undertaking to decide that question *for others,* without allowing them to hear what can be said on the contrary side. And I denounce and reprobate this pretension not the less if put forth on the side of my most solemn convictions. However positive anyone's persuasion may be, not only of the falsity but of the pernicious consequences—not only of the pernicious consequences, but (to adopt expressions which I altogether condemn) the immorality and impiety of an opinion—yet if, in pursuance of that private judgment, though backed by the public judgment of his country or his contemporaries, he prevents the opinion from being heard in its defense, he assumes infallibility. And so far from the assumption being less objectionable or less dangerous because the opinion is called immoral or impious, this is the case of all others in which it is most fatal. These are exactly the occasions on which the men of one generation commit those dreadful mistakes which excite the astonishment and horror of posterity. It is among such that we find the instances memorable in history, when the arm of the law has been employed to root out the best men and the noblest doctrines; with deplorable success as to the men, though some of the doctrines have survived to be (as if in mockery) invoked in defense of similar conduct toward those who dissent from *them,* or from their received interpretation.

Mankind can hardly be too often reminded that there was once a man called Socrates, between whom and the legal authorities and public opinion of this time there took place a memorable collision. Born in an age and country abounding in individual greatness, this man has been handed down to us by those who best knew both him and the age as the most virtuous man in it; while *we* know him as the head and

prototype of all subsequent teachers of virtue, the source
equally of the lofty inspiration of Plato and the judicious utilitarianism of Aristotle, *"i maestri di color che sanno,"* the
two headsprings of ethical as of all other philosophy. This
acknowledged master of all the eminent thinkers who have
since lived—whose fame, still growing after more than two
thousand years, all but outweighs the whole remainder of
the names which make his native city illustrious—was put to
death by his countrymen, after a judicial conviction, for impiety and immorality. Impiety, in denying the gods recognized by the State; indeed, his accuser asserted (see the
Apologia) that he believed in no gods at all. Immorality, in
being, by his doctrines and instructions, a "corruptor of
youth." Of these charges the tribunal, there is every ground
for believing, honestly found him guilty, and condemned
the man who probably of all then born had deserved best of
mankind to be put to death as a criminal.

To pass from this to the only other instance of judicial
iniquity, the mention of which, after the condemnation of
Socrates, would not be an anticlimax: the event which took
place on Calvary rather more than eighteen hundred years
ago. The man who left on the memory of those who witnessed his life and conversation such an impression of his
moral grandeur that eighteen subsequent centuries have done
homage to him as the Almighty in person, was ignominiously
put to death, as what? As a blasphemer. Men did not merely
mistake their benefactor, they mistook him for the exact contrary of what he was and treated him as that prodigy of impiety which they themselves are now held to be for their
treatment of him. The feelings with which mankind now
regard these lamentable transactions, especially the later of
the two, render them extremely unjust in their judgment of
the unhappy actors. These were, to all appearance, not bad
men—not worse than men commonly are, but rather the
contrary; men who possessed in a full, or somewhat more than
a full measure, the religious, moral, and patriotic feelings of
their time and people: the very kind of men who, in all times,
our own included, have every chance of passing through life

blameless and respected. The high priest who rent his garments when the words were pronounced, which, according to all the ideas of his country, constituted the blackest guilt, was in all probability quite as sincere in his horror and indignation as the generality of respectable and pious men now are in the religious and moral sentiments they profess; and most of those who now shudder at his conduct, if they had lived in his time, and been born Jews, would have acted precisely as he did. Orthodox Christians who are tempted to think that those who stoned to death the first martyrs must have been worse men than they themselves are ought to remember that one of those persecutors was Saint Paul.

Let us add one more example, the most striking of all, if the impressiveness of an error is measured by the wisdom and virtue of him who falls into it. If ever anyone possessed of power had grounds for thinking himself the best and most enlightened among his contemporaries, it was the Emperor Marcus Aurelius. Absolute monarch of the whole civilized world, he preserved through life not only the most unblemished justice, but what was less to be expected from his Stoical breeding, the tenderest heart. The few failings which are attributed to him were all on the side of indulgence, while his writings, the highest ethical product of the ancient mind, differ scarcely perceptibly, if they differ at all, from the most characteristic teachings of Christ. This man, a better Christian in all but the dogmatic sense of the word than almost any of the ostensibly Christian sovereigns who have since reigned, persecuted Christianity. Placed at the summit of all the previous attainments of humanity, with an open, unfettered intellect, and a character which led him of himself to embody in his moral writings the Christian ideal, he yet failed to see that Christianity was to be a good and not an evil to the world, with his duties to which he was so deeply penetrated. Existing society he knew to be in a deplorable state. But such as it was, he saw, or thought he saw, that it was held together, and prevented from being worse, by belief and reverence of the received divinities. As a ruler of mankind, he deemed it his duty not to suffer society to fall in pieces; and saw not how, if its existing ties were removed, any others could be formed which could again knit it together. The new religion openly aimed at dissolving these ties; unless, therefore, it was his duty to adopt that religion, it seemed to be his duty to put it down. Inasmuch then as the theology of Christianity did not appear to him true or of divine origin, inasmuch as this strange history of a crucified God was not credible to him, and a system which purported to rest entirely upon a foundation to him so wholly unbelievable, could not be foreseen by him to be that renovating agency which, after all abatements, it has in fact proved to be; the gentlest and most amiable of philosophers and rulers, under a solemn sense of duty, authorized the persecution of Christianity. To my mind this is one of the most tragical facts in all history. It is a bitter thought how different a thing the Christianity of the world might have been if the Christian faith had been adopted as the religion of the empire under the auspices of Marcus Aurelius instead of those of Constantine. But it would be equally unjust to him and false to truth to deny that no one plea which can be urged for punishing anti-Christian teaching was wanting to Marcus Aurelius for punishing, as he did, the propagation of Christianity. No Christian more firmly believes that atheism is false and tends to the dissolution of society than Marcus Aurelius believed the same things of Christianity; he who, of all men then living, might have been thought the most capable of appreciating it. Unless anyone who approves of punishment for the promulgation of opinions flatters himself that he is a wiser and better man than Marcus Aurelius—more deeply versed in the wisdom of his time, more elevated in his intellect above it, more earnest in his search for truth, or more single-minded in his devotion to it when found—let him abstain from that assumption of the joint infallibility of himself and the multitude which the great Antoninus [Aurelius] made with so unfortunate a result.

Aware of the impossibility of defending the use of punishment for restraining irreligious opinions by any argument which will not justify Marcus Antoninus, the enemies of religious freedom, when hard pressed, occasionally accept this consequence and say, with Dr. Johnson, that the persecutors of Christianity were in the right, that persecution is an ordeal through which truth ought to pass, and always passes successfully, legal penalties being, in the end, powerless against truth, though sometimes beneficially effective against mischievous errors. This is a form of the argument for religious intolerance sufficiently remarkable not to be passed without notice.

A theory which maintains that truth may justifiably be persecuted because persecution cannot possibly do it any harm cannot be charged with being intentionally hostile to the reception of new truths; but we cannot commend the generosity of its dealing with the persons to whom mankind are indebted for them. To discover to the world something which deeply concerns it, and of which it was previously ignorant, to prove to it that it had been mistaken on some vital point of temporal or spiritual interest, is as important a service as a human being can render to his fellow creatures, and in certain cases, as in those of the early Christians and of the Reformers, those who think with Dr. Johnson believe it to have been the most precious gift which could be bestowed on mankind. That the authors of such spendid benefits should be requited by martyrdom, that their reward should be to be dealt with as the vilest of criminals, is not, upon this theory, a deplorable error and misfortune for which humanity should mourn in sackcloth and ashes, but the normal and justifiable state of things. The propounder of a new truth, according to this doctrine, should stand, as stood, in the legislation of the Locrians, the proposer of a new law, with a halter round his neck, to be instantly tightened if the public assembly did not, on hearing his reasons, then and there adopt his proposition. People who defend this mode of treating benefactors cannot be supposed to set much value on the benefit; and I believe this view of the subject is mostly confined to the sort of persons who think that new truths may have been desirable once, but that we have had enough of them now.

But, indeed, the dictum that truth always triumphs over

persecution is one of those pleasant falsehoods which men
repeat after one another till they pass into commonplaces, but
which all experience refutes. History teems with instances
of truth put down by persecution. If not suppressed forever,
it may be thrown back for centuries. To speak only of religious opinions: the Reformation broke out at least twenty
times before Luther, and was put down. Arnold of Brescia
was put down. Fra Dolcino was put down. Savonarola was
put down. The Albigeois were put down. The Vaudois were
put down. The Lollards were put down. The Hussites were
put down. Even after the era of Luther, wherever persecution was persisted in, it was successful. In Spain, Italy, Flan-
ders, the Austrian empire, Protestantism was rooted out;
and, most likely, would have been so in England had Queen
Mary lived or Queen Elizabeth died. Persecution has always
succeeded save where the heretics were too strong a party to
be effectually persecuted. No reasonable person can doubt
that Christianity might have been extirpated in the Roman
Empire. It spread and became predominant because the persecutions were only occasional, lasting but a short time, and
separated by long intervals of almost undisturbed propagan-
dism. It is a piece of idle sentimentality that truth, merely as
truth, has any inherent power denied to error of prevailing
against the dungeon and the stake. Men are not more zealous
for truth than they often are for error, and a sufficient application of legal or even of social penalties will generally succeed in stopping the propagation of either. The real advantage which truth has consists in this, that when an opinion is
true, it may be extinguished once, twice, or many times, but
in the course of ages there will generally be found persons
to rediscover it, until some one of its reappearances falls on a
time when from favorable circumstances it escapes persecution until it has made such head as to withstand all subsequent attempts to suppress it.

It will be said that we do not now put to death the intro-
ducers of new opinions: we are not like our fathers who slew
the prophets; we even build sepulchers to them. It is true
we no longer put heretics to death; and the amount of penal

infliction which modern feeling would probably tolerate, even against the most obnoxious opinions, is not sufficient to extirpate them. But let us not flatter persecution. Penalties for opinion, or at least for its expression, still exist by law; and their enforcement is not, even in these times, so unexampled as to make it at all incredible that they may some day be revived in full force. In the year 1857, at the summer assizes of the county of Cornwall, an unfortunate man, said to be of unexceptionable conduct in all relations of life, was sentenced to twenty-one months' imprisonment for uttering, and writing on a gate, some offensive words concerning Christianity.* Within a month of the same time, at the Old Bailey, two persons, on two separate occasions,† were rejected as jurymen, and one of them grossly insulted by the judge and by one of the counsel, because they honestly declared that they had no theological belief; and a third, a foreigner,‡ for the same reason, was denied justice against a thief. This refusal of redress took place in virtue of the legal doctrine that no person can be allowed to give evidence in a court of justice who does not profess belief in a God (any god is sufficient) and in a future state, which is equivalent to declaring such persons to be outlaws, excluded from the protection of the tribunals; who may not only be robbed or assaulted with impunity, if no one but themselves, or persons of similar opinions, be present, but anyone else may be robbed or assaulted with impunity if the proof of the fact depends on their evidence. The assumption on which this is grounded is that the oath is worthless of a person who does not believe in a future state—a proposition which betokens much ignorance of history in those who assent to it (since it is historically true that a large proportion of infidels in all ages have been persons of distinguished integrity and honor), and would be maintained by no one who had the smallest conception how many of the persons in greatest repute with the

---

* Thomas Pooley, Bodmin Assizes, July 31, 1857. In December following, he received a free pardon from the Crown.

† George Jacob Holyoake, August 17, 1857; Edward Truelove, July, 1857.

‡ Baron de Gleichen, Marlborough Street Police Court, August 4, 1857.

world, both for virtues and attainments, are well known, at least to their intimates, to be unbelievers. The rule, besides, is suicidal and cuts away its own foundation. Under pretense that atheists must be liars, it admits the testimony of all atheists who are willing to lie, and rejects only those who brave the obloquy of publicly confessing a detested creed rather than affirm a falsehood. A rule thus self-convicted of absurdity so far as regards its professed purpose can be kept in force only as a badge of hatred, a relic of persecution—a persecution, too, having the peculiarity that the qualification for undergoing it is the being clearly proved not to deserve it. The rule and the theory it implies are hardly less insulting to believers than to infidels. For if he who does not believe in a future state necessarily lies, it follows that they who do believe are only prevented from lying, if prevented they are, by the fear of hell. We will not do the authors and abettors of the rule the injury of supposing that the conception which they have formed of Christian virtue is drawn from their own consciousness.

These, indeed, are but rags and remnants of persecution, and may be thought to be not so much an indication of the wish to persecute, as an example of that very frequent infirmity of English minds, which makes them take a preposterous pleasure in the assertion of a bad principle, when they are no longer bad enough to desire to carry it really into practice. But unhappily there is no security in the state of the public mind that the suspension of worse forms of legal persecution, which has lasted for about the space of a generation, will continue. In this age the quiet surface of routine is as often ruffled by attempts to resuscitate past evils as to introduce new benefits. What is boasted of at the present time as the revival of religion is always, in narrow and uncultivated minds, at least as much the revival of bigotry; and where there is the strong permanent leaven of intolerance in the feelings of a people, which at all times abides in the middle classes of this country, it needs but little to provoke them into actively persecuting those whom they have never ceased to think proper objects of persecution.* For it is this—it is the opinions men entertain, and the feelings they cherish, respecting those who disown the beliefs they deem important which makes this country not a place of mental freedom. For a long time past, the chief mischief of the legal penalties is that they strengthen the social stigma. It is that stigma which is really effective, and so effective is it that the profession of opinions which are under the ban of society is much less common in England than is, in many other countries, the avowal of those which incur risk of judicial punishment. In respect to all persons but those whose pecuniary circumstances make them independent of the good will of other people, opinion, on this subject, is as efficacious as law; men might as well be imprisoned as excluded from the means of earning their bread. Those whose bread is already secured, and who desire no favors from men in power, or from bodies of men, or from the public, have nothing to fear from the open avowal of any opinions but to be ill-thought of and ill-spoken of, and this it ought not to require a very heroic mold to enable

* Ample warning may be drawn from the large infusion of the passions of a persecutor, which mingled with the general display of the worst parts of our national character on the occasion of the Sepoy insurrection. The ravings of fanatics or charlatans from the pulpit may be unworthy of notice; but the heads of the Evangelical party have announced as their principle for the government of Hindus and Mohammedans that no schools be supported by public money in which the Bible is not taught, and by necessary consequence that no public employment be given to any but real or pretended Christians. An Undersecretary of State, in a speech delivered to his constituents on the 12th of November, 1857, is reported to have said: "Toleration of their faith" (the faith of a hundred millions of British subjects), "the superstition which they called religion, by the British Government, had had the effect of retarding the ascendancy of the British name, and preventing the salutary growth of Christianity. . . . Toleration was the great cornerstone of the religious liberties of this country; but do not let them abuse that precious word 'toleration.' As he understood it, it meant the complete liberty to all, freedom of worship, *among Christians, who worshiped upon the same foundation*. It meant toleration of all sects and denominations of *Christians who believed in the one mediation*." I desire to call attention to the fact that a man who has been deemed fit to fill a high office in the government of this country under a liberal ministry maintains the doctrine that all who do not believe in the divinity of Christ are beyond the pale of toleration. Who, after this imbecile display, can indulge the illusion that religious persecution has passed away, never to return?

them to bear. There is no room for any appeal *ad misericor-diam* in behalf of such persons. But though we do not now inflict so much evil on those who think differently from us as it was formerly our custom to do, it may be that we do our-selves as much evil as ever by our treatment of them. Soc-rates was put to death, but the Socratic philosophy rose like the sun in heaven and spread its illumination over the whole intellectual firmament. Christians were cast to the lions, but the Christian church grew up a stately and spreading tree, overtopping the older and less vigorous growths, and stifling them by its shade. Our merely social intolerance kills no one, roots out no opinions, but induces men to disguise them or to abstain from any active effort for their diffusion. With us, heretical opinions do not perceptibly gain, or even lose, ground in each decade or generation; they never blaze out far and wide, but continue to smolder in the narrow circles of thinking and studious persons among whom they originate, without ever lighting up the general affairs of mankind with either a true or a deceptive light. And thus is kept up a state of things very satisfactory to some minds, because, without the unpleasant process of fining or imprisoning anybody, it maintains all prevailing opinions outwardly un-disturbed, while it does not absolutely interdict the exercise of reason by dissentients afflicted with the malady of thought. A convenient plan for having peace in the intellectual world, and keeping all things going on therein very much as they do already. But the price paid for this sort of intellec-tual pacification is the sacrifice of the entire moral courage of the human mind. A state of things in which a large portion of the most active and inquiring intellects find it advisable to keep the general principles and grounds of their convictions within their own breasts, and attempt, in what they address to the public, to fit as much as they can of their own conclu-sions to premises which they have internally renounced, can-not send forth the open, fearless characters and logical, con-sistent intellects who once adorned the thinking world. The sort of men who can be looked for under it are either mere conformers to commonplace, or timeservers for truth, whose arguments on all great subjects are meant for their hearers, and are not those which have convinced themselves. Those who avoid this alternative do so by narrowing their thoughts and interest to things which can be spoken of without venturing within the region of principles, that is, to small practical matters which would come right of themselves, if but the minds of mankind were strengthened and enlarged, and which will never be made effectually right until then, while that which would strengthen and enlarge men's minds—free and daring speculation on the highest subjects—is abandoned.

Those in whose eyes this reticence on the part of heretics is no evil should consider, in the first place, that in consequence of it there is never any fair and thorough discussion of heretical opinions; and that such of them as could not stand such a discussion, though they may be prevented from spreading, do not disappear. But it is not the minds of heretics that are deteriorated most by the ban placed on all inquiry which does not end in the orthodox conclusions. The greatest harm done is to those who are not heretics, and whose whole mental development is cramped and their reason cowed by the fear of heresy. Who can compute what the world loses in the multitude of promising intellects combined with timid characters, who dare not follow out any bold, vigorous, independent train of thought, lest it should land them in something which would admit of being considered irreligious or immoral? Among them we may occasionally see some man of deep conscientiousness and subtle and refined understanding, who spends a life in sophisticating with an intellect which he cannot silence, and exhausts the resources of ingenuity in attempting to reconcile the promptings of his conscience and reason with orthodoxy, which yet he does not, perhaps, to the end succeed in doing. No one can be a great thinker who does not recognize that as a thinker it is his first duty to follow his intellect to whatever conclusions it may lead. Truth gains more even by the errors of one who, with due study and preparation, thinks for himself than by the true opinions of those who only hold

them because they do not suffer themselves to think. Not
that it is solely, or chiefly, to form great thinkers that freedom
of thinking is required. On the contrary, it is as much and
even more indispensable to enable average human beings to
attain the mental stature which they are capable of. There
have been, and may again be, great individual thinkers in
a general atmosphere of mental slavery. But there never has
been, nor ever will be, in that atmosphere an intellectually
active people. Where any people has made a temporary approach to such a character, it has been because the dread of
heterodox speculation was for a time suspended. Where
there is a tacit convention that principles are not to be disputed, where the discussion of the greatest questions which
can occupy humanity is considered to be closed, we cannot
hope to find that generally high scale of mental activity
which has made some periods of history so remarkable.
Never when controversy avoided the subjects which are large
and important enough to kindle enthusiasm was the mind of
a people stirred up from its foundations, and the impulse
given which raised even persons of the most ordinary intellect to something of the dignity of thinking beings. Of such
we have had an example in the condition of Europe during
the times immediately following the Reformation; another,
though limited to the Continent and to a more cultivated
class, in the speculative movement of the latter half of the
eighteenth century; and a third, of still briefer duration,
in the intellectual fermentation of Germany during the
Goethian and Fichtean period. These periods differed
widely in the particular opinions which they developed, but
were alike in this, that during all three the yoke of authority
was broken. In each, an old mental despotism had been
thrown off, and no new one had yet taken its place. The impulse given at these three periods has made Europe what it
now is. Every single improvement which has taken place
either in the human mind or in institutions may be traced
distinctly to one or other of them. Appearances have for
some time indicated that all three impulses are well-nigh

spent; and we can expect no fresh start until we again assert our mental freedom.

Let us now pass to the second division of the argument, and dismissing the supposition that any of the received opinions may be false, let us assume them to be true and examine into the worth of the manner in which they are likely to be held when their truth is not freely and openly canvassed. However unwillingly a person who has a strong opinion may admit the possibility that his opinion may be false, he ought to be moved by the consideration that, however true it may be, if it is not fully, frequently, and fearlessly discussed, it will be held as a dead dogma, not a living truth.

There is a class of persons (happily not quite so numerous as formerly) who think it enough if a person assents undoubtingly to what they think true, though he has no knowledge whatever of the grounds of the opinion and could not make a tenable defense of it against the most superficial objections. Such persons, if they can once get their creed taught from authority, naturally think that no good, and some harm, comes of its being allowed to be questioned. Where their influence prevails, they make it nearly impossible for the received opinion to be rejected wisely and considerately, though it may still be rejected rashly and ignorantly; for to shut out discussion entirely is seldom possible, and when it once gets in, beliefs not grounded on conviction are apt to give way before the slightest semblance of an argument. Waiving, however, this possibility—assuming that the true opinion abides in the mind, but abides as a prejudice, a belief independent of, and proof against, argument—this is not the way in which truth ought to be held by a rational being. This is not knowing the truth. Truth, thus held, is but one superstition the more, accidentally clinging to the words which enunciate a truth.

If the intellect and judgment of mankind ought to be cultivated, a thing which Protestants at least do not deny, on what can these faculties be more appropriately exercised by anyone than on the things which concern him so much that it is considered necessary for him to hold opinions on them? If the cultivation of the understanding consists in one thing more than in another, it is surely in learning the grounds of one's own opinions. Whatever people believe, on subjects on which it is of the first importance to believe rightly, they ought to be able to defend against at least the common objections. But, someone may say, "Let them be *taught* the grounds of their opinions. It does not follow that opinions must be merely parroted because they are never heard controverted. Persons who learn geometry do not simply commit the theorems to memory, but understand and learn likewise the demonstrations; and it would be absurd to say that they remain ignorant of the grounds of geometrical truths because they never hear anyone deny and attempt to disprove them." Undoubtedly; and such teaching suffices on a subject like mathematics, where there is nothing at all to be said on the wrong side of the question. The peculiarity of the evidence of mathematical truths is that all the argument is on one side. There are no objections, and no answers to objections. But on every subject on which difference of opinion is possible, the truth depends on a balance to be struck between two sets of conflicting reasons. Even in natural philosophy, there is always some other explanation possible of the same facts; some geocentric theory instead of heliocentric, some phlogiston instead of oxygen; and it has to be shown why that other theory cannot be the true one; and until this is shown, and until we know how it is shown, we do not understand the grounds of our opinion. But when we turn to subjects infinitely more complicated, to morals, religion, politics, social relations, and the business of life, three-fourths of the arguments for every disputed opinion consist in dispelling the appearances which favor some opinion different from it. The greatest orator, save one, of antiquity, has left it on record that he always studied his adversary's case with as great, if not still greater, intensity than even his own. What Cicero practiced as the means of forensic success requires to be imitated by all who study any subject in order to arrive at the truth. He who knows only his own side of the case knows little of that. His reasons may be good, and no one may have been able to refute them. But if he is equally unable to refute the reasons on the opposite side, if he does not so much as know what they are, he has no ground for preferring either opinion. The rational position for him would be suspension of judgment, and unless he contents himself with that, he is either led by authority or adopts, like the generality of the world, the side to which he feels most inclination. Nor is it enough that he should hear the arguments of adversaries from his own teachers, presented as they state them, and accompanied by what they offer as refutations. That is not the way to do justice to the arguments or bring them into real contact with his own mind. He must be able to hear them from persons who actually believe them, who defend them in earnest and do their very utmost for them. He must know them in their most plausible and persuasive form; he must feel the whole force of the difficulty which the true view of the subject has to encounter and dispose of, else he will never really possess himself of the portion of truth which meets and removes that difficulty. Ninety-nine in a hundred of what are called educated men are in this condition, even of those who can argue fluently for their opinions. Their conclusion may be true, but it might be false for anything they know; they have never thrown themselves into the mental position of those who think differently from them, and considered what such persons may have to say; and, consequently, they do not, in any proper sense of the word, know the doctrine which they themselves profess. They do not know those parts of it which explain and justify the remainder—the considerations which show that a fact which seemingly conflicts with another is reconcilable with it, or that, of two apparently strong reasons, one and not the other ought to be preferred. All that part of the truth which turns the scale and decides the judgment of a completely informed mind, they are strangers to; nor is it ever really known but to those who have attended equally and impartially to both sides and endeavored to see the reasons of both in the strongest light. So essential is this discipline to a real understanding of moral and human subjects that, if opponents of all-important truths do not exist, it is indispensable to imagine them and supply them with the strongest arguments which the most skillful devil's advocate can conjure up.

To abate the force of these considerations, an enemy of free discussion may be supposed to say that there is no necessity for mankind in general to know and understand all that can be said against or for their opinions by philosophers and theologians. That it is not needful for common men to be able to expose all the misstatements or fallacies of an ingenious opponent. That it is enough if there is always somebody capable of answering them, so that nothing likely to mislead uninstructed persons remains unrefuted. That simple minds, having been taught the obvious grounds of the truths inculcated in them, may trust to authority for the rest and, being aware that they have neither knowledge nor talent to resolve every difficulty which can be raised, may repose in the assurance that all those which have been raised have been or can be answered by those who are specially trained to the task.

Conceding to this view of the subject the utmost that can be claimed for it by those most easily satisfied with the amount of understanding of truth which ought to accompany the belief of it, even so, the argument for free discussion is no way weakened. For even this doctrine acknowledges that mankind ought to have a rational assurance that all objections have been satisfactorily answered; and how are they to be answered if that which requires to be answered is not spoken? Or how can the answer be known to be satisfactory if the objectors have no opportunity of showing that it is unsatisfactory? If not the public, at least the philosophers and theologians who are to resolve the difficulties must make themselves familiar with those difficulties in their most puzzling form; and this cannot be accomplished unless they are freely stated and placed in the most advantageous light which they admit of. The Catholic Church has its own way of dealing with this embarrassing problem. It makes a broad separation between those who can be permitted to receive its doctrines on conviction and those who must accept them on trust. Neither, indeed, are allowed any choice as to what they will accept; but the clergy, such at least as can be fully confided in, may admissibly and meritoriously make themselves acquainted with the arguments of opponents, in order to answer them, and may, therefore, read heretical books; the laity, not unless by special permission, hard to be obtained. This discipline recognizes a knowledge of the enemy's case as beneficial to the teachers, but finds means, consistent with this, of denying it to the rest of the world, thus giving to the *élite* more mental culture, though not more mental freedom, than it allows to the mass. By this device it succeeds in obtaining the kind of mental superiority which its purposes require; for though culture without freedom never made a large and liberal mind, it can make a clever *nisi prius* advocate of a cause. But in countries professing Protestantism, this resource is denied, since Protestants hold, at least in theory, that the responsibility for the choice of a religion must be borne by each for himself and cannot be thrown off upon teachers. Besides, in the present state of the world, it is practically impossible that writings which are read by the instructed can be kept from the uninstructed. If the teachers of mankind are to be cognizant of all that they ought to know, everything must be free to be written and published without restraint.

If, however, the mischievous operation of the absence of free discussion, when the received opinions are true, were confined to leaving men ignorant of the grounds of those opinions, it might be thought that this, if an intellectual, is no moral evil and does not affect the worth of the opinions, regarded in their influence on the character. The fact, however, is that not only the grounds of the opinion are forgotten in the absence of discussion, but too often the meaning of the opinion itself. The words which convey it cease to suggest ideas, or suggest only a small portion of those they were originally employed to communicate. Instead of a vivid conception and a living belief, there remain only a few phrases retained by rote; or, if any part, the shell and husk only of the meaning is retained, the finer essence being lost. The great chapter in human history which this fact occupies and fills cannot be too earnestly studied and meditated on.

It is illustrated in the experience of almost all ethical doctrines and religious creeds. They are all full of meaning and vitality to those who originate them, and to the direct disciples of the originators. Their meaning continues to be felt in undiminished strength, and is perhaps brought out into even fuller consciousness, so long as the struggle lasts to give the doctrine or creed an ascendancy over other creeds. At last it either prevails and becomes the general opinion, or its progress stops; it keeps possession of the ground it has gained, but ceases to spread further. When either of these results has become apparent, controversy on the subject flags, and gradually dies away. The doctrine has taken its place, if not as a received opinion, as one of the admitted sects or divisions of opinion; those who hold it have generally inherited, not adopted it; and conversion from one of these doctrines to another, being now an exceptional fact, occupies little place in the thoughts of their professors. Instead of being, as at first, constantly on the alert either to defend themselves against the world or to bring the world over to them, they have subsided into acquiescence and neither listen, when they can help it, to arguments against their creed, nor trouble dissentients (if there be such) with arguments in its favor. From this time may usually be dated the decline in the living power of the doctrine. We often hear the teachers of all creeds lamenting the difficulty of keeping up in the minds of believers a lively apprehension of the truth which they nominally recognize, so that it may penetrate the feelings and acquire a real mastery over the conduct. No such difficulty is complained of while the creed is still fighting for its existence; even the weaker combatants then know and feel what they are fighting for, and the difference between it and other doctrines; and in that period of every creed's existence not a few persons may be found who have realized its fundamental principles in all the forms

of thought, have weighed and considered them in all their
important bearings, and have experienced the full effect on
the character which belief in that creed ought to produce in a
mind thoroughly imbued with it. But when it has come to
be an hereditary creed, and to be received passively, not actively—when the mind is no longer compelled, in the same
degree as at first, to exercise its vital powers on the questions which its belief presents to it, there is a progressive
tendency to forget all of the belief except the formularies, or
to give it a dull and torpid assent, as if accepting it on trust
dispensed with the necessity of realizing it in consciousness,
or testing it by personal experience, until it almost ceases to
connect itself at all with the inner life of the human being.
Then are seen the cases, so frequent in this age of the world
as almost to form the majority, in which the creed remains
as it were outside the mind, incrusting and petrifying it
against all other influences addressed to the higher parts of
our nature; manifesting its power by not suffering any fresh
and living conviction to get in, but itself doing nothing for
the mind or heart except standing sentinel over them to
keep them vacant.

To what an extent doctrines intrinsically fitted to make
the deepest impression upon the mind may remain in it
as dead beliefs, without being ever realized in the imagination, the feelings, or the understanding, is exemplified by
the manner in which the majority of believers hold the doctrines of Christianity. By Christianity, I here mean what is
accounted such by all churches and sects—the maxims and
precepts contained in the New Testament. These are considered sacred, and accepted as laws, by all professing Christians. Yet it is scarcely too much to say that not one Christian in a thousand guides or tests his individual conduct
by reference to those laws. The standard to which he does
refer it is the custom of his nation, his class, or his religious
profession. He has thus, on the one hand, a collection of
ethical maxims which he believes to have been vouchsafed
to him by infallible wisdom as rules for his government; and,
on the other, a set of everyday judgments and practices which

go a certain length with some of those maxims, not so great a
length with others, stand in direct opposition to some, and
are, on the whole, a compromise between the Christian creed
and the interests and suggestions of worldly life. To the first
of these standards he gives his homage; to the other his real
allegiance. All Christians believe that the blessed are the
poor and humble, and those who are ill-used by the world;
that it is easier for a camel to pass through the eye of a needle
than for a rich man to enter the kingdom of heaven; that
they should judge not, lest they be judged; that they should
swear not at all; that they should love their neighbor as themselves; that if one take their cloak, they should give him
their coat also; that they should take no thought for the mor-
row; that if they would be perfect they should sell all that
they have and give it to the poor. They are not insincere
when they say that they believe these things. They do believe them, as people believe what they have always heard
lauded and never discussed. But in the sense of that living
belief which regulates conduct, they believe these doctrines
just up to the point to which it is usual to act upon them. The
doctrines in their integrity are serviceable to pelt adversaries with; and it is understood that they are to be put forward (when possible) as the reasons for whatever people do
that they think laudable. But anyone who reminded them
that the maxims require an infinity of things which they
never even think of doing would gain nothing but to be
classed among those very unpopular characters who affect
to be better than other people. The doctrines have no hold
on ordinary believers—are not a power in their minds.
They have an habitual respect for the sound of them, but no
feeling which spreads from the words to the things signified
and forces the mind to take *them* in and make them conform
to the formula. Whenever conduct is concerned, they look
round for Mr. A and B to direct them how far to go in obey-
ing Christ.

Now we may be well assured that the case was not thus,
but far otherwise, with the early Christians. Had it been
thus, Christianity never would have expanded from an ob-

scure sect of the despised Hebrews into the religion of the
Roman empire. When their enemies said, "See how these
Christians love one another" (a remark not likely to be
made by anybody now), they assuredly had a much livelier
feeling of the meaning of their creed than they have ever
had since. And to this cause, probably, it is chiefly owing
that Christianity now makes so little progress in extending
its domain, and after eighteen centuries is still nearly confined to Europeans and the descendants of Europeans. Even
with the strictly religious, who are much in earnest about
their doctrines and attach a greater amount of meaning to
many of them than people in general, it commonly happens
that the part which is thus comparatively active in their
minds is that which was made by Calvin, or Knox, or some
such person much nearer in character to themselves. The
sayings of Christ coexist passively in their minds, producing
hardly any effect beyond what is caused by mere listening to
words so amiable and bland. There are many reasons, doubtless, why doctrines which are the badge of a sect retain more
of their vitality than those common to all recognized sects,
and why more pains are taken by teachers to keep their
meaning alive; but one reason certainly is that the peculiar
doctrines are more questioned, and have to be oftener defended against open gainsayers. Both teachers and learners go to
sleep at their post as soon as there is no enemy in the field.

The same thing holds true, generally speaking, of all
traditional doctrines—those of prudence and knowledge of
life as well as of morals or religion. All languages and litera-
tures are full of general observations on life, both as to what
it is and how to conduct oneself in it—observations which
everybody knows, which everybody repeats or hears with
acquiescence, which are received as truisms, yet of which
most people first truly learn the meaning when experience,
generally of a painful kind, has made it a reality to them.
How often, when smarting under some unforeseen misfortune or disappointment, does a person call to mind some
proverb or common saying, familiar to him all his life, the
meaning of which, if he had ever before felt it as he does

now, would have saved him from the calamity. There are indeed reasons for this, other than the absence of discussion; there are many truths of which the full meaning *cannot* be realized until personal experience has brought it home. But much more of the meaning even of these would have been understood, and what was understood would have been far more deeply impressed on the mind, if the man had been accustomed to hear it argued *pro* and *con* by people who did understand it. The fatal tendency of mankind to leave off thinking about a thing when it is no longer doubtful is the cause of half their errors. A contemporary author has well spoken of "the deep slumber of a decided opinion."

But what! (it may be asked), Is the absence of unanimity an indispensable condition of true knowledge? Is it necessary that some part of mankind should persist in error to enable any to realize the truth? Does a belief cease to be real and vital as soon as it is generally received—and is a proposition never thoroughly understood and felt unless some doubt of it remains? As soon as mankind have unanimously accepted a truth, does the truth perish within them? The highest aim and best result of improved intelligence, it has hitherto been thought, is to unite mankind more and more in the acknowledgment of all-important truths; and does the intelligence only last as long as it has not achieved its object? Do the fruits of conquest perish by the very completeness of victory?

I affirm no such thing. As mankind improve, the number of doctrines which are no longer disputed or doubted will be constantly on the increase; and the well-being of mankind may almost be measured by the number and gravity of the truths which have reached the point of being uncontested. The cessation, on one question after another, of serious controversy is one of the necessary incidents of the consolidation of opinion—a consolidation as salutary in the case of true opinions as it is dangerous and noxious when the opinions are erroneous. But though this gradual narrowing of the bounds of diversity of opinion is necessary in both senses of the term, being at once inevitable and indispensable, we are not therefore obliged to conclude that all its consequences must be beneficial. The loss of so important an aid to the intelligent and living apprehension of a truth as is afforded by the necessity of explaining it to, or defending it against, opponents, though not sufficient to outweigh, is no trifling drawback from the benefit of its universal recognition. Where this advantage can no longer be had, I confess I should like to see the teachers of mankind endeavoring to provide a substitute for it—some contrivance for making the difficulties of the question as present to the learner's consciousness as if they were pressed upon him by a dissentient champion, eager for his conversion.

But instead of seeking contrivances for this purpose, they have lost those they formerly had. The Socratic dialectics, so magnificently exemplified in the dialogues of Plato, were a contrivance of this description. They were essentially a negative discussion of the great questions of philosophy and life, directed with consummate skill to the purpose of convincing anyone who had merely adopted the commonplaces of received opinion that he did not understand the subject—that he as yet attached no definite meaning to the doctrines he professed; in order that, becoming aware of his ignorance, he might be put in the way to obtain a stable belief, resting on a clear apprehension both of the meaning of doctrines and of their evidence. The school disputations of the Middle Ages had a somewhat similar object. They were intended to make sure that the pupil understood his own opinion, and (by necessary correlation) the opinion opposed to it, and could enforce the grounds of the one and confute those of the other. These last-mentioned contests had indeed the incurable defect that the premises appealed to were taken from authority, not from reason; and, as a discipline to the mind, they were in every respect inferior to the powerful dialectics which formed the intellects of the "*Socratici viri*"; but the modern mind owes far more to both than it is generally willing to admit, and the present modes of education contain nothing which in the smallest degree supplies the place either of the one or of the other. A person who derives all his instruction from teachers of books, even if he escape the besetting temptation of contenting himself with cram, is under no compulsion to hear both sides; accordingly it is far from a frequent accomplishment, even among thinkers, to know both sides; and the weakest part of what everybody says in defense of his opinion is what he intends as a reply to antagonists. It is the fashion of the present time to disparage negative logic—that which points out weaknesses in theory or errors in practice without establishing positive truths. Such negative criticism would indeed be poor enough as an ultimate result, but as a means to attaining any positive knowledge or conviction worthy the name it cannot be valued too highly; and until people are again systematically trained to it, there will be few great thinkers and a low general average of intellect in any but the mathematical and physical departments of speculation. On any other subject no one's opinions deserve the name of knowledge, except so far as he has either had forced upon him by others or gone through of himself the same mental process which would have been required of him in carrying on an active controversy with opponents. That, therefore, which, when absent, it is so indispensable, but so difficult, to create, how worse than absurd it is to forego when spontaneously offering itself! If there are any persons who contest a received opinion, or who will do so if law or opinion will let them, let us thank them for it, open our minds to listen to them, and rejoice that there is someone to do for us what we otherwise ought, if we have any regard for either the certainty or the vitality of our convictions, to do with much greater labor for ourselves.

It still remains to speak of one of the principal causes which make diversity of opinion advantageous, and will continue to do so until mankind shall have entered a stage of intellectual advancement which at present seems at an incalculable distance. We have hitherto considered only two possibilities: that the received opinion may be false, and some other opinion, consequently, true; or that, the received opin-

ion being true, a conflict with the opposite error is essential
to a clear apprehension and deep feeling of its truth. But
there is a commoner case than either of these: when the conflicting doctrines, instead of being one true and the other
false, share the truth between them, and the nonconforming
opinion is needed to supply the remainder of the truth of
which the received doctrine embodies only a part. Popular
opinions, on subjects not palpable to sense, are often true,
but seldom or never the whole truth. They are a part of the
truth, sometimes a greater, sometimes a smaller part, but
exaggerated, distorted, and disjointed from the truths by
which they ought to be accompanied and limited. Heretical
opinions, on the other hand, are generally some of these
suppressed and neglected truths, bursting the bonds which
kept them down, and either seeking reconciliation with the
truth contained in the common opinion, or fronting it as
enemies, and setting themselves up, with similar exclusive-
ness, as the whole truth. The latter case is hitherto the most
frequent, as, in the human mind, one-sidedness has always
been the rule, and many-sidedness the exception. Hence,
even in revolutions of opinion, one part of the truth usually
sets while another rises. Even progress, which ought to superadd, for the most part only substitutes one partial and incomplete truth for another; improvement consisting chiefly in
this, that the new fragment of truth is more wanted, more
adapted to the needs of the time than that which it displaces.
Such being the partial character of prevailing opinions, even
when resting on a true foundation, every opinion which em-
bodies somewhat of the portion of truth which the common
opinion omits ought to be considered precious, with whatever amount of error and confusion that truth may be
blended. No sober judge of human affairs will feel bound
to be indignant because those who force on our notice truths
which we should otherwise have overlooked, overlook some
of those which we see. Rather, he will think that so long as
popular truth is one-sided, it is more desirable than otherwise that unpopular truth should have one-sided assertors,
too, such being usually the most energetic and the most likely

to compel reluctant attention to the fragment of wisdom which they proclaim as if it were the whole.

Thus, in the eighteenth century, when nearly all the instructed, and all those of the uninstructed who were led by them, were lost in admiration of what is called civilization, and of the marvels of modern science, literature, and philosophy, and while greatly overrating the amount of unlikeness between the men of modern and those of ancient times, indulged the belief that the whole of the difference was in their own favor; with what a salutary shock did the paradoxes of Rousseau explode like bombshells in the midst, dislocating the compact mass of one-sided opinion and forcing its elements to recombine in a better form and with additional ingredients. Not that the current opinions were on the whole farther from the truth than Rousseau's were; on the contrary, they were nearer to it; they contained more of positive, truth, and very much less of error. Nevertheless there lay in Rousseau's doctrine, and has floated down the stream of opinion along with it, a considerable amount of exactly those truths which the popular opinion wanted; and these are the deposit which was left behind them when the flood subsided. The superior worth of simplicity of life, the enervating and demoralizing effect of the trammels and hypocrisies of artificial society are ideas which have never been entirely absent from cultivated minds since Rousseau wrote; and they will in time produce their due effect, though at present needing to be asserted as much as ever, and to be asserted by deeds; for words, on this subject, have nearly exhausted their power.

In politics, again, it is almost a commonplace that a party of order or stability and a party of progress or reform are both necessary elements of a healthy state of political life, until the one or the other shall have so enlarged its mental grasp as to be a party equally of order and of progress, knowing and distinguishing what is fit to be preserved from what ought to be swept away. Each of these modes of thinking derives its utility from the deficiencies of the other; but it is in a great measure the opposition of the other that keeps each within the limits of reason and sanity. Unless opinions favorable to democracy and to aristocracy, to property and to equality, to co-operation and to competition, to luxury and to abstinence, to sociality and individuality, to liberty and discipline, and all the other standing antagonisms of practical life, are expressed with equal freedom and enforced and defended with equal talent and energy, there is no chance of both elements obtaining their due; one scale is sure to go up, and the other down. Truth, in the great practical concerns of life, is so much a question of the reconciling and combining of opposites that very few have minds sufficiently capacious and impartial to make the adjustment with an approach to correctness, and it has to be made by the rough process of a struggle between combatants fighting under hostile banners. On any of the great open questions just enumerated, if either of the two opinions has a better claim than the other, not merely to be tolerated, but to be encouraged and countenanced, it is the one which happens at the particular time and place to be in a minority. That is the opinion which, for the time being, represents the neglected interests, the side of human well-being which is in danger of obtaining less than its share. I am aware that there is not, in this country, any intolerance of differences of opinion on most of these topics. They are adduced to show, by admitted and multiplied examples, the universality of the fact that only through diversity of opinion is there, in the existing state of human intellect, a chance of fair play to all sides of the truth. When there are persons to be found who form an exception to the apparent unanimity of the world on any subject, even if the world is in the right, it is always probable that dissentients have something worth hearing to say for themselves, and that truth would lose something by their silence.

It may be objected, "But *some* received principles, especially on the highest and most vital subjects, are more than half-truths. The Christian morality, for instance, is the whole truth on that subject, and if anyone teaches a morality which varies from it, he is wholly in error." As this is of all cases the most important in practice, none can be fitter to test the general maxim. But before pronouncing what Chrisitan morality is or is not, it would be desirable to decide what is meant by Christian morality. If it means the morality of the New Testament, I wonder that any one who derives his knowledge of this from the book itself can suppose that it was announced, or intended, as a complete doctrine of morals. The Gospel always refers to a pre-existing morality and confines its precepts to the particulars in which that morality was to be corrected or superseded by a wider and higher, expressing itself, moreover, in terms most general, often impossible to be interpreted literally, and possessing rather the impressiveness of poetry or eloquence than the precision of legislation. To extract from it a body of ethical doctrine has never been possible without eking it out from the Old Testament, that is, from a system elaborate indeed, but in many respects barbarous, and intended only for a barbarous people. St. Paul, a declared enemy to this Judaical mode of interpreting the doctrine and filling up the scheme of his Master, equally assumes a pre-existing morality, namely that of the Greeks and Romans; and his advice to Christians is in a great measure a system of accommodation to that, even to the extent of giving an apparent sanction to slavery. What is called Christian, but should rather be termed theological, morality was not the work of Christ or the Apostles, but is of much later origin, having been gradually built up by the Catholic Church of the first five centuries, and though not implicitly adopted by moderns and Protestants, has been much less modified by them than might have been expected. For the most part, indeed, they have contented themselves with cutting off the additions which had been made to it in the Middle Ages, each sect supplying the place by fresh additions, adapted to its own character and tendencies. That mankind owe a great debt to this morality, and to its early teachers, I should be the last person to deny, but I do not scruple to say of it that it is, in many important points, incomplete and one-sided, and that, unless ideas and feelings not sanctioned by it had contributed to the formation of European life and character, human affairs would have been in a worse condition than they now are. Christian morality (so called) has all the characters of a reaction; it is, in great part, a protest against paganism. Its ideal is negative rather than positive; passive rather than active; innocence rather than nobleness; abstinence from evil rather than energetic pursuit of good; in its precepts (as has been well said) "thou shalt not" predominates unduly over "thou shalt." In its horror of sensuality, it made an idol of asceticism which has been gradually compromised away into one of legality. It holds out the hope of heaven and the threat of hell as the appointed and appropriate motives to a virtuous life: in this falling far below the best of the ancients, and doing what lies in it to give to human morality an essentially selfish character, by disconnecting each man's feelings of duty from the interests of his fellow creatures, except so far as a self-interested inducement is offered to him for consulting them. It is essentially a doctrine of passive obedience; it inculcates submission to all authorities found established; who indeed are not to be actively obeyed when they command what religion forbids, but who are not to be resisted, far less rebelled against, for any amount of wrong to ourselves. And while, in the morality of the best pagan nations, duty to the State holds even a disproportionate place, infringing on the just liberty of the individual, in purely Christian ethics that grand department of duty is scarcely noticed or acknowledged. It is in the Koran, not the New Testament, that we read the maxim: "A ruler who appoints any man to an office, when there is in his dominions another man better qualified for it, sins against God and against the State." What little recognition the idea of obligation to the public obtains in modern morality is derived from Greek and Roman sources, not from Christian; as, even in the morality of private life, whatever exists of magnanimity, high-mindedness, personal dignity, even the sense of honor, is derived from the purely

human, not the religious part of our education, and never
could have grown out of a standard of ethics in which the
only worth, professedly recognized, is that of obedience.

I am as far as anyone from pretending that these defects
are necessarily inherent in the Christian ethics in every manner in which it can be conceived, or that the many requisites
of a complete moral doctrine which it does not contain do
not admit of being reconciled with it. Far less would I insinuate this out of the doctrines and precepts of Christ himself. I believe that the sayings of Christ are all that I can see
any evidence of their having been intended to be; that they
are irreconcilable with nothing which a comprehensive
morality requires; that everything which is excellent in
ethics may be brought within them, with no greater violence
to their language than has been done to it by all who have
attempted to deduce from them any practical system of conduct whatever. But it is quite consistent with this to believe
that they contain, and were meant to contain, only a part of
the truth; that many essential elements of the highest morality are among the things which are not provided for, nor intended to be provided for, in the recorded deliverances of
the Founder of Christianity, and which have been entirely
thrown aside in the system of ethics erected on the basis of
those deliverances by the Christian Church. And this
being so, I think it a great error to persist in attempting to
find in the Christian doctrine that complete rule for our
guidance which its Author intended it to sanction and enforce, but only partially to provide. I believe, too, that this
narrow theory is becoming a grave practical evil, detracting
greatly from the moral training and instruction which so
many well-meaning persons are now at length exerting themselves to promote. I much fear that by attempting to form
the mind and feelings on an exclusively religious type, and
discarding those secular standards (as for want of a better
name they may be called) which heretofore coexisted with
and supplemented the Christian ethics, receiving some of its
spirit, and infusing into it some of theirs, there will result,
and is even now resulting, a low, abject, servile type of char-

acter which, submit itself as it may to what it deems the Supreme Will, is incapable of rising to or sympathizing in the conception of Supreme Goodness. I believe that other ethics than any which can be evolved from exclusively Christian sources must exist side by side with Christian ethics to produce the moral regeneration of mankind; and that the Christian system is no exception to the rule that in an imperfect state of the human mind the interests of truth require a diversity of opinions. It is not necessary that in ceasing to ignore the moral truths not contained in Christianity men should ignore any of those which it does contain. Such prejudice or oversight, when it occurs, is altogether an evil, but it is one from which we cannot hope to be always exempt, and must be regarded as the price paid for an inestimable good. The exclusive pretension made by a part of the truth to be the whole must and ought to be protested against; and if a reactionary impulse should make the protestors unjust in their turn, this one-sidedness, like the other, may be lamented but must be tolerated. If Christians would teach infidels to be just to Christianity, they should themselves be just to infidelity. It can do truth no service to blink the fact, known to all who have the most ordinary acquaintance with literary history, that a large portion of the noblest and most valuable moral teaching has been the work, not only of men who did not know, but of men who knew and rejected, the Christian faith.

I do not pretend that the most unlimited use of the freedom of enunciating all possible opinions would put an end to the evils of religious or philosophical sectarianism. Every truth which men of narrow capacity are in earnest about is sure to be asserted, inculcated, and in many ways even acted on, as if no other truth existed in the world, or at all events none that could limit or qualify the first. I acknowledge that the tendency of all opinions to become sectarian is not cured by the freest discussion, but is often heightened and exacerbated thereby; the truth which ought to have been, but was not, seen, being rejected all the more violently because proclaimed by persons regarded as opponents. But it is not on the impassioned partisan, it is on the calmer and more disinterested bystander, that this collision of opinions works its salutary effect. Not the violent conflict between parts of the truth, but the quiet suppression of half of it, is the formidable evil; there is always hope when people are forced to listen to both sides; it is when they attend only to one that errors harden into prejudices, and truth itself ceases to have the effect of truth by being exaggerated into false-hood. And since there are few mental attributes more rare than that judicial faculty which can sit in intelligent judg-ment between two sides of a question, of which only one is represented by an advocate before it, truth has no chance but in proportion as every side of it, every opinion which em-bodies any fraction of the truth, not only finds advocates, but is so advocated as to be listened to.

We have now recognized the necessity to the mental well-being of mankind (on which all their other well-being depends) of freedom of opinion, and freedom of the expres-sion of opinion, on four distinct grounds, which we will now briefly recapitulate:

First, if any opinion is compelled to silence, that opin-ion may, for aught we can certainly know, be true. To deny this is to assume our own infallibility.

Secondly, though the silenced opinion be an error, it may, and very commonly does, contain a portion of truth; and since the general or prevailing opinion on any subject is rarely or never the whole truth, it is only by the collision of adverse opinions that the remainder of the truth has any chance of being supplied.

Thirdly, even if the received opinion be not only true, but the whole truth; unless it is suffered to be, and actually is, vigorously and earnestly contested, it will, by most of those who receive it, be held in the manner of a prejudice, with little comprehension or feeling of its rational grounds. And not only this, but, fourthly, the meaning of the doc-trine itself will be in danger of being lost or enfeebled, and deprived of its vital effect on the character and conduct:

the dogma becoming a mere formal profession, inefficacious for good, but cumbering the ground and preventing the growth of any real and heartfelt conviction from reason or personal experience.

Before quitting the subject of freedom of opinion, it is fit to take some notice of those who say that the free expression of all opinions should be permitted on condition that the manner be temperate, and do not pass the bounds of fair discussion. Much might be said on the impossibility of fixing where these supposed bounds are to be placed; for if the test be offense to those whose opinions are attacked, I think experience testifies that this offense is given whenever the attack is telling and powerful, and that every opponent who pushes them hard, and whom they find it difficult to answer, appears to them, if he shows any strong feeling on the subject, an intemperate opponent. But this, though an important consideration in a practical point of view, merges in a more fundamental objection. Undoubtedly, the manner of asserting an opinion, even though it be a true one, may be very objectionable and may justly incur severe censure. But the principal offenses of the kind are such as it is mostly impossible, unless by accidental self-betrayal, to bring home to conviction. The gravest of them is, to argue sophistically, to suppress facts or arguments, to misstate the elements of the case, or misrepresent the opposite opinion. But all this, even to the most aggravated degree, is so continually done in perfect good faith by persons who are not considered, and in many other respects may not deserve to be considered, ignorant or incompetent, that it is rarely possible, on adequate grounds, conscientiously to stamp the misrepresentation as morally culpable, and still less could law presume to interfere with this kind of controversial misconduct. With regard to what is commonly meant by intemperate discussion, namely invective, sarcasm, personality, and the like, the denunciation of these weapons would deserve more sympathy if it were ever proposed to interdict them equally to both sides; but it is only desired to restrain the employment of them against the prevailing opinion;

against the unprevailing they may not only be used without general disapproval, but will be likely to obtain for him who uses them the praise of honest zeal and righteous indignation. Yet whatever mischief arises from their use is greatest when they are employed against the comparatively defenseless; and whatever unfair advantage can be derived by any opinion from this mode of asserting it accrues almost exclusively to received opinions. The worst offense of this kind which can be committed by a polemic is to stigmatize those who hold the contrary opinion as bad and immoral men. To calumny of this sort, those who hold any unpopular opinion are peculiarly exposed, because they are in general few and uninfluential, and nobody but themselves feels much interested in seeing justice done them; but this weapon is, from the nature of the case, denied to those who attack a prevailing opinion: they can neither use it with safety to themselves, nor, if they could, would it do anything but recoil on their own cause. In general, opinions contrary to those commonly received can only obtain a hearing by studied moderation of language and the most cautious avoidance of unnecessary offense, from which they hardly ever deviate even in a slight degree without losing ground, while unmeasured vituperation employed on the side of the prevailing opinion really does deter people from professing contrary opinions and from listening to those who profess them. For the interest, therefore, of truth and justice it is far more important to restrain this employment of vituperative language than the other; and, for example, if it were necessary to choose, there would be much more need to discourage offensive attacks on infidelity than on religion. It is, however, obvious that law and authority have no business with restraining either, while opinion ought, in every instance, to determine its verdict by the circumstances of the individual case—condemning everyone, on whichever side of the argument he places himself, in whose mode of advocacy either want of candor, or malignity, bigotry, or intolerance of feeling manifest themselves; but not inferring these vices from the side which a person takes, though it be the contrary side of the question to our own; and giving merited honor to everyone, whatever opinion he may hold, who has calmness to see and honesty to state what his opponents and their opinions really are, exaggerating nothing to their discredit, keeping nothing back which tells, or can be supposed to tell, in their favor. This is the real morality of public discussion; and if often violated, I am happy to think that there are many controversialists who to a great extent observe it, and a still greater number who conscientiously strive toward it.

III OF INDIVIDUALITY, AS ONE OF THE ELEMENTS OF WELL-BEING

Such being the reasons which make it imperative that human beings should be free to form opinions and to express their opinions without reserve; and such the baneful consequences to the intellectual, and through that to the moral nature of man, unless this liberty is either conceded or asserted in spite of prohibition; let us next examine whether the same reasons do not require that men should be free to act upon their opinions—to carry these out in their lives without hindrance, either physical or moral, from their fellow men, so long as it is at their own risk and peril. This last proviso is of course indispensable. No one pretends that actions should be as free as opinions. On the contrary, even opinions lose their immunity when the circumstances in which they are expressed are such as to constitute their expression a positive instigation to some mischievous act. An opinion that corn dealers are starvers of the poor, or that private property is robbery, ought to be unmolested when simply circulated through the press, but may justly incur punishment when delivered orally to an excited mob assembled before the house of a corn dealer, or when handed about among the same mob in the form of a placard. Acts, of whatever kind, which without justifiable cause do harm to others may be, and in the more important cases absolutely require to be, controlled by the unfavorable sentiments, and, when needful, by the active interference of mankind. The liberty of the individual must be thus far limited; he must not make himself a nuisance to other people. But if he refrains from molesting others in what concerns them, and merely acts according to his own inclination and judgment in things which concern himself, the same reasons which show that opinion should be free prove also that he should be allowed, without molestation, to carry his opinions into practice at his own cost. That mankind are not infallible; that their truths, for the most part, are only half-truths; that unity of opinion, unless resulting from the fullest and freest comparison of opposite opinions, is not desirable, and diversity not an evil, but a good, until mankind are much more capable than at present of recognizing all sides of the truth, are principles applicable to men's modes of action not less than to their opinions. As it is useful that while mankind are imperfect there should be different opinions, so it is that there should be different experiments of living; that free scope should be given to varieties of character, short of injury to others; and that the worth of different modes of life should be proved practically, when anyone thinks fit to try them. It is desirable, in short, that in things which do not primarily concern others individuality should assert itself. Where not the person's own character but the traditions or customs of other people are the rule of conduct, there is wanting one of the principal ingredients of human happiness, and quite the chief ingredient of individual and social progress.

In maintaining this principle, the greatest difficulty to be encountered does not lie in the appreciation of means toward an acknowledged end, but in the indifference of persons in general to the end itself. If it were felt that the free development of individuality is one of the leading essentials of well-being; that it is not only a co-ordinate element with all that is designated by the terms civilization, instruction, education, culture, but is itself a necessary part and condition of all those things, there would be no danger that liberty should be undervalued, and the adjustment of the boundaries between it and social control would present no extraordinary difficulty. But the evil is that individual spontaneity is hardly recognized by the common modes of thinking as having any intrinsic worth, or deserving any regard on its own account. The majority, being satisfied with the ways of mankind as they now are (for it is they who make them what they are), cannot comprehend why those ways should not be good enough for everybody; and what is more, spontaneity forms no part of the ideal of the majority of moral and social reformers, but is rather looked on with jealousy, as a troublesome and perhaps rebellious obstruction to the general acceptance of what these reformers, in their own judgment, think would be best for mankind. Few persons, out of Germany, even comprehend the meaning of the doctrine which Wilhelm von Humboldt, so eminent both as a *savant* and as a politician, made the text of a treatise—that "the end of man, or that which is prescribed by the eternal or immutable dictates of reason, and not suggested by vague and transient desires, is the highest and most harmonious development of his powers to a complete and consistent whole"; that, therefore, the object "toward which every human being must ceaselessly direct his efforts, and on which especially those who design to influence their fellow men must ever keep their eyes, is the individuality of power and development"; that for this there are two requisites, "freedom, and variety of situations"; and that from the union of these arise "individual vigor and manifold diversity," which combine themselves in "originality." *

Little, however, as people are accustomed to a doctrine like that of von Humboldt, and surprising as it may be to them to find so high a value attached to individuality, the question, one must nevertheless think, can only be one of degree. No one's idea of excellence in conduct is that people should do absolutely nothing but copy one another. No one would assert that people ought not to put into their mode of life, and into the conduct of their concerns, any impress whatever of their own judgment or of their own

* *The Sphere and Duties of Government,* from the German of Baron Wilhelm von Humboldt, pp. 11-13.

individual character. On the other hand, it would be absurd to pretend that people ought to live as if nothing whatever had been known in the world before they came into
it; as if experience had as yet done nothing toward showing
that one mode of existence, or of conduct, is preferable to
another. Nobody denies that people should be so taught
and trained in youth as to know and benefit by the ascertained results of human experience. But it is the privilege
and proper condition of a human being, arrived at the maturity of his faculties, to use and interpret experience in his
own way. It is for him to find out what part of recorded experience is properly applicable to his own circumstances and
character. The traditions and customs of other people are,
to a certain extent, evidence of what their experience has
taught *them*—presumptive evidence, and as such, have a
claim to his deference: but, in the first place, their experience may be too narrow, or they may have not interpreted it
rightly. Secondly, their interpretation of experience may
be correct, but unsuitable to him. Customs are made for
customary circumstances and customary characters; and
his circumstances or his character may be uncustomary.
Thirdly, though the customs be both good as customs and
suitable to him, yet to conform to custom merely *as* custom
does not educate or develop in him any of the qualities which
are the distinctive endowment of a human being. The human faculties of perception, judgment, discriminative feeling, mental activity, and even moral preference are exercised
only in making a choice. He who does anything because it is
the custom makes no choice. He gains no practice either in
discerning or in desiring what is best. The mental and
moral, like the muscular, powers are improved only by
being used. The faculties are called into no exercise by doing a thing merely because others do it, no more than by
believing a thing only because others believe it. If the
grounds of an opinion are not conclusive to the person's own
reason, his reason cannot be strengthened, but is likely to be
weakened, by his adopting it: and if the inducements to an
act are not such as are consentaneous to his own feelings

and character (where affection, or the rights of others, are not concerned), it is so much done toward rendering his feelings and character inert and torpid instead of active and energetic.

He who lets the world, or his own portion of it, choose his plan of life for him has no need of any other faculty than the ape-like one of imitation. He who chooses his plan for himself employs all his faculties. He must use observation to see, reasoning and judgment to foresee, activity to gather materials for decision, discrimination to decide, and when he has decided, firmness and self-control to hold to his deliberate decision. And these qualities he requires and exercises exactly in proportion as the part of his conduct which he determines according to his own judgment and feelings is a large one. It is possible that he might be guided in some good path, and kept out of harm's way, without any of these things. But what will be his comparative worth as a human being? It really is of importance, not only what men do, but also what manner of men they are that do it. Among the works of man which human life is rightly employed in perfecting and beautifying, the first in importance surely is man himself. Supposing it were possible to get houses built, corn grown, battles fought, causes tried, and even churches erected and prayers said by machinery—by automatons in human form—it would be a considerable loss to exchange for these automatons even the men and women who at present inhabit the more civilized parts of the world, and who assuredly are but starved specimens of what nature can and will produce. Human nature is not a machine to be built after a model, and set to do exactly the work prescribed for it, but a tree, which requires to grow and develop itself on all sides, according to the tendency of the inward forces which make it a living thing.

It will probably be conceded that it is desirable people should exercise their understandings, and that an intelligent following of custom, or even occasionally an intelligent deviation from custom, is better than a blind and simply mechanical adhesion to it. To a certain extent it is admitted that our understanding should be our own; but there is not the same willingness to admit that our desires and impulses should be our own likewise, or that to possess impulses of our own, and of any strength, is anything but a peril and a snare. Yet desires and impulses are as much a part of a perfect human being as beliefs and restraints; and strong impulses are only perilous when not properly balanced, when one set of aims and inclinations is developed into strength, while others, which ought to coexist with them, remain weak and inactive. It is not because men's desires are strong that they act ill; it is because their consciences are weak. There is no natural connection between strong impulses and a weak conscience. The natural connection is the other way. To say that one person's desires and feelings are stronger and more various than those of another is merely to say that he has more of the raw material of human nature and is therefore capable, perhaps of more evil, but certainly of more good. Strong impulses are but another name for energy. Energy may be turned to bad uses; but more good may always be made of an energetic nature than of an indolent and impassive one. Those who have most natural feeling are always those whose cultivated feelings may be made the strongest. The same strong susceptibilities which make the personal impulses vivid and powerful are also the source from whence are generated the most passionate love of virtue and the sternest self-control. It is through the cultivation of these that society both does its duty and protects its interests, not by rejecting the stuff of which heroes are made, because it knows not how to make them. A person whose desires and impulses are his own—are the expression of his own nature, as it has been developed and modified by his own culture—is said to have a character. One whose desires and impulses are not his own has no character, no more than a steam engine has a character. If, in addition to being his own, his impulses are strong and are under the government of a strong will, he has an energetic character. Whoever thinks that individuality of desires and impulses should not be encouraged to unfold itself must maintain that society has no need of strong

natures—is not the better for containing many persons who
have much character—and that a high general average of
energy is not desirable.

In some early states of society, these forces might be,
and were, too much ahead of the power which society then
possessed of disciplining and controlling them. There has
been a time when the element of spontaneity and individuality was in excess, and the social principle had a hard
struggle with it. The difficulty then was to induce men of
strong bodies or minds to pay obedience to any rules which
required them to control their impulses. To overcome this
difficulty, law and discipline, like the Popes struggling
against the Emperors, asserted a power over the whole man,
claiming to control all his life in order to control his character—which society had not found any other sufficient
means of binding. But society has now fairly got the better
of individuality; and the danger which threatens human
nature is not the excess, but the deficiency, of personal impulses and preferences. Things are vastly changed since the
passions of those who were strong by station or by personal
endowment were in a state of habitual rebellion against
laws and ordinances, and required to be rigorously chained
up to enable the persons within their reach to enjoy any
particle of security. In our times, from the highest class of
society down to the lowest, everyone lives as under the eye
of a hostile and dreaded censorship. Not only in what concerns others, but in what concerns only themselves, the
individual or the family do not ask themselves, what do I
prefer? or, what would suit my character and disposition?
or, what would allow the best and highest in me to have
fair play and enable it to grow and thrive? They ask themselves, what is suitable to my position? what is usually done
by persons of my station and pecuniary circumstances? or
(worse still) what is usually done by persons of a station
and circumstances superior to mine? I do not mean that
they choose what is customary in preference to what suits
their own inclination. It does not occur to them to have any
inclination except for what is customary. Thus the mind

itself is bowed to the yoke: even in what people do for pleasure, conformity is the first thing thought of; they like in crowds; they exercise choice only among things commonly done; peculiarity of taste, eccentricity of conduct are shunned equally with crimes, until by dint of not following their own nature they have no nature to follow: their human capacities are withered and starved; they become incapable of any strong wishes or native pleasures, and are generally without either opinions or feelings of home growth, or properly their own. Now is this, or is it not, the desirable condition of human nature?

It is so, on the Calvinistic theory. According to that, the one great offense of man is self-will. All the good of which humanity is capable is comprised in obedience. You have no choice; thus you must do, and no otherwise: "Whatever is not a duty is a sin." Human nature being radically corrupt, there is no redemption for anyone until human nature is killed within him. To one holding this theory of life, crushing out any of the human faculties, capacities, and susceptibilities is no evil: man needs no capacity but that of surrendering himself to the will of God; and if he uses any of his faculties for any other purpose but to do that supposed will more effectually, he is better without them. This is the theory of Calvinism; and it is held, in a mitigated form, by many who do not consider themselves Calvinists; the mitigation consisting in giving a less ascetic interpretation to the alleged will of God, asserting it to be his will that mankind should gratify some of their inclinations, of course not in the manner they themselves prefer, but in the way of obedience, that is, in a way prescribed to them by authority, and, therefore, by the necessary condition of the case, the same for all.

In some such insidious form there is at present a strong tendency to this narrow theory of life, and to the pinched and hidebound type of human character which it patronizes. Many persons, no doubt, sincerely think that human beings thus cramped and dwarfed are as their Maker designed them to be, just as many have thought that trees are a much finer thing when clipped into pollards, or cut out into figures of animals, than as nature made them. But if it be any part of religion to believe that man was made by a good Being, it is more consistent with that faith to believe that this Being gave all human faculties that they might be cultivated and unfolded, not rooted out and consumed, and that he takes delight in every nearer approach made by his creatures to the ideal conception embodied in them, every increase in any of their capabilities of comprehension, of action, or of enjoyment. There is a different type of human excellence from the Calvinistic: a conception of humanity as having its nature bestowed on it for other purposes than merely to be abnegated. "Pagan self-assertion" is one of the elements of human worth, as well as "Christian self-denial." * There is a Greek ideal of self-development, which the Platonic and Christian ideal of self-government blends with, but does not supersede. It may be better to be a John Knox than an Alcibiades, but it is better to be a Pericles than either; nor would a Pericles, if we had one in these days, be without anything good which belonged to John Knox.

It is not by wearing down into uniformity all that is individual in themselves, but by cultivating it and calling it forth, within the limits imposed by the rights and interests of others, that human beings become a noble and beautiful object of contemplation; and as the works partake the character of those who do them, by the same process human life also becomes rich, diversified, and animating, furnishing more abundant aliment to high thoughts and elevating feelings, and strengthening the tie which binds every individual to the race, by making the race infinitely better worth belonging to. In proportion to the development of his individuality, each person becomes more valuable to himself, and is, therefore, capable of being more valuable to others. There is a greater fullness of life about his own existence, and when there is more life in the units there is more in the mass which is composed of them. As much compression as is necessary to prevent the stronger specimens of

* Sterling's *Essays*.

human nature from encroaching on the rights of others cannot be dispensed with; but for this there is ample compensation even in the point of view of human development. The means of development which the individual loses by being prevented from gratifying his inclinations to the injury of others are chiefly obtained at the expense of the development of other people. And even to himself there is a full equivalent in the better development of the social part of his nature, rendered possible by the restraint put upon the selfish part. To be held to rigid rules of justice for the sake of others develops the feelings and capacities which have the good of others for their object. But to be restrained in things not affecting their good, by their mere displeasure, develops nothing valuable except such force of character as may unfold itself in resisting the restraint. If acquiesced in, it dulls and blunts the whole nature. To give any fair play to the nature of each, it is essential that different persons should be allowed to lead different lives. In proportion as this latitude has been exercised in any age has that age been noteworthy to posterity. Even despotism does not produce its worst effects so long as individuality exists under it; and whatever crushes individuality is despotism, by whatever name it may be called and whether it professes to be enforcing the will of God or the injuctions of men.

Having said that the individuality is the same thing with development, and that it is only the cultivation of individuality which produces, or can produce, well-developed human beings, I might here close the argument; for what more or better can be said of any condition of human affairs than that it brings human beings themselves nearer to the best thing they can be? Or what worse can be said of any obstruction to good than that it prevents this? Doubtless, however, these considerations will not suffice to convince those who most need convincing; and it is necessary further to show that these developed human beings are of some use to the undeveloped—to point out to those who do not desire liberty, and would not avail themselves of it, that they may be in some intelligible manner rewarded for allowing other people to make use of it without hindrance.

In the first place, then, I would suggest that they might possibly learn something from them. It will not be denied by anybody that originality is a valuable element in human affairs. There is always need of persons not only to discover new truths and point out when what were once truths are true no longer, but also to commence new practices and set the example of more enlightened conduct and better taste and sense in human life. This cannot well be gainsaid by anybody who does not believe that the world has already attained perfection in all its ways and practices. It is true that this benefit is not capable of being rendered by everybody alike; there are but few persons, in comparison with the whole of mankind, whose experiments, if adopted by others, would be likely to be any improvement on established practice. But these few are the salt of the earth; without them, human life would become a stagnant pool. Not only is it they who introduce good things which did not before exist; it is they who keep the life in those which already exist. If there were nothing new to be done, would human intellect cease to be necessary? Would it be a reason why those who do the old things should forget why they are done, and do them like cattle, not like human beings? There is only too great a tendency in the best beliefs and practices to degenerate into the mechanical; and unless there were a succession of persons whose ever-recurring originality prevents the grounds of those beliefs and practices from becoming merely traditional, such dead matter would not resist the smallest shock from anything really alive, and there would be no reason why civilization should not die out, as in the Byzantine Empire. Persons of genius, it is true, are, and are always likely to be, a small minority; but in order to have them, it is necessary to preserve the soil in which they grow. Genius can only breathe freely in an *atmosphere* of freedom. Persons of genius are, *ex vi termini*, more individual than any other people—less capable, consequently, of fitting themselves, without hurtful compression, into any of the small number of molds which society provides in order to save its members the trouble of forming their own character. If from timidity they consent to be forced into one of these molds, and to let all that part of themselves which cannot expand under the pressure remain unexpanded, society will be little the better for their genius. If they are of a strong character and break their fetters, they become a mark for the society which has not succeeded in reducing them to commonplace, to point out with solemn warning as "wild," "erratic," and the like—much as if one should complain of the Niagara river for not flowing smoothly between its banks like a Dutch canal.

I insist thus emphatically on the importance of genius and the necessity of allowing it to unfold itself freely both in thought and in practice, being well aware that no one will deny the position in theory, but knowing also that almost everyone, in reality, is totally indifferent to it. People think genius a fine thing if it enables a man to write an exciting poem or paint a picture. But in its true sense, that of originality in thought and action, though no one says that it is not a thing to be admired, nearly all, at heart, think that they can do very well without it. Unhappily this is too natural to be wondered at. Originality is the one thing which unoriginal minds cannot feel the use of. They cannot see what it is to do for them: how should they? If they could see what it would do for them, it would not be originality. The first service which originality has to render them is that of opening their eyes: which being once fully done, they would have a chance of being themselves original. Meanwhile, recollecting that nothing was ever done which someone was not the first to do, and that all good things which exist are the fruits of originality, let them be modest enough to believe that there is something still left for it to accomplish, and assure themselves that they are more in need of originality, the less they are conscious of the want.

In sober truth, whatever homage may be professed, or even paid, to real or supposed mental superiority, the general tendency of things throughout the world is to render mediocrity the ascendant power among mankind. In ancient history, in the Middle Ages, and in a diminishing degree through the long transition from feudality to the present time, the individual was a power in himself; and if he had either great talents or a high social position, he was a considerable power. At present individuals are lost in the crowd. In politics it is almost a triviality to say that public opinion now rules the world. The only power deserving the name is that of masses, and of governments while they make themselves the organ of the tendencies and instincts of masses. This is as true in the moral and social relations of private life as in public transactions. Those whose opinions go by the name of public opinion are not always the same sort of public: in America, they are the whole white population; in England, chiefly the middle class. But they are always a mass, that is to say, collective mediocrity. And what is a still greater novelty, the mass do not now take their opinions from dignitaries in Church or State, from ostensible leaders, or from books. Their thinking is done for them by men much like themselves, addressing them or speaking in their name, on the spur of the moment, through the newspapers. I am not complaining of all this. I do not assert that anything better is compatible, as a general rule, with the present low state of the human mind. But that does not hinder the government of mediocrity from being mediocre government. No government by a democracy or a numerous aristocracy, either in its political acts or in the opinions, qualities, and tone of mind which it fosters, ever did or could rise above mediocrity, except in so far as the sovereign. Many have let themselves be guided (which in their best times they always have done) by the counsels and influence of a more highly gifted and instructed *one* or *few*. The initiation of all wise or noble things comes and must come from individuals; generally at first from some one individual. The honor and glory of the average man is that he is capable of following that initiative; that he can respond internally to wise and noble things, and be led to them with his eyes open. I am not countenancing the sort of "hero-worship" which applauds the strong man of genius for forcibly seizing on the government of the world and making it do his bidding in spite of itself. All he can claim is freedom to point out the way. The power of compelling others into it is not only inconsistent with the freedom and development of all the rest, but corrupting to the strong man himself. It does seem, however, that when the opinions of masses of merely average men are everywhere become or becoming the dominant power, the counterpoise and corrective to that tendency would be the more and more pronounced individuality of those who stand on the higher eminences of thought. It is in these circumstances most especially that exceptional individuals, instead of being deterred, should be encouraged in acting differently from the mass. In other times there was no advantage in their doing so, unless they acted not only differently but better. In this age, the mere example of nonconformity, the mere refusal to bend the knee to custom, is itself a service. Precisely because the tyranny of opinion is such as to make eccentricity a reproach, it is desirable, in order to break through that tyranny, that people should be eccentric. Eccentricity has always abounded when and where strength of character has abounded; and the amount of eccentricity in a society has generally been proportional to the amount of genius, mental vigor, and moral courage it contained. That so few now dare to be eccentric marks the chief danger of the time.

I have said that it is important to give the freest scope possible to uncustomary things, in order that it may in time appear which of these are fit to be converted into customs. But independence of action and disregard of custom are not solely deserving of encouragement for the chance they afford that better modes of action, and customs more worthy of general adoption, may be struck out; nor is it only persons of decided mental superiority who have a just claim to carry on their lives in their own way. There is no reason that all human existence should be constructed on some

one or some small number of patterns. If a person possesses
any tolerable amount of common sense and experience, his
own mode of laying out his existence is the best, not because
it is the best in itself, but because it is his own mode. Human beings are not like sheep; and even sheep are not un-
distinguishably alike. A man cannot get a coat or a pair of
boots to fit him unless they are either made to his measure
or he has a whole warehouseful to choose from; and is it
easier to fit him with a life than with a coat, or are human
beings more like one another in their whole physical and
spiritual conformation than in the shape of their feet? If it
were only that people have diversities of taste, that is reason
enough for not attempting to shape them all after one model.
But different persons also require different conditions for
their spiritual development; and can no more exist healthily
in the same moral than all the variety of plants can in the
same physical, atmosphere and climate. The same things
which are helps to one person toward the cultivation of his
higher nature are hindrances to another. The same mode
of life is a healthy excitement to one, keeping all his faculties of action and enjoyment in their best order, while to
another it is a distracting burden which suspends or crushes
all internal life. Such are the differences among human
beings in their sources of pleasure, their susceptibilities of
pain, and the operation on them of different physical and
moral agencies that, unless there is a corresponding diversity
in their modes of life, they neither obtain their fair share of
happiness, nor grow up to the mental, moral, and aesthetic
stature of which their nature is capable. Why then should
tolerance, as far as the public sentiment is concerned, extend only to tastes and modes of life which extort acquiescence by the multitude of their adherents? Nowhere (except in some monastic institutions) is diversity of taste entirely unrecognized; a person may, without blame, either
like or dislike rowing, or smoking, or music, or athletic
exercises, or chess, or cards, or study, because both those
who like each of these things and those who dislike them are
too numerous to be put down. But the man, and still more

the woman, who can be accused either of doing "what nobody does," or of not doing "what everybody does," is the
subject of as much depreciatory remark as if he or she had
committed some grave moral delinquency. Persons require
to possess a title, or some other badge of rank, or of the
consideration of people of rank, to be able to indulge somewhat in the luxury of doing as they like without detriment
to their estimation. To indulge somewhat, I repeat: for
whoever allow themselves much of that indulgence incur
the risk of something worse than disparaging speeches—
they are in peril of a commission *de lunatico* and of having
their property taken from them and given to their relations.*

There is one characteristic of the present direction of
public opinion peculiarly calculated to make it intolerant
of any marked demonstration of individuality. The general average of mankind are not only moderate in intellect,
but also moderate in inclinations; they have no tastes or
wishes strong enough to incline them to do anything unusual, and they consequently do not understand those who

* There is something both contemptible and frightful in the sort of
evidence on which, of late years, any person can be judicially declared unfit
for the management of his affairs; and after his death, his disposal of his
property can be set aside if there is enough of it to pay the expenses of
litigation—which are charged on the property itself. All the minute details
of his daily life are pried into, and whatever is found which, seen through
the medium of the perceiving and describing faculties of the lowest of the
low, bears an appearance unlike absolute commonplace, is laid before the
jury as evidence of insanity, and often with success; the jurors being little,
if at all, less vulgar and ignorant than the witnesses, while the judges, with
that extraordinary want of knowledge of human nature and life which
continually astonishes us in English lawyers, often help to mislead them.
These trials speak volumes as to the state of feeling and opinion among the
vulgar with regard to human liberty. So far from setting any value on individuality—so far from respecting the right of each individual to act, in
things indifferent, as seems good to his own judgment and inclinations, judges
and juries cannot even conceive that a person in a state of sanity can desire
such freedom. In former days, when it was proposed to burn atheists, charitable people used to suggest putting them in a madhouse instead; it would
be nothing surprising nowadays were we to see this done, and the doers ap-
plauding themselves because, instead of persecuting for religion, they had
adopted so humane and Christian a mode of treating these unfortunates,
not without a silent satisfaction at their having thereby obtained their deserts.

have, and class all such with the wild and intemperate whom they are accustomed to look down upon. Now, in addition to this fact which is general, we have only to suppose that a strong movement has set in toward the improvement of morals, and it is evident what we have to expect. In these days such a movement has set in; much has actually been effected in the way of increased regularity of conduct and discouragement of excesses; and there is a philanthropic spirit abroad for the exercise of which there is no more inviting fields than the moral and prudential improvement of our fellow creatures. These tendencies of the times cause the public to be more disposed than at most former periods to prescribe general rules of conduct and endeavor to make everyone conform to the approved standard. And that standard, express or tacit, is to desire nothing strongly. Its ideal of character is to be without any marked character— to maim by compression, like a Chinese lady's foot, every part of human nature which stands out prominently and tends to make the person markedly dissimilar in outline to commonplace humanity.

As is usually the case with ideals which exclude one-half of what is desirable, the present standard of approbation produces only an inferior imitation of the other half. Instead of great energies guided by vigorous reason and strong feelings strongly controlled by a conscientious will, its result is weak feelings and weak energies, which therefore can be kept in outward conformity to rule without any strength either of will or of reason. Already energetic characters on any large scale are becoming merely traditional. There is now scarcely any outlet for energy in this country except business. The energy expended in this may still be regarded as considerable. What little is left from that employment is expended on some hobby, which may be a useful, even a philanthropic, hobby, but is always some one thing, and generally a thing of small dimensions. The greatness of England is now all collective; individually small, we only appear capable of anything great by our habit of combining; and with this our moral and religious philanthro-

pists are perfectly contented. But it was men of another
stamp than this that made England what it has been; and
men of another stamp will be needed to prevent its decline.

The despotism of custom is everywhere the standing
hindrance to human advancement, being in unceasing an-
tagonism to that disposition to aim at something better than
customary, which is called, according to circumstances, the
spirit of liberty, or that of progress or improvement. The
spirit of improvement is not always a spirit of liberty, for
it may aim at forcing improvements on an unwilling people; and the spirit of liberty, in so far as it resists such attempts, may ally itself locally and temporarily with the
opponents of improvement; but the only unfailing and
permanent source of improvement is liberty, since by it
there are as many possible independent centers of improvement as there are individuals. The progressive principle,
however, in their shape, whether as the love of liberty or
of improvement, is antagonistic to the sway of custom, involving at least emancipation from that yoke; and the contest between the two constitutes the chief interest of the
history of mankind. The greater part of the world has,
properly speaking, no history, because the despotism of
Custom is complete. This is the case over the whole East.
Custom is there, in all things, the final appeal; justice and
right mean conformity to custom; the argument of custom
no one, unless some tyrant intoxicated with power, thinks
of resisting. And we see the result. Those nations must once
have had originality; they did not start out of the ground
populous, lettered, and versed in many of the arts of life;
they made themselves all this, and were then the greatest
and most powerful nations of the world. What are they
now? The subjects or dependents of tribes whose forefathers
wandered in the forest when theirs had magnificent palaces
and gorgeous temples, but over whom custom exercised
only a divided rule with liberty and progress. A people, it
appears, may be progressive for a certain length of time,
and then stop: when does it stop? When it ceases to possess individuality. If a similar change should befall the

nations of Europe, it will not be in exactly the same shape: the despotism of custom with which these nations are threatened is not precisely stationariness. It proscribes singularity, but it does not preclude change, provided all change together. We have discarded the fixed costumes of our forefathers; everyone must still dress like other people, but the fashion may change once or twice a year. We thus take care that when there is a change, it shall be for change's sake, and not from any idea of beauty or convenience; for the same idea of beauty or convenience would not strike all the world at the same moment, and be simultaneously thrown aside by all at another moment. But we are progressive as well as changeable: we continually make new inventions in mechanical things, and keep them until they are again superseded by better; we are eager for improvement in politics, in education, even in morals, though in this last our idea of improvement chiefly consists in persuading or forcing other people to be as good as ourselves. It is not progress that we object to; on the contrary, we flatter ourselves that we are the most progressive people who ever lived. It is individuality that we war against: we should think we had done wonders if we had made ourselves all alike, forgetting that the unlikeness of one person to another is generally the first thing which draws the attention of either to the imperfection of his own type and the superiority of another, or the possibility, by combining the advantages of both, of producing something better than either. We have a warning example in China—a nation of much talent and, in some respects, even wisdom, owing to the rare good fortune of having been provided at an early period with a particularly good set of customs, the work, in some measure, of men to whom even the most enlightened European must accord, under certain limitations, the title of sages and philosophers. They are remarkable, too, in the excellence of their apparatus for impressing, as far as possible, the best wisdom they possess upon every mind in the community, and securing that those who have appropriated most of it shall occupy the posts of honor and power. Surely the people who did this have discovered the secret of human progressiveness and must have kept themselves steadily at the head of the movement of the world. On the contrary, they have become stationary—have remained so for thousands of years; and if they are ever to be further improved, it must be by foreigners. They have succeeded beyond all hope in what English philanthropists are so industriously working at—in making a people all alike, all governing their thoughts and conduct by the same maxims and rules; and these are the fruits. The modern *régime* of public opinion is, in an unorganized form, what the Chinese educational and political systems are in an organized; and unless individuality shall be able successfully to assert itself against this yoke, Europe, notwithstanding its noble antecedents and its professed Christianity, will tend to become another China.

What is it that has hitherto preserved Europe from this lot? What has made the European family of nations an improving, instead of a stationary, portion of mankind? Not any superior excellence in them, which, when it exists, exists as the effect, not as the cause, but their remarkable diversity of character and culture. Individuals, classes, nations have been extremely unlike one another: they have struck out a great variety of paths, each leading to something valuable; and although at every period those who traveled in different paths have been intolerant of one another, and each would have thought it an excellent thing if all the rest could have been compelled to travel his road, their attempts to thwart each other's development have rarely had any permanent success, and each has in time endured to receive the good which the others have offered. Europe is, in my judgment, wholly indebted to this plurality of paths for its progressive and many-sided development. But it already begins to possess this benefit in a considerably less degree. It is decidedly advancing toward the Chinese ideal of making all people alike. M. de Tocqueville, in his last important work, remarks how much more the Frenchmen of the present day resemble one another than did those even of the last generation. The same remark might be made of Englishmen in a far greater degree. In a passage already quoted from Wilhelm von Humboldt, he points out two things as necessary conditions of human development—because necessary to render people unlike one another—namely, freedom and variety of situations. The second of these two conditions is in this country every day diminishing. The circumstances which surround different classes and individuals, and shape their characters, are daily becoming more assimilated. Formerly, different ranks, different neighborhoods, different trades and professions lived in what might be called different worlds; at present, to a great degree in the same. Comparatively speaking, they now read the same things, listen to the same things, see the same things, go to the same places, have their hopes and fears directed to the same objects, have the same rights and liberties, and the same means of asserting them. Great as are the differences of position which remain, they are nothing to those which have ceased. And the assimilation is still proceeding. All the political changes of the age promote it, since they all tend to raise the low and to lower the high. Every extension of education promotes it, because education brings people under common influences and gives them access to the general stock of facts and sentiments. Improvement in the means of communication promotes it, by bringing the inhabitants of distant places into personal contact, and keeping up a rapid flow of changes of residence between one place and another. The increase of commerce and manufactures promotes it, by diffusing more widely the advantages of easy circumstances and opening all objects of ambition, even the highest, to general competition, whereby the desire of rising becomes no longer the character of a particular class, but of all classes. A more powerful agency than even all these, in bringing about a general similarity among mankind, is the complete establishment, in this and other free countries, of the ascendancy of public opinion in the State. As the various social eminences which enabled persons entrenched on them to disregard the opinion of the multitude gradually become leveled; as the very idea of resisting the will of the public, when it is positively known that they have a will, disappears more and more from the minds of practical politicians, there ceases to be any social support for nonconformity—any substantive power in society which, itself opposed to the ascendancy of numbers, is interested in taking under its protection opinions and tendencies at variance with those of the public.

The combination of all these causes forms so great a mass of influences hostile to individuality that it is not easy to see how it can stand its ground. It will do so with increasing difficulty unless the intelligent part of the public can be made to feel its value—to see that it is good there should be differences, even though not for the better, even though, as it may appear to them, some should be for the worse. If the claims of individuality are ever to be asserted, the time is now while much is still wanting to complete the enforced assimilation. It is only in the earlier stages that any stand can be successfully made against the encroachment. The demand that all other people shall resemble ourselves grows by what it feeds on. If resistance waits till life is reduced *nearly* to one uniform type, all deviations from that type will come to be considered impious, immoral, even monstrous and contrary to nature. Mankind speedily become unable to conceive diversity when they have been for some time unaccustomed to see it.

IV OF THE LIMITS TO THE AUTHORITY OF SOCIETY OVER THE INDIVIDUAL

What, then, is the rightful limit to the sovereignty of the individual over himself? Where does the authority of society begin? How much of human life should be assigned to individuality, and how much to society?

Each will receive its proper share if each has that which more particularly concerns it. To individuality should belong the part of life in which it is chiefly the individual that is interested; to society, the part which chiefly interests society.

Though society is not founded on a contract, and though no good purpose is answered by inventing a contract in order to deduce social obligations from it, everyone who receives the protection of society owes a return for the benefit, and the fact of living in society renders it indispensable that each should be bound to observe a certain line of conduct toward the rest. This conduct consists, first, in not injuring the interests of one another, or rather certain interests which, either by express legal provision or by tacit understanding, ought to be considered as rights; and secondly, in each person's bearing his share (to be fixed on some equitable principle) of the labors and sacrifices incurred for defending the society or its members from injury and molestation. These conditions society is justified in enforcing at all costs to those who endeavor to withhold fulfillment. Nor is this all that society may do. The acts of an individual may be hurtful to others or wanting in due consideration for their welfare, without going to the length of violating any of their constituted rights. The offender may then be justly punished by opinion, though not by law. As soon as any part of a person's conduct affects prejudicially the interests of others, society has jurisdiction over it, and the question whether the general welfare will or will not be promoted by interfering with it becomes open to discussion. But there is no room for entertaining any such question when a person's conduct affects the interests of no persons besides himself, or needs not affect them unless they like (all the persons concerned being of full age and the ordinary amount of understanding). In all such cases, there should be perfect freedom, legal and social, to do the action and stand the consequences.

It would be a great misunderstanding of this doctrine to suppose that it is one of selfish indifference which pretends that human beings have no business with each other's conduct in life, and that they should not concern themselves about the well-doing or well-being of one another, unless their own interest is involved. Instead of any diminution, there is need of a great increase of disinterested exertion to promote the good of others. But disinterested benevolence can find other instruments to persuade people to their good than whips and scourges, either of the literal or the metaphorical sort. I am the last person to undervalue the self-regarding virtues; they are only second in importance, if even second, to the social. It is equally the business of education to cultivate both. But even education works by conviction and persuasion as well as by compulsion, and it is by the former only that, when the period of education is passed, the self-regarding virtues should be inculcated. Human beings owe to each other help to distinguish the better from the worse, and encouragement to choose the former and avoid the latter. They should be forever stimulating each other to increased exercise of their higher faculties and increased direction of their feelings and aims toward wise instead of foolish, elevating instead of degrading, objects and contemplations. But neither one person, nor any number of persons, is warranted in saying to another human creature of ripe years that he shall not do with his life for his own benefit what he chooses to do with it. He is the person most interested in his own well-being: the interest which any other person, except in cases of strong personal attachment, can have in it is trifling compared with that which he himself has; the interest which society has in him individually (except as to his conduct to others) is fractional and altogether indirect, while with respect to his own feelings and circumstances the most ordinary man or woman has means of knowledge immeasurably surpassing those that can be possessed by anyone else. The interference of society to overrule his judgment and purposes in what only regards himself must be grounded on general presumptions which may be altogether wrong and, even if right, are as likely as not to be misapplied to individual cases, by persons no better acquainted with the circumstances of such cases than those are who look at them merely from without. In this department, therefore, of human affairs, individuality

has its proper field of action. In the conduct of human beings toward one another it is necessary that general rules
should for the most part be observed in order that people
may know what they have to expect; but in each person's
own concerns his individual spontaneity is entitled to free
exercise. Considerations to aid his judgment, exhortations
to strengthen his will may be offered to him, even obtruded
on him, by others; but he himself is the final judge. All
errors which he is likely to commit against advice and warn-
ings are far outweighed by the evil of allowing others to
constrain him to what they deem his good.

I do not mean that the feelings with which a person is
regarded by others ought not to be in any way affected by
his self-regarding qualities or deficiencies. This is neither
possible nor desirable. If he is eminent in any of the qualities which conduce to his own good, he is, so far, a proper
object of admiration. He is so much the nearer to the ideal
perfection of human nature. If he is grossly deficient in
those qualities, a sentiment the opposite of admiration will
follow. There is a degree of folly, and a degree of what may
be called (though the phrase is not unobjectionable) low-
ness or depravation of taste, which, though it cannot
justify doing harm to the person who manifests it, renders
him necessarily and properly a subject of distaste, or, in extreme cases, even of contempt: a person could not have the
opposite qualities in due strength without entertaining
these feelings. Though doing no wrong to anyone, a person
may so act as to compel us to judge him, and feel to him, as
a fool or as a being of an inferior order; and since this judgment and feeling are a fact which he would prefer to avoid,
it is doing him a service to warn him of it beforehand, as of
any other disagreeable consequence to which he exposes
himself. It would be well, indeed, if this good office were
much more freely rendered than the common notions of
politeness at present permit, and if one person could
honestly point out to another that he thinks him in fault,
without being considered unmannerly or presuming. We
have a right, also, in various ways, to act upon our unfavor-

able opinion of anyone, not to the oppression of his individuality, but in the exercise of ours. We are not bound, for example, to seek his society; we have a right to avoid it (though not to parade the avoidance), for we have a right to choose the society most acceptable to us. We have a right, and it may be our duty, to caution others against him if we think his example or conversation likely to have a pernicious effect on those with whom he associates. We may give others a preference over him in optional good offices, except those which tend to his improvement. In these various modes a person may suffer very severe penalties at the hands of others for faults which directly concern only himself; but he suffers these penalties only in so far as they are the natural and, as it were, the spontaneous consequences of the faults themselves, not because they are purposely inflicted on him for the sake of punishment. A person who shows rashness, obstinacy, self-conceit—who cannot live within moderate means; who cannot restrain himself from hurtful indulgence; who pursues animal pleasures at the expense of those of feeling and intellect—must expect to be lowered in the opinion of others, and to have a less share of their favorable sentiments; but of this he has no right to complain unless he has merited their favor by special excellence in his social relations and has thus established a title to their good offices, which is not affected by his demerits toward himself.

What I contend for is that the inconveniences which are strictly inseparable from the unfavorable judgment of others are the only ones to which a person should ever be subjected for that portion of his conduct and character which concerns his own good, but which does not affect the interest of others in their relations with him. Acts injurious to others require a totally different treatment. Encroachment on their rights; infliction on them of any loss or damage not justified by his own rights; falsehood or duplicity in dealing with them; unfair or ungenerous use of advantages over them; even selfish abstinence from defending them against injury —these are fit objects of moral reprobation and, in grave cases, of moral retribution and punishment. And not only these acts, but the dispositions which lead to them, are properly immoral and fit subjects of disapprobation which may rise to abhorrence. Cruelty of disposition; malice and ill-nature; that most antisocial and odious of all passions, envy; dissimulation and insincerity, irascibility on insufficient cause, and resentment disproportioned to the provocation; the love of domineering over others; the desire to engross more than one's share of advantages (the *pleonexia* of the Greeks); the pride which derives gratification from the abasement of others; the egotisim which thinks self and its concerns more important than everything else, and decides all doubtful questions in its own favor—these are moral vices and constitute a bad and odious moral character; unlike the self-regarding faults previously mentioned, which are not properly immoralities and, to whatever pitch they may be carried, do not constitute wickedness. They may be proofs of any amount of folly or want of personal dignity and self-respect, but they are only a subject of moral reprobation when they involve a breach of duty to others, for whose sake the individual is bound to have care of himself. What are called duties to ourselves are not socially obligatory unless circumstances render them at the same time duties to others. The term duty to oneself, when it means anything more than prudence, means self-respect or self-development, and for none of these is anyone accountable to his fellow creatures, because for none of them is it for the good of mankind that he be held accountable to them.

The distinction between the loss of consideration which a person may rightly incur by defect of prudence or of personal dignity, and the reprobation which is due to him for an offense against the rights of others, is not a merely nominal distinction. It makes a vast difference both in our feelings and in our conduct toward him whether he displeases us in things in which we think we have a right to control him or in things in which we know that we have not. If he displeases us, we may express our distaste, and we may stand aloof from a person as well as from a thing that displeases us; but we shall not therefore feel called on to make

his life uncomfortable. We shall reflect that he already
bears, or will bear, the whole penalty of his error; if he
spoils his life by mismanagement, we shall not, for that reason, desire to spoil it still further; instead of wishing to
punish him, we shall rather endeavor to alleviate his punishment by showing him how he may avoid or cure the evils
his conduct tends to bring upon him. He may be to us an
object of pity, perhaps of dislike, but not of anger or resentment; we shall not treat him like an enemy of society; the
worst we shall think ourselves justified in doing is leaving
him to himself, if we do not interfere benevolently by showing interest or concern for him. It is far otherwise if he has
infringed the rules necessary for the protection of his fellow
creatures, individually or collectively. The evil consequences of his acts do not then fall on himself, but on others;
and society, as the protector of all its members, must retaliate
on him, must inflict pain on him for the express purpose of
punishment, and must take care that it be sufficiently severe.
In the one case, he is an offender at our bar, and we are
called on not only to sit in judgment on him, but, in one
shape or another, to execute our own sentence; in the other
case, it is not our part to inflict any suffering on him, except
what may incidentally follow from our using the same liberty
in the regulation of our own affairs which we allow to him
in his.

The distinction here pointed out between the part of a
person's life which concerns only himself and that which
concerns others, many persons will refuse to admit. How
(it may be asked) can any part of the conduct of a member
of society be a matter of indifference to the other members?
No person is an entirely isolated being; it is impossible for
a person to do anything seriously or permanently hurtful to
himself without mischief reaching at least to his near con-
nections, and often far beyond them. If he injures his property, he does harm to those who directly or indirectly derived support from it, and usually diminishes, by a greater
or less amount, the general resources of the community. If

he deteriorates his bodily or mental faculties, he not only brings evil upon all who depended on him for any portion of their happiness, but disqualifies himself for rendering the services which he owes to his fellow creatures generally, perhaps becomes a burden on their affection or benevolence; and if such conduct were very frequent hardly any offense that is committed would detract more from the general sum of good. Finally, if by his vices or follies a person does no direct harm to others, he is nevertheless (it may be said), injurious by his example, and ought to be compelled to control himself for the sake of those whom the sight of knowledge of his conduct might corrupt or mislead.

And even (it will be added) if the consequences of misconduct could be confined to the vicious or thoughtless individual, ought society to abandon to their own guidance those who are manifestly unfit for it? If protection against themselves is confessedly due to children and persons under age, is not society equally bound to afford it to persons of mature years who are equally incapable of self-government? If gambling, or drunkenness, or incontinence, or idleness, or uncleanliness are as injurious to happiness, and as great a hindrance to improvement, as many or most of the acts prohibited by law, why (it may be asked) should not law, so far as is consistent with practicability and social convenience, endeavor to repress these also? And as a supplement to the unavoidable imperfections of law, ought not opinion at least to organize a powerful police against these vices and visit rigidly with social penalties those who are known to practice them? There is no question here (it may be said) about restricting individuality, or impeding the trial of new and original experiments in living. The only things it is sought to prevent are things which have been tried and condemned from the beginning of the world until now—things which experience has shown not to be useful or suitable to any person's individuality. There must be some length of time and amount of experience after which a moral or prudential truth may be regarded as established;

and it is merely desired to prevent generation after generation from falling over the same precipice which has been
fatal to their predecessors.

I fully admit that the mischief which a person does to
himself may seriously affect, both through their sympathies
and their interests, those nearly connected with him and,
in a minor degree, society at large. When, by conduct of
this sort, a person is led to violate a distinct and assignable
obligation to any other person or persons, the case is taken
out of the self-regarding class and becomes amenable to
moral disapprobation in the proper sense of the term. If,
for example, a man, through intemperance or extravagance,
becomes unable to pay his debts, or, having undertaken the
moral responsibility of a family, becomes from the same
cause incapable of supporting or educating them, he is deservedly reprobated and might be justly punished; but it is
for the breach of duty to his family or creditors, not for the
extravagance. If the resources which ought to have been
devoted to them had been diverted from them for the most
prudent investment, the moral culpability would have been
the same. George Barnwell murdered his uncle to get
money for his mistress, but if he had done it to set himself
up in business, he would equally have been hanged. Again,
in the frequent case of a man who causes grief to his family
by addiction to bad habits, he deserves reproach for his
unkindness or ingratitude; but so he may for cultivating
habits not in themselves vicious, if they are painful to those
with whom he passes his life, or who from personal ties
are dependent on him for their comfort. Whoever fails in
the consideration generally due to the interests and feelings
of others, not being compelled by some more imperative
duty, or justified by allowable self-preference, is a subject of moral disapprobation for that failure, but not for the
cause of it, nor for the errors, merely personal to himself,
which may have remotely led to it. In like manner, when a
person disables himself, by conduct purely self-regarding,
from the performance of some definite duty incumbent on
him to the public, he is guilty of a social offense. No person

ought to be punished simply for being drunk; but a soldier or a policeman should be punished for being drunk on duty. Whenever, in short, there is a definite damage, or a definite risk of damage, either to an individual or to the public, the case is taken out of the province of liberty and placed in that of morality or law.

But with regard to the merely contingent or, as it may be called, constructive injury which a person causes to society by conduct which neither violates any specific duty to the public, nor occasions perceptible hurt to any assignable individual except himself, the inconvenience is one which society can afford to bear, for the sake of the greater good of human freedom. If grown persons are to be punished for not taking proper care of themselves, I would rather it were for their own sake than under pretense of preventing them from impairing their capacity or rendering to society benefits which society does not pretend it has a right to exact. But I cannot consent to argue the point as if society had no means of bringing its weaker members up to its ordinary standard of rational conduct, except waiting till they do something irrational, and then punishing them, legally or morally, for it. Society has had absolute power over them during all the early portion of their existence; it has had the whole period of childhood and nonage in which to try whether it could make them capable of rational conduct in life. The existing generation is master both of the training and the entire circumstances of the generation to come; it cannot indeed make them perfectly wise and good, because it is itself so lamentably deficient in goodness and wisdom; and its best efforts are not always, in individual cases, its most successful ones; but it is perfectly well able to make the rising generation, as a whole, as good as, and a little better than, itself. If society lets any considerable number of its members grow up mere children, incapable of being acted on by rational consideration of distant motives, society has itself to blame for the consequences. Armed not only with all the powers of education, but with the ascendancy which the authority of a received opinion always exercises over the minds who are least fitted to judge for themselves, and aided by the *natural* penalties which cannot be prevented from falling on those who incur the distaste or the contempt of those who know them—let not society pretend that it needs, besides all this, the power to issue commands and enforce obedience in the personal concerns of individuals in which, on all principles of justice and policy, the decision ought to rest with those who are to abide the consequences. Nor is there anything which tends more to discredit and frustrate the better means of influencing conduct than a resort to the worse. If there be among those whom it is attempted to coerce into prudence or temperance any of the material of which vigorous and independent characters are made, they will infallibly rebel against the yoke. No such person will ever feel that others have a right to control him in his concerns, such as they have to prevent him from injuring them in theirs; and it easily comes to be considered a mark of spirit and courage to fly in the face of such usurped authority and do with ostentation the exact opposite of what it enjoins, as in the fashion of grossness which succeeded, in the time of Charles II, to the fanatical moral intolerance of the Puritans. With respect to what is said of the necessity of protecting society from the bad example set to others by the vicious or the self-indulgent, it is true that bad example may have a pernicious effect, especially the example of doing wrong to others with impunity to the wrong-doer. But we are now speaking of conduct which, while it does no wrong to others, is supposed to do great harm to the agent himself; and I do not see how those who believe this can think otherwise than that the example, on the whole, must be more salutary than hurtful, since, if it displays the misconduct, it displays also the painful or degrading consequences which, if the conduct is justly censured, must be supposed to be in all or most cases attendant on it.

But the strongest of all the arguments against the interference of the public with purely personal conduct is that, when it does interfere, the odds are that it interferes wrongly and in the wrong place. On questions of social morality, of duty to others, the opinion of the public, that is, of an over-ruling majority, though often wrong, is likely to be still oftener right, because on such questions they are only re-quired to judge of their own interests, of the manner in which some mode of conduct, if allowed to be practiced, would affect themselves. But the opinion of a similar ma-jority, imposed as a law on the minority, on questions of self-regarding conduct is quite as likely to be wrong as right, for in these cases public opinion means, at the best, some people's opinion of what is good or bad for other people, while very often it does not even mean that—the public, with the most perfect indifference, passing over the pleasure or convenience of those whose conduct they censure and con-sidering only their own preference. There are many who consider as an injury to themselves any conduct which they have a distaste for, and resent it as an outrage to their feel-ings; as a religious bigot, when charged with disregarding the religious feelings of others, has been known to retort that they disregard his feelings by persisting in their abomi-nable worship or creed. But there is no parity between the feeling of a person for his own opinion and the feeling of another who is offended at his holding it, no more than be-tween the desire of a thief to take a purse and the desire of the right owner to keep it. And a person's taste is as much his own peculiar concern as his opinion or his purse. It is easy for anyone to imagine an ideal public which leaves the freedom and choice of individuals in all uncertain mat-ters undisturbed and only requires them to abstain from modes of conduct which universal experience has con-demned. But where has there been seen a public which set any such limit to its censorship? Or when does the pub-lic trouble itself about universal experience? In its inter-ferences with personal conduct it is seldom thinking of any-thing but the enormity of acting or feeling differently from itself; and this standard of judgment, thinly disguised, is held up to mankind as the dictate of religion and philosophy by nine-tenths of all moralists and speculative writers. These teach that things are right because they are right; because we feel them to be so. They tell us to search in our own minds and hearts for laws of conduct binding on ourselves and on all others. What can the poor public do but apply these instructions and make their own personal feelings of good and evil, if they are tolerably unanimous in them, obligatory on all the world?

The evil here pointed out is not one which exists only in theory; and it may perhaps be expected that I should specify the instances in which the public of this age and country improperly invests its own preferences with the character of moral laws. I am not writing an essay on the aberrations of existing moral feeling. That is too weighty a subject to be discussed parenthetically, and by way of illustration. Yet examples are necessary to show that the principle I maintain is of serious and practical moment, and that I am not endeavoring to erect a barrier against imaginary evils. And it is not difficult to show, by abundant instances, that to extend the bounds of what may be called moral police until it encroaches on the most unquestionably legitimate liberty of the individual is one of the most universal of all human propensities.

As a first instance, consider the antipathies which men cherish on no better grounds than that persons whose religious opinions are different from theirs do not practice their religious observances, especially their religious abstinences. To cite a rather trivial example, nothing in the creed or practice of Christians does more to envenom the hatred of Mohammedans against them than the fact of their eating pork. There are few acts which Christians and Europeans regard with more unaffected disgust than Mussulmans regard this particular mode of satisfying hunger. It is, in the first place, an offense against their religion; but this circumstance by no means explains either the degree or the kind of their repugnance; for wine also is forbidden by their religion, and to partake of it is by all Mussulmans accounted wrong, but not disgusting. Their aversion to the flesh of the "unclean beast" is, on the contrary, of that peculiar character, resembling an instinctive antipathy, which the idea of uncleanness, when once it thoroughly sinks into the feelings, seems always to excite even in those whose personal habits are anything but scrupulously cleanly, and of which the sentiment of religious impurity, so intense in the Hindus, is a remarkable example. Suppose now that in a people of whom the majority were Mussulmans, that majority should insist upon not permitting pork to be eaten within the limits of the country. This would be nothing new in Mohammedan countries.* Would it be a legitimate exercise of the moral authority of public opinion, and if not, why not? The practice is really revolting to such a public. They also sincerely think that it is forbidden and abhorred by the Deity. Neither could the prohibition be censured as religious persecution. It might be religious in its origin, but it would not be persecution for religion, since nobody's religion makes it a duty to eat pork. The only tenable ground of condemnation would be that with the personal tastes and self-regarding concerns of individuals the public has no business to interfere.

To come somewhat nearer home: the majority of Spaniards consider it a gross impiety, offensive in the highest degree to the Supreme Being, to worship him in any other manner than the Roman Catholic; and no other public worship is lawful on Spanish soil. The people of all southern Europe look upon a married clergy as not only irreligious, but unchaste, indecent, gross, disgusting. What do Protestants think of these perfectly sincere feelings, and of the attempt to enforce them against non-Catholics? Yet, if man-

* The case of the Bombay Parsees is a curious instance in point. When this industrious and enterprising tribe, the descendants of the Persian fire-worshipers, flying from their native country before the Caliphs, arrived in western India, they were admitted to toleration by the Hindu sovereigns, on condition of not eating beef. When those regions afterward fell under the dominion of Mohammedan conquerors, the Parsees obtained from them a continuance of indulgence, on condition of refraining from pork. What was at first obedience to authority became a second nature, and the Parsees to this day abstain both from beef and pork. Though not required by their religion, the double abstinence has had time to grow into a custom of their tribe; and custom, in the East, is a religion.

kind are justified in interfering with each other's liberty in things which do not concern the interests of others, on what principle is it possible consistently to exclude these cases? Or who can blame people for desiring to suppress what they regard as a scandal in the sight of God and man? No stronger case can be shown for prohibiting anything which is regarded as a personal immorality than is made out for suppressing these practices in the eyes of those who regard them as impieties; and unless we are willing to adopt the logic of persecutors, and to say that we may persecute others because we are right, and that they must not persecute us because they are wrong, we must beware of admitting a principle of which we should resent as a gross injustice the application to ourselves.

The preceding instances may be objected to, although unreasonably, as drawn from contingencies impossible among us—opinion, in this country, not being likely to enforce abstinence from meats or to interfere with people for worshiping and for either marrying or not marrying, according to their creed or inclination. The next example, however, shall be taken from an interference with liberty which we have by no means passed all danger of. Wherever the Puritans have been sufficiently powerful, as in New England, and in Great Britain at the time of the Commonwealth, they have endeavored, with considerable success, to put down all public, and nearly all private, amusements: especially music, dancing, public games, or other assemblages for purposes of diversion, and the theater. There are still in this country large bodies of persons by whose notions of morality and religion these recreations are condemned; and those persons belonging chiefly to the middle class, who are the ascendant power in the present social and political condition of the kingdom, it is by no means impossible that persons of these sentiments may at some time or other command a majority in Parliament. How will the remaining portion of the community like to have the amusements that shall be permitted to them regulated by the religious and moral sentiments of the stricter Calvinists and Methodists? Would

they not, with considerable peremptoriness, desire these in-
trusively pious members of society to mind their own business? This is precisely what should be said to every government and every public who have the pretension that no person shall enjoy any pleasure which they think wrong. But
if the principle of the pretension be admitted, no one can
reasonably object to its being acted on in the sense of the
majority, or other preponderating power in the country;
and all persons must be ready to conform to the idea of a
Christian commonwealth as understood by the early settlers
in New England, if a religious profession similar to theirs
should ever succeed in regaining its lost ground, as religions
supposed to be declining have so often been known to do.

To imagine another contingency, perhaps more likely
to be realized than the one last mentioned. There is
confessedly a strong tendency in the modern world toward
a democratic constitution of society, accompanied or not by
popular political institutions. It is affirmed that in the country where this tendency is most completely realized—where
both society and the government are most democratic: the
United States—the feeling of the majority, to whom any
appearance of a more showy or costly style of living than they
can hope to rival is disagreeable, operates as a tolerably effectual sumptuary law, and that in many parts of the Union
it is really difficult for a person possessing a very large income
to find any mode of spending it which will not incur popular
disapprobation. Though such statements as these are doubtless much exaggerated as a representation of existing facts,
the state of things they describe is not only a conceivable
and possible, but a probable result of democratic feeling
combined with the notion that the public has a right to a
veto on the manner in which individuals shall spend their
incomes. We have only further to suppose a considerable
diffusion of Socialist opinions, and it may become infamous
in the eyes of the majority to possess more property than
some very small amount, or any income not earned by manual labor. Opinions similar in principle to these already
prevail widely among the artisan class and weigh oppres-

sively on those who are amenable to the opinion chiefly of that class, namely, its own members. It is known that the bad workmen who form the majority of the operatives in many branches of industry are decidedly of opinion that bad workmen ought to receive the same wages as good, and that no one ought to be allowed, through piecework or otherwise, to earn by superior skill or industry more than others can without it. And they employ a moral police, which occasionally becomes a physical one, to deter skillful workmen from receiving, and employers from giving, a larger remuneration for a more useful service. If the public have any jurisdiction over private concerns, I cannot see that these people are in fault, or that any individual's particular public can be blamed for asserting the same authority over his individual conduct which the general public asserts over people in general.

But, without dwelling upon supposititious cases, there are, in our own day, gross usurpations upon the liberty of private life actually practiced, and still greater ones threatened with some expectation of success, and opinons propounded which assert an unlimited right in the public not only to prohibit by law everything which it thinks wrong, but, in order to get at what it thinks wrong, to prohibit a number of things which it admits to be innocent.

Under the name of preventing intemperance, the people of one English colony, and of nearly half the United States, have been interdicted by law from making any use whatever of fermented drinks, except for medical purposes, for prohibition of their sale is in fact, as it is intended to be, prohibition of their use. And though the impracticability of executing the law has caused its repeal in several of the States which had adopted it, including the one from which it derives its name, an attempt has notwithstanding been commenced, and is prosecuted with considerable zeal by many of the professed philanthropists, to agitate for a similar law in this country. The association, or "Alliance," as it terms itself, which has been formed for this purpose, has acquired some notoriety through the publicity given to a

correspondence between its secretary and one of the very
few English public men who hold that a politician's opinions ought to be founded on principles. Lord Stanley's share
in this correspondence is calculated to strengthen the hopes
already built on him by those who know how rare such qualities as are manifested in some of his public appearances unhappily are among those who figure in political life. The
organ of the Alliance, who would "deeply deplore the recognition of any principle which could be wrested to justify
bigotry and persecution," undertakes to point out the "broad
and impassable barrier" which divides such principles from
those of the association. "All matters relating to thought,
opinion, conscience, appear to me," he says, "to be without
the sphere of legislation; all pertaining to social act, habit,
relation, subject only to a discretionary power vested in the
State itself, and not in the individual, to be within it." No
mention is made of a third class, different from either of
these, viz., acts and habits which are not social, but individual; although it is to this class, surely, that the act of drinking fermented liquors belongs. Selling fermented liquors,
however, is trading, and trading is a social act. But the infringement complained of is not on the liberty of the seller,
but on that of the buyer and consumer; since the State might
just as well forbid him to drink wine as purposely make it
impossible for him to obtain it. The secretary, however,
says, "I claim, as a citizen, a right to legislate whenever my
social rights are invaded by the social act of another." And
now for the definition of these "social rights": "If anything
invades my social rights, certainly the traffic in strong drink
does. It destroys my primary right of security by constantly
creating and stimulating social disorder. It invades my right
of equality by deriving a profit from the creation of a misery
I am taxed to support. It impedes my right to free moral
and intellectual development by surrounding my path with
dangers and by weakening and demoralizing society, from
which I have a right to claim mutual aid and intercourse."
A theory of "social rights" the like of which probably never
before found its way into distinct language: being nothing

short of this—that it is the absolute social right of every individual that every other individual shall act in every respect exactly as he ought; that whosoever fails thereof in the smallest particular violates my social right and entitles me to demand from the legislature the removal of the grievance. So monstrous a principle is far more dangerous than any single interference with liberty; there is no violation of liberty which it would not justify; it acknowledges no right to any freedom whatever, except perhaps to that of holding opinions in secret, without ever disclosing them; for the moment an opinion which I consider noxious passes anyone's lips, it invades all the "social rights" attributed to me by the Alliance. The doctrine ascribes to all mankind a vested interest in each other's moral, intellectual, and even physical perfection, to be defined by each claimant according to his own standard.

Another important example of illegitimate interference with the rightful liberty of the individual, not simply threatened, but long since carried into triumphant effect, is Sabbatarian legislation. Without doubt, abstinence on one day in the week, so far as the exigencies of life permit, from the usual daily occupation, though in no respect religiously binding on any except Jews, is a highly beneficial custom. And inasmuch as this custom cannot be observed without a general consent to that effect among the industrious classes, therefore, in so far as some persons by working may impose the same necessity on others, it may be allowable and right that the law should guarantee to each the observance by others of the custom, by suspending the greater operations of industry on a particular day. But this justification, grounded on the direct interest which others have in each individual's observance of the practice, does not apply to the self-chosen occupations in which a person may think fit to employ his leisure, nor does it hold good, in the smallest degree, for legal restrictions on amusements. It is true that the amusement of some is the day's work of others; but the pleasure, not to say the useful recreation, of many is worth the labor of a few, provided the occupation is freely chosen and can be freely resigned. The operatives are perfectly right in thinking that if all worked on Sunday, seven days' work would have to be given for six days' wages; but so long as the great mass of employments are suspended, the small number who for the enjoyment of others must still work obtain a proportional increase of earnings; and they are not obliged to follow those occupations if they prefer leisure to emolument. If a further remedy is sought, it might be found in the establishment by custom of a holiday on some other day of the week for those particular classes of persons. The only ground, therefore, on which restrictions on Sunday amusements can be defended must be that they are religiously wrong—a motive of legislation which can never be too earnestly protested against. *"Deorum injuriae Diis curae."* It remains to be proved that society or any of its officers holds a commission from on high to avenge any supposed offense to Omnipotence which is not also a wrong to our fellow creatures. The notion that it is one man's duty that another should be religious was the foundation of all the religious persecutions ever perpetrated, and, if admitted, would fully justify them. Though the feeling which breaks out in the repeated attempts to stop railway traveling on Sunday, in the resistance to the opening of museums, and the like, has not the cruelty of the old persecutors, the state of mind indicated by it is fundamentally the same. It is a determination not to tolerate others in doing what is permitted by their religion, because it is not permitted by the persecutor's religion. It is a belief that God not only abominates the act of the misbeliever, but will not hold us guiltless if we leave him unmolested.

I cannot refrain from adding to these examples of the little account commonly made of human liberty the language of downright persecution which breaks out from the press of this country whenever it feels called on to notice the remarkable phenomenon of Mormonism. Much might be said on the unexpected and instructive fact that an alleged new revelation and a religion founded on it—the product

of palpable imposture, not even supported by the *prestige*
of extraordinary qualities in its founder—is believed by
hundreds of thousands, and has been made the foundation
of a society in the age of newspapers, railways, and the elec-
tric telegraph. What here concerns us is that this religion,
like other and better religions, has its martyrs: that its
prophet and founder was, for his teaching, put to death by a
mob; that others of its adherents lost their lives by the same
lawless violence; that they were forcibly expelled, in a body,
from the country in which they first grew up, while, now
that they have been chased into a solitary recess in the midst
of a desert, many in this country openly declare that it would
be right (only that it is not convenient) to send an expedi-
tion against them and compel them by force to conform to
the opinions of other people. The article of the Mormonite
doctrine which is the chief provocative to the antipathy
which thus breaks through the ordinary restraints of religious tolerance is its sanction of polygamy; which, though permitted to Mohammedans, and Hindus, and Chinese, seems
to excite unquenchable animosity when practiced by persons
who speak English and profess to be a kind of Christians.
No one has a deeper disapprobation than I have of this Mor-
mon institution; both for other reasons and because, far
from being in any way countenanced by the principle of
liberty, it is a direct infraction of that principle, being a mere
riveting of the chains of one half of the community, and an
emancipation of the other from reciprocity of obligation toward them. Still, it must be remembered that this relation
is as much voluntary on the part of the women concerned
in it, and who may be deemed the sufferers by it, as is the
case with any other form of the marriage institution; and
however surprising this fact may appear, it has its explanation in the common ideas and customs of the world, which,
teaching women to think marriage the one thing needful,
make it intelligible that many a woman should prefer being
one of several wives to not being a wife at all. Other countries are not asked to recognize such unions, or release any
portion of their inhabitants from their own laws on the score

of Mormonite opinions. But when the dissentients have
conceded to the hostile sentiments of others far more than
could justly be demanded; when they have left the countries
to which their doctrines were unacceptable and established
themselves in a remote corner of the earth, which they have
been the first to render habitable to human beings, it is difficult to see on what principles but those of tyranny they can
be prevented from living there under what laws they please,
provided they commit no aggression on other nations and
allow perfect freedom of departure to those who are dis-
satisfied with their ways. A recent writer, in some respects
of considerable merit, proposes (to use his own words) not
a crusade, but a *civilizade,* against this polygamous community, to put an end to what seems to him a retrograde step
in civilization. It also appears so to me, but I am not aware
that any community has a right to force another to be
civilized. So long as the sufferers by the bad law do not in-
voke assistance from other communities, I cannot admit that
persons entirely unconnected with them ought to step in
and require that a condition of things with which all who are
directly interested appear to be satisfied should be put an
end to because it is a scandal to persons some thousands of
miles distant who have no part or concern in it. Let them
send missionaries, if they please, to preach against it; and let
them, by any fair means (of which silencing the teachers is
not one), oppose the progress of similar doctrines among
their own people. If civilization has got the better of barbarism when barbarism had the world to itself, it is too much
to profess to be afraid lest barbarism, after having been fairly
got under, should revive and conquer civilization. A civilization that can thus succumb to its vanquished enemy must
first have become so degenerate that neither its appointed
priests and teachers, nor anybody else has the capacity, or
will take the trouble, to stand up for it. If this be so, the
sooner such a civilization receives notice to quit, the better.
It can only go on from bad to worse until destroyed and re-
generated (like the Western Empire) by energetic barbarians.

V   APPLICATIONS

The principles asserted in these pages must be more generally admitted as the basis for discussion of details before a consistent application of them to all the various departments of government and morals can be attempted with any prospect of advantage. The few observations I propose to make on questions of detail are designed to illustrate the principles rather than to follow them out to their consequences. I offer not so much applications as specimens of application, which may serve to bring into greater clearness the meaning and limits of the two maxims which together form the entire doctrine of this essay, and to assist the judgment in holding the balance between them in the cases where it appears doubtful which of them is applicable to the case.

The maxims are, first, that the individual is not accountable to society for his actions in so far as these concern the interests of no person but himself. Advice, instruction, persuasion, and avoidance by other people, if thought necessary by them for their own good, are the only measures by which society can justifiably express its dislike or disapprobation of his conduct. Secondly, that for such actions as are prejudicial to the interests of others, the individual is accountable and may be subjected either to social or to legal punishment if society is of opinion that the one or the other is requisite for its protection.

In the first place, it must by no means be supposed, because damage, or probability of damage, to the interests of others can alone justify the interference of society, that therefore it always does justify such interference. In many cases an individual, in pursuing a legitimate object, necessarily and therefore legitimately causes pain or loss to others, or intercepts a good which they had a reasonable hope of obtaining. Such oppositions of interest between individuals often arise from bad social institutions, but are unavoidable while those institutions last; and some would be unavoidable under any institutions. Whoever succeeds in an overcrowded profession or in a competitive examination, whoever is preferred to another in any contest for an object which both desire, reaps benefit from the loss of others, from their wasted exertion and their disappointment. But it is, by common admission, better for the general interest of mankind that persons should pursue their objects undeterred by this sort of consequences. In other words, society admits no right, either legal or moral, in the disappointed competitors to immunity from this kind of suffering, and feels called on to interfere only when means of success have been employed which it is contrary to the general interest to permit—namely, fraud or treachery, and force.

Again, trade is a social act. Whoever undertakes to sell any description of goods to the public does what affects the interest of other persons, and of society in general; and thus his conduct, in principle, comes within the jurisdiction of society; accordingly, it was once held to be the duty of governments, in all cases which were considered of importance, to fix prices and regulate the processes of manufacture. But it is now recognized, though not till after a long struggle, that both the cheapness and the good quality of commodities are most effectually provided for by leaving the producers and sellers perfectly free, under the sole check of equal freedom to the buyers for supplying themselves elsewhere. This is the so-called doctrine of "free trade," which rests on grounds different from, though equally, solid with, the principle of individual liberty asserted in this essay. Restrictions on trade, or on production for purposes of trade, are indeed restraints; and all restraint, *qua* restraint, is an evil; but the restraints in question affect only that part of conduct which society is competent to restrain, and are wrong solely because they do not really produce the results which it is desired to produce by them. As the principle of individual liberty is not involved in the doctrine of free trade, so neither is it in most of the questions which arise respecting the limits of that doctrine, as, for example, what amount of public control is admissible for the prevention of fraud by adulteration; how far sanitary precautions, or arrangements to protect workpeople employed in dangerous occupations, should be enforced on employers. Such questions involve considerations of liberty only in so far as leaving people to themselves is always better, *caeteris paribus*, than controlling them; but that they may be legitimately controlled for these ends is in principle undeniable. On the other hand, there are questions relating to interference with trade which are essentially questions of liberty, such as the Maine Law, already touched upon; the prohibition of the importation of opium into China; the restriction of the sale of poisons—all cases, in short, where the object of the interference is to make it impossible or difficult to obtain a particular commodity. These interferences are objectionable, not as infringements on the liberty of the producer or seller, but on that of the buyer.

One of these examples, that of the sale of poisons, opens a new question: the proper limits of what may be called the functions of police; how far liberty may legitimately be invaded for the prevention of crime, or of accident. It is one of the undisputed functions of government to take precautions against crime before it has been committed, as well as to detect and punish it afterwards. The preventive function of government, however, is far more liable to be abused, to the prejudice of liberty, than the punitory function; for there is hardly any part of the legitimate freedom of action of a human being which would not admit of being represented, and fairly, too, as increasing the facilities for some form or other of delinquency. Nevertheless, if a public authority, or even a private person, sees anyone evidently preparing to commit a crime, they are not bound to look on inactive until the crime is committed, but may interfere to prevent it. If poisons were never bought or used for any purpose except the commission of murder, it would be right to prohibit their manufacture and sale. They may, however, be wanted not only for innocent but for useful purposes, and restrictions cannot be imposed in the one case without operating in the other. Again, it is a proper office of public authority to guard against accidents. If either a public officer or anyone else saw a person attempting to cross a bridge which had been ascertained to be unsafe, and there were no time to warn him of his danger, they might seize him and turn him back, without any real infringement of his liberty; for liberty consists in doing what one desires, and he does not desire to fall into the river. Nevertheless, when there is not a certainty, but only a danger of mischief, no one but the person himself can judge of the sufficiency of the motive which may prompt him to incur the risk; in this case, therefore (unless he is a child, or delirious, or in some state of excitement or absorption incompatible with the full use of the reflecting faculty), he ought, I conceive, to be only warned of the danger; not forcibly prevented from exposing himself to it. Similar considerations, applied to such a question as the sale of poisons, may enable us to decide which among the possible modes of regulation are or are not contrary to principle. Such a precaution, for example, as that of labeling the drug with some word expressive of its dangerous character may be enforced without violation of liberty: the buyer cannot wish not to know that the thing he possesses has poisonous qualities. But to require in all cases the certificate of a medical practitioner would make it sometimes impossible, always expensive, to obtain the article for legitimate uses. The only mode apparent to me, in which difficulties may be thrown in the way of crime committed through this means, without any infringement worth taking into account upon the liberty of those who desire the poisonous substance for other purposes, consists in providing what, in the apt language of Bentham, is called "preappointed evidence." This provision is familiar to everyone in the case of contracts. It is usual and right that the law, when a contract is entered into, should require as the condition of its enforcing performance that certain formalities should be observed, such as signatures, attestation of witnesses, and the like, in order that in case of subsequent dispute there may be evidence to prove that the contract was really entered into, and that there was nothing in the circumstances to render it legally invalid, the effect being to throw great obstacles in the way of fictitious contracts, or contracts made in circumstances which, if known, would destroy their validity. Precautions of a similar nature might be enforced in the sale of articles adapted to be instruments of crime. The seller, for example, might be required to enter in a register the exact time of the transaction, the name and address of the buyer, the precise quality and quantity sold; to ask the purpose for which it was wanted, and record the answer he received. When there was no medical prescription, the presence of some third person might be required to bring home the fact to the purchaser, in case there should afterwards be reason to believe that the article had been applied to criminal purposes. Such regulations would in general be no material impediment to obtaining the article, but a very considerable one to making an improper use of it without detection.

The right inherent in society to ward off crimes against itself by antecedent precautions suggests the obvious limitations to the maxim that purely self-regarding misconduct cannot properly be meddled with in the way of prevention or punishment. Drunkenness, for example, in ordinary cases, is not a fit subject for legislative interference, but I should deem it perfectly legitimate that a person who had once been convicted of any act of violence to others under the influence of drink should be placed under a special legal restriction, personal to himself; that if he were afterwards found drunk, he should be liable to a penalty, and that if, when in that state, he committed another offense, the punishment to which he would be liable for that other offense should be increased in severity. The making himself drunk, in a person whom drunkenness excites to do harm to others, is a crime against others. So, again, idleness, except in a person receiving support from the public, or except when it constitutes a breach of contract, cannot without tyranny be made a subject of legal punishment; but if, either from idleness or from any other avoidable cause, a man fails to perform his legal duties to others, as for instance to support his children, it is no tyranny to force him to fulfill that obligation by compulsory labor if no other means are available.

Again, there are many acts which, being directly injurious only to the agents themselves, ought not to be legally interdicted, but which, if done publicly, are a violation of good manners and, coming thus within the category of offenses against others, may rightly be prohibited. Of this kind are offenses against decency; on which it is unnecessary to dwell, the rather as they are only connected indirectly with our subject, the objection to publicity being equally strong in the case of many actions not in themselves condemnable, nor supposed to be so.

There is another question to which an answer must be found, consistent with the principles which have been laid down. In cases of personal conduct supposed to be blamable, but which respect for liberty precludes society from preventing or punishing because the evil directly resulting falls wholly on the agent; what the agent is free to do, ought other persons to be equally free to counsel or instigate? This question is not free from difficulty. The case of a person who solicits another to do an act is not strictly a case of self-regarding conduct. To give advice or offer inducements to anyone is a social act and may, therefore, like actions in general which affect others, be supposed amenable to social control. But a little reflection corrects the first impression, by showing that if the case is not strictly within the definition of individual liberty, yet the reasons on which the principle of individual liberty is grounded are applicable to it. If people must be allowed, in whatever concerns only themselves, to act as seems best to themselves, at their own peril, they must equally be free to consult with one another about what is fit to be so done; to exchange opinions, and give and receive suggestions. Whatever it is permitted to do, it must be permitted to advise to do. The question is doubtful only when the instigator derives a personal benefit from his advice, when he makes it his occupation, for subsistence or pecuniary gain, to promote what society and the State consider to be an evil. Then, indeed, a new element of complication

is introduced—namely, the existence of classes of persons
with an interest opposed to what is considered as the public
weal, and whose mode of living is grounded on the counter-
action of it. Ought this to be interfered with, or not? Fornication, for example, must be tolerated, and so must gambling; but should a person be free to be a pimp, or to keep a
gambling house? The case is one of those which lie on the
exact boundary line between two principles, and it is not at
once apparent to which of the two it properly belongs. There
are arguments on both sides. On the side of toleration it may
be said that the fact of following anything as an occupation,
and living or profiting by the practice of it, cannot make that
criminal which would otherwise be admissible; that the act
should either be consistently permitted or consistently prohibited; that if the principles which we have hitherto defended are true, society has no business, *as* society, to decide
anything to be wrong which concerns only the individual;
that it cannot go beyond dissuasion, and that one person
should be as free to persuade as another to dissuade. In opposition to this it may be contended that, although the public, or the State, are not warranted in authoritatively deciding, for purposes of repression or punishment, that such
or such conduct affecting only the interests of the individual
is good or bad, they are fully justified in assuming, if they
regard it as bad, that its being so or not is at least a disputable
question: that, this being supposed, they cannot be acting
wrongly in endeavoring to exclude the influence of solicita-
tions which are not disinterested, of instigators who cannot
possibly be impartial—who have a direct personal interest
on one side, and that side the one which the State believes
to be wrong, and who confessedly promote it for personal
objects only. There can surely, it may be urged, be nothing
lost, no sacrifice of good, by so ordering matters that persons
shall make their election, either wisely or foolishly, on their
own prompting, as free as possible from the arts of persons
who stimulate their inclinations for interested purposes of
their own. Thus (it may be said), though the statutes respecting unlawful games are utterly indefensible—though

all persons should be free to gamble in their own or each other's houses, or in any place of meeting established by their own subscriptions and open only to the members and their visitors—yet public gambling houses should not be permitted. It is true that the prohibition is never effectual, and that, whatever amount of tyrannical power may be given to the police, gambling houses can always be maintained under other pretenses; but they may be compelled to conduct their operations with a certain degree of secrecy and mystery, so that nobody knows anything about them but those who seek them; and more than this society ought not to aim at. There is considerable force in these arguments. I will not venture to decide whether they are sufficient to justify the moral anomaly of punishing the accessory when the principal is (and must be) allowed to go free; of fining or imprisoning the procurer, but not the fornicator—the gambling-house keeper, but not the gambler. Still less ought the common operations of buying and selling to be interfered with on analogous grounds. Almost every article which is bought and sold may be used in excess, and the sellers have a pecuniary interest in encouraging that excess; but no argument can be founded on this in favor, for instance, of the Maine Law; because the class of dealers in strong drinks, though interested in their abuse, are indispensably required for the sake of their legitimate use. The interest, however, of these dealers in promoting intemperance is a real evil and justifies the State in imposing restrictions and requiring guarantees which, but for that justification, would be infringements of legitimate liberty.

A further question is whether the State, while it permits, should nevertheless indirectly discourage conduct which it deems contrary to the best interests of the agent; whether, for example, it should take measures to render the means of drunkenness more costly, or add to the difficulty of procuring them by limiting the number of the places of sale. On this, as on most other practical questions, many distinctions require to be made. To tax stimulants for the sole purpose of making them more difficult to be obtained is a measure differing only in degree from their entire prohibition, and would be justifiable only if that were justifiable. Every increase of cost is a prohibition to those whose means do not come up to the augmented price; and to those who do, it is a penalty laid on them for gratifying a particular taste. Their choice of pleasures and their mode of expending their income, after satisfying their legal and moral obligations to the State and to individuals, are their own concern and must rest with their own judgment. These considerations may seem at first sight to condemn the selection of stimulants as special subjects of taxation for purposes of revenue. But it must be remembered that taxation for fiscal purposes is absolutely inevitable; that in most countries it is necessary that a considerable part of that taxation should be indirect; that the State, therefore, cannot help imposing penalties, which to some persons may be prohibitory, on the use of some articles of consumption. It is hence the duty of the State to consider, in the imposition of taxes, what commodities the consumers can best spare; and *a fortiori*, to select in preference those of which it deems the use, beyond a very moderate quantity, to be positively injurious. Taxation, therefore, of stimulants up to the point which produces the largest amount of revenue (supposing that the State needs all the revenue which it yields) is not only admissible, but to be approved of.

The question of making the sale of these commodities a more or less exclusive privilege must be answered differently, according to the purposes to which the restriction is intended to be subservient. All places of public resort require the restraint of a police, and places of this kind peculiarly, because offenses against society are especially apt to originate there. It is, therefore, fit to confine the power of selling these commodities (at least for consumption on the spot) to persons of known or vouched-for respectability of conduct; to make such regulations respecting hours of opening and closing as may be requisite for public surveillance, and to withdraw the license if breaches of the peace repeatedly take place through the connivance or incapacity of the keeper of the house, or if it becomes a rendezvous for concocting and preparing offenses against the law. Any further restriction I do not conceive to be, in principle, justifiable. The limitation in number, for instance, of beer and spirit houses, for the express purpose of rendering them more difficult of access and diminishing the occasions of temptation, not only exposes all to an inconvenience because there are some by whom the facility would be abused, but is suited only to a state of society in which the laboring classes are avowedly treated as children or savages, and placed under an education of restraint, to fit them for future admission to the privileges of freedom. This is not the principle on which the laboring classes are professedly governed in any free country; and no person who sets due value on freedom will give his adhesion to their being so governed, unless after all efforts have been exhausted to educate them for freedom and govern them as freemen, and it has been definitively proved that they can only be governed as children. The bare statement of the alternative shows the absurdity of supposing that such efforts have been made in any case which needs be considered here. It is only because the institutions of this country are a mass of inconsistencies, that things find admittance into our practice which belong to the system of despotic, or what is called paternal, government, while the general freedom of our institutions precludes the exercise of the amount of control necessary to render the restraint of any real efficacy as a moral education.

It was pointed out in an early part of this essay that the liberty of the individual, in things wherein the individual is alone concerned, implies a corresponding liberty in any number of individuals to regulate by mutual agreement such things as regard them jointly, and regard no persons but themselves. This question presents no difficulty so long as the will of all the persons implicated remains unaltered; but since that will may change, it is often necessary, even in things in which they alone are concerned, that they should enter into engagements with one another; and when they do, it is fit, as a general rule, that those engagements should be kept. Yet, in the laws, probably, of every country, this general rule has some exceptions. Not only persons are not held to engagements which violate the rights of third parties but it is sometimes considered a sufficient reason for releasing them from an engagement that it is injurious to themselves. In this and most other civilized countries, for example, an engagement by which a person should sell himself, or allow himself to be sold, as a slave would be null and void, neither enforced by law nor by opinion. The ground for thus limiting his power of voluntarily disposing of his own lot in life is apparent, and is very clearly seen in this extreme case. The reason for not interfering, unless for the sake of others, with a person's voluntary acts is consideration for his liberty. His voluntary choice is evidence that what he so chooses is desirable, or at least endurable, to him, and his good is on the whole best provided for by allowing him to take his own means of pursuing it. But by selling himself for a slave, he abdicates his liberty; he foregoes any future use of it beyond that single act. He therefore defeats, in his own case, the very purpose which is the justification of allowing him to dispose of himself. He is no longer free, but is thenceforth in a position which has no longer the presumption in its favor that would be afforded by his voluntarily remaining in it. The principle of freedom cannot require that he should be free not to be free. It is not freedom to be allowed to alienate his freedom. These reasons, the force of which is so conspicuous in this peculiar case, are evidently of far wider application, yet a limit is everywhere set to them by the necessities of life, which continually require, not indeed that we should resign our freedom, but that we should consent to this and the other limitation of it. The principle, however, which demands uncontrolled freedom of action in all that concerns only the agents themselves requires that those who have become bound to one another, in things which concern no third party, should be able to release one another from the engagement; and even without such voluntary release there are perhaps no contracts or engagements, except those that relate to money or money's worth, of which one can venture to say that there ought to be no liberty whatever of retractation. Baron Wilhelm von Humboldt, in the excellent essay from which I have already quoted, states it as his conviction that engagements which involve personal relations or services should never be legally binding beyond a limited duration of time; and that the most important of these engagements, marriage, having the peculiarity that its objects are frustrated unless the feelings of both the parties are in harmony with it, should require nothing more than the declared will of either party to dissolve it. This subject is too important and too complicated to be discussed in a parenthesis, and I touch on it only so far as is necessary for purposes of illustration. If the conciseness and generality of Baron Humboldt's dissertation had not obliged him in this instance to content himself with enunciating his conclusion without discussing the premises, he would doubtless have recognized that the question cannot be decided on grounds so simple as those to which he confines himself. When a person, either by express promise or by conduct, has encouraged another to rely upon his continuing to act in a certain way—to build expectations and calculations, and stake any part of his plan of life upon that supposition—a new series of moral obligations arises on his part toward that person, which may possibly be overruled, but cannot be ignored. And again, if the relation between two contracting parties has been followed by consequences to others; if it has placed third parties in any peculiar position, or, as in the case of marriage, has even called third parties into existence, obligations arise on the part of both the contracting parties toward those third persons, the fulfillment of which, or at all events the mode of fulfillment, must be greatly affected by the continuance or disruption of the relation between the original parties to the contract. It does not follow, nor can I admit, that these obligations extend to requiring the fulfillment of the contract at all costs to the happiness of the reluctant party; but they are a necessary element in the question; and even if, as von Humboldt maintains, they ought to make no difference in the *legal* freedom of the parties to release themselves from the engagement (and I also hold that they ought not to make *much* difference), they necessarily make a great difference in the *moral* freedom. A person is bound to take all these circumstances into account before resolving on a step which may affect such important interests of others; and if he does not allow proper weight to those interests, he is morally responsible for the wrong. I have made these obvious remarks for the better illustration of the general principle of liberty, and not because they are at all needed on the particular question, which, on the contrary, is usually discussed as if the interest of children was everything, and that of grown persons nothing.

I have already observed that, owing to the absence of any recognized general principles, liberty is often granted where it should be withheld, as well as withheld where it should be granted; and one of the cases in which, in the modern European world, the sentiment of liberty is the strongest is a case where, in my view, it is altogether misplaced. A person should be free to do as he likes in his own concerns, but he ought not to be free to do as he likes in acting for another, under the pretext that the affairs of the other are his own affairs. The State, while it respects the liberty of each in what specially regards himself, is bound to maintain a vigilant control over his exercise of any power which it allows him to possess over others. This obligation is almost entirely disregarded in the case of the family relations—a case, in its direct influence on human happiness, more important than all others taken together. The almost despotic power of husbands over wives needs not be enlarged upon here, because nothing more is needed for the complete removal of the evil than that wives should have the same rights and should receive the protection of law in the same manner as all other persons; and because, on this subject, the defenders of established injustice do not avail themselves of the plea of liberty but stand forth openly as the champions of power. It is in the case of children that misapplied notions of liberty are a real obstacle to the fulfillment by the State of its duties. One would almost think that a man's children were supposed to be literally, and not metaphorically, a part of himself, so jealous is opinion of the smallest interference of law with his absolute and exclusive control over them, more jealous than of almost any interference with his own freedom of action: so much less do the generality of mankind value liberty than power. Consider, for example, the case of education. Is it not almost a self-evident axiom that the State should require and compel the education, up to a certain standard, of every human being who is born its citizen? Yet who is there that is not afraid to recognize and assert this truth? Hardly anyone, indeed, will deny that it is one of the most sacred duties of the parents (or, as law and usage now stand, the father), after summoning a human being into the world, to give to that being an education fitting him to perform his part well in life toward others and toward himself. But while this is unanimously declared to be the father's duty, scarcely anybody, in this country, will bear to hear of obliging him to perform it. Instead of his being required to make any exertion or sacrifice for securing education to his child, it is left to his choice to accept it or not when it is provided gratis! It still remains unrecognized that to bring a child into existence without a fair prospect of being able, not only to provide food for its body, but instruction and training for its mind is a moral crime, both against the unfortunate offspring and against society; and that if the parent does not fulfill this obligation, the State ought to see it fulfilled at the charge, as far as possible, of the parent.

Were the duty of enforcing universal education once admitted there would be an end to the difficulties about what the State should teach, and how it should teach, which now convert the subject into a mere battlefield for sects and parties, causing the time and labor which should have been spent in education to be wasted in quarreling about education. If the government would make up its mind to require for every child a good education, it might save itself the trouble of providing one. It might leave to parents to obtain

the education where and how they pleased, and content
itself with helping to pay the school fees of the poorer classes
of children, and defraying the entire school expenses of
those who have no one else to pay for them. The objections
which are urged with reason against State education do not
apply to the enforcement of education by the State, but to
the State's taking upon itself to direct that education; which
is a totally different thing. That the whole or any large
part of the education of the people should be in State hands,
I go as far as anyone in deprecating. All that has been said
of the importance of individuality of character, and diversity
in opinions and modes of conduct, involves, as of the same
unspeakable importance, diversity of education. A general
State education is a mere contrivance for molding people to
be exactly like one another; and as the mold in which it casts
them is that which pleases the predominant power in the
government—whether this be a monarch, a priesthood, an
aristocracy, or the majority of the existing generation—in
proportion as it is efficient and successful, it establishes a
despotism over the mind, leading by natural tendency to
one over the body. An education established and controlled
by the State should only exist, if it exist at all, as one among
many competing experiments, carried on for the purpose
of example and stimulus to keep the others up to a certain
standard of excellence. Unless, indeed, when society in
general is in so backward a state that it could not or would
not provide for itself any proper institutions of education
unless the government undertook the task, then, indeed,
the government may, as the less of two great evils, take upon
itself the business of schools and universities, as it may that
of joint stock companies when private enterprise in a shape
fitted for undertaking great works of industry does not exist
in the country. But in general, if the country contains a
sufficient number of persons qualified to provide education
under government auspices, the same persons would be able
and willing to give an equally good education on the voluntary principle, under the assurance of remuneration afforded

by a law rendering education compulsory, combined with
State aid to those unable to defray the expense.

The instrument for enforcing the law could be no
other than public examinations, extending to all children
and beginning at an early age. An age might be fixed at
which every child must be examined, to ascertain if he (or
she) is able to read. If a child proves unable, the father,
unless he has some sufficient ground of excuse, might be subjected to a moderate fine, to be worked out, if necessary, by
his labor, and the child might be put to school at his expense.
Once in every year the examination should be renewed, with
a gradually extending range of subjects, so as to make the
universal acquisition and, what is more, retention of a
certain minimum of general knowledge virtually compulsory. Beyond that minimum there should be voluntary examinations on all subjects, at which all who come up to a
certain standard of proficiency might claim a certificate. To
prevent the State from exercising, through these arrangements, an improper influence over opinion, the knowledge
required for passing an examination (beyond the merely
instrumental parts of knowledge, such as languages and
their use) should, even in the higher classes of examinations,
be confined to facts and positive science exclusively. The
examinations on religion, politics, or other disputed topics
should not turn on the truth or falsehood of opinions, but
in the matter of fact that such and such an opinion is held,
on such grounds, by such authors, or schools, or churches.
Under this system, the rising generation would be no worse
off in regard to all disputed truths than they are at present;
they would be brought up either churchmen or dissenters
as they now are, the State merely taking care that they
should be instructed churchmen, or instructed dissenters.
There would be nothing to hinder them from being taught
religion, if their parents chose, at the same schools where
they were taught other things. All attempts by the State to
bias the conclusions of its citizens on disputed subjects are
evil; but it may very properly offer to ascertain and certify

that a person possesses the knowledge requisite to make his conclusions on any given subject worth attending to. A student of philosophy would be the better for being able to stand an examination both in Locke and in Kant, whichever of the two he takes up with, or even if with neither: and there is no reasonable objection to examining an atheist in the evidences of Christianity, provided he is not required to profess a belief in them. The examinations, however, in the higher branches of knowledge should, I conceive, be entirely voluntary. It would be giving too dangerous a power to governments were they allowed to exclude anyone from professions, even from the profession of teacher, for alleged deficiency of qualifications; and I think, with Wilhelm von Humboldt, that degrees or other public certificates of scientific or professional acquirements should be given to all who present themselves for examination and stand the test, but that such certificates should confer no advantage over competitors other than the weight which may be attached to their testimony by public opinion.

It is not in the matter of education only that misplaced notions of liberty prevent moral obligations on the part of parents from being recognized, and legal obligations from being imposed, where there are the strongest grounds for the former always, and in many cases for the latter also. The fact itself, of causing the existence of a human being, is one of the most responsible actions in the range of human life. To undertake this responsibility—to bestow a life which may be either a curse or a blessing—unless the being on whom it is to be bestowed will have at least the ordinary chances of a desirable existence, is a crime against that being. And in a country, either overpeopled or threatened with being so, to produce children, beyond a very small number, with the effect of reducing the reward of labor by their competition is a serious offense against all who live by the remuneration of their labor. The laws which, in many countries on the Continent, forbid marriage unless the parties can show that they have the means of supporting a family do not exceed the legitimate powers of the State; and whether such laws be expedient or not (a question mainly dependent on local circumstances and feelings), they are not objectionable as violations of liberty. Such laws are interferences of the State to prohibit a mischievous act—an act injurious to others, which ought to be a subject of reprobation and social stigma, even when it is not deemed expedient to superadd legal punishment. Yet the current ideas of liberty, which bend so easily to real infringements of the freedom of the individual in things which concern only himself, would repel the attempt to put any restraint upon his inclinations when the consequence of their indulgence is a life or lives of wretchedness and depravity to the offspring, with manifold evils to those sufficiently within reach to be in any way affected by their actions. When we compare the strange respect of mankind for liberty with their strange want of respect for it, we might imagine that a man had an indispensable right to do harm to others, and no right at all to please himself without giving pain to anyone.

I have reserved for the last place a large class of questions respecting the limits of government interference, which, though closely connected with the subject of this essay, do not, in strictness, belong to it. These are cases in which the reasons against interference do not turn upon the the principle of liberty: the question is not about restraining the actions of individuals, but about helping them; it is asked whether the government should do, or cause to be done, something for their benefit instead of leaving it to be done by themselves, individually or in voluntary combination.

The objections to government interference, when it is not such as to involve infringement of liberty, may be of three kinds:

The first is when the thing to be done is likely to be better done by individuals than by the government. Speaking generally, there is no one so fit to conduct any business, or to determine how or by whom it shall be conducted, as those who are personally interested in it. This principle

condemns the interferences, once so common, of the legislature, or the officers of government, with the ordinary
processes of industry. But this part of the subject has been
sufficiently enlarged upon by political economists, and is
not particularly related to the principles of this essay.

The second objection is more nearly allied to our subject. In many cases, though individuals may not do the particular thing so well, on the average, as the officers of government, it is nevertheless desirable that it should be done by
them, rather than by the government, as a means to their
own mental education—a mode of strengthening their
active faculties, exercising their judgment, and giving them
a familiar knowledge of the subjects with which they are
thus left to deal. This is a principal, though not the sole,
recommendation of jury trial (in cases not political); of free
and popular local and municipal institutions; of the conduct of industrial and philanthropic enterprises by voluntary associations. These are not questions of liberty,
and are connected with that subject only by remote tendencies, but they are questions of development. It belongs
to a different occasion from the present to dwell on these
things as parts of national education, as being, in truth,
the peculiar training of a citizen, the practical part of the
political education of a free people, taking them out of the
narrow circle of personal and family selfishness, and accus-
toming them to the comprehension of joint interests, the
management of joint concerns—habituating them to act
from public or semi-public motives, and guide their conduct
by aims which unite instead of isolating them from one another. Without these habits and powers, a free constitution
can neither be worked nor preserved, as is exemplified by
the too-often transitory nature of political freedom in countries where it does not rest upon a sufficient basis of local
liberties. The management of purely local business by the
localities, and of the great enterprises of industry by the
union of those who voluntarily supply the pecuniary means,
is further recommended by all the advantages which have
been set forth in this essay as belonging to individuality of

development and diversity of modes of action. Government operations tend to be everywhere alike. With individuals and voluntary associations, on the contrary, there are varied experiments and endless diversity of experience. What the State can usefully do is to make itself a central depository, and active circulator and diffuser, of the experience resulting from many trials. Its business is to enable each experimentalist to benefit by the experiments of others, instead of tolerating no experiments but its own.

The third and most cogent reason for restricting the interference of government is the great evil of adding unnecessarily to its power. Every function superadded to those already exercised by the government causes its influence over hopes and fears to be more widely diffused, and converts, more and more, the active and ambitious part of the public into hangers-on of the government, or of some party which aims at becoming the government. If the roads, the railways, the banks, the insurance offices, the great joint-stock companies, the universities, and the public charities were all of them branches of the government; if, in addition, the municipal corporations and local boards, with all that now devolves on them, became departments of the central administration; if the employees of all these different enterprises were appointed and paid by the government and looked to the government for every rise in life, not all the freedom of the press and popular constitution of the legislature would make this or any other country free otherwise than in name. And the evil would be greater, the more efficiently and scientifically the administrative machinery was constructed—the more skillful the arrangements for obtaining the best qualified hands and heads with which to work it. In England it has of late been proposed that all the members of the civil service of government should be selected by competitive examination, to obtain for these employments the most intelligent and instructed persons procurable; and much has been said and written for and against this proposal. One of the arguments most insisted on by its opponents is that the occupation of a permanent official servant

of the State does not hold out sufficient prospects of emolument and importance to attract the highest talents, which
will always be able to find a more inviting career in the professions or in the service of companies and other public
bodies. One would not have been surprised if this argument
had been used by the friends of the proposition as an answer
to its principal difficulty. Coming from the opponents it is
strange enough. What is urged as an objection is the safety
valve of the proposed system. If, indeed, all the high talent
of the country *could* be drawn into the service of the government, a proposal tending to bring about that result might
well inspire uneasiness. If every part of the business of society which required organized concert, or large and comprehensive views, were in the hands of the government,
and if government offices were universally filled by the
ablest men, all the enlarged culture and practiced intelligence in the country, except the purely speculative, would
be concentrated in a numerous bureaucracy, to whom alone
the rest of the community would look for all things—the
multitude for direction and dictation in all they had to do;
the able and aspiring for personal advancement. To be
admitted into the ranks of this bureaucracy, and when
admitted, to rise therein, would be the sole objects of ambition. Under this *régime* not only is the outside public ill-
qualified, for want of practical experience, to criticize or
check the mode of operation of the bureaucracy, but even
if the accidents of despotic or the natural working of popular institutions occasionally raise to the summit a ruler or
rulers of reforming inclinations, no reform can be effected
which is contrary to the interest of the bureaucracy. Such is
the melancholy condition of the Russian empire, as shown
in the accounts of those who have had sufficient opportunity
of observation. The Czar himself is powerless against the
bureaucratic body; he can send any one of them to Siberia,
but he cannot govern without them, or against their will.
On every decree of his they have a tacit veto, by merely
refraining from carrying it into effect. In countries of more
advanced civilization and of a more insurrectionary spirit,

the public, accustomed to expect everything to be done for them by the State, or at least to do nothing for themselves without asking from the State not only leave to do it, but even how it is to be done, naturally hold the State responsible for all evil which befalls them, and when the evil exceeds their amount of patience, they rise against the government and make what is called a revolution; whereupon somebody else, with or without legitimate authority from the nation, vaults into the seat, issues his orders to the bureaucracy, and everything goes on much as it did before; the bureaucracy being unchanged, and nobody else being capable of taking their place.

A very different spectacle is exhibited among a people accustomed to transact their own business. In France, a large part of the people, having been engaged in military service, many of whom have held at least the rank of noncommissioned officers, there are in every popular insurrection several persons competent to take the lead and improvise some tolerable plan of action. What the French are in military affairs, the Americans are in every kind of civil business; let them be left without a government, every body of Americans is able to improvise one and to carry on that or any other public business with a sufficient amount of intelligence, order, and decision. This is what every free people ought to be; and a people capable of this is certain to be free; it will never let itself be enslaved by any man or body of men because these are able to seize and pull the reins of the central administration. No bureaucracy can hope to make such a people as this do or undergo anything that they do not like. But where everything is done through the bureaucracy, nothing to which the bureaucracy is really adverse can be done at all. The constitution of such countries is an organization of the experience and practical ability of the nation into a disciplined body for the purpose of governing the rest; and the more perfect that organization is in itself, the more successful in drawing to itself and educating for itself the persons of greatest capacity from all ranks of the community, the more complete is the bondage

of all, the members of the bureaucracy included. For the
governors are as much the slaves of their organization and
discipline as the governed are of the governors. A Chinese
mandarin is as much the tool and creature of a despotism
as the humblest cultivator. An individual Jesuit is to the
utmost degree of abasement the slave of his order, though
the order itself exists for the collective power and importance of its members.

It is not, also, to be forgotten that the absorption of all
the principal ability of the country into the governing body
is fatal, sooner or later, to the mental activity and progressiveness of the body itself. Banded together as they are—
working a system which, like all systems, necessarily proceeds in a great measure by fixed rules—the official body
are under the constant temptation of sinking into indolent
routine, or, if they now and then desert that mill-horse
round, of rushing into some half-examined crudity which
has struck the fancy of some leading member of the corps;
and the sole check to these closely allied, though seemingly
opposite, tendencies, the only stimulus which can keep the
ability of the body itself up to a high standard, is liability
to the watchful criticism of equal ability outside the body.
It is indispensable, therefore, that the means should exist,
independently of the government, of forming such ability
and furnishing it with the opportunities and experience
necessary for a correct judgment of great practical affairs.
If we would possess permanently a skillful and efficient body
of functionaries—above all a body able to originate and willing to adopt improvements—if we would not have our bureaucracy degenerate into a pedantocracy, this body must
not engross all the occupations which form and cultivate
the faculties required for the government of mankind.

To determine the point at which evils, so formidable
to human freedom and advancement, begin, or rather at
which they begin to predominate over the benefits attending the collective application of the force of society, under
its recognized chiefs, for the removal of the obstacles which
stand in the way of its well-being; to secure as much of the

advantages of centralized power and intelligence as can be had without turning into governmental channels too great a proportion of the general activity—is one of the most difficult and complicated questions in the art of government. It is, in a great measure, a question of detail in which many and various considerations must be kept in view, and no absolute rule can be laid down. But I believe that the practical principle in which safety resides, the ideal to be kept in view, the standard by which to test all arrangements intended for overcoming the difficulty, may be conveyed in these words: the greatest dissemination of power consistent with efficiency; but the greatest possible centralization of information and diffusion of it from the center. Thus, in municipal administration, there would be, as in the New England states, a very minute division among separate officers, chosen by the localities, of all business which is not better left to the persons directly interested; but besides this, there would be, in each department of local affairs, a central superintendence, forming a branch of the general government. The organ of this superintendence would concentrate, as in a focus, the variety of information and experience derived from the conduct of that branch of public business in all the localities, from everything analogous which is done in foreign countries, and from the general principles of political science. This central organ should have a right to know all that is done, and its special duty should be that of making the knowledge acquired in one place available for others. Emancipated from the petty prejudices and narrow views of a locality by its elevated position and comprehensive sphere of observation, its advice would naturally carry much authority; but its actual power, as a permanent institution, should, I conceive, be limited to compelling the local officers to obey the laws laid down for their guidance. In all things not provided for by general rules, those officers should be left to their own judgment, under responsibility to their constituents. For the violation of rules, they should be responsible to law, and the rules themselves should be laid down by the legislature; the central administrative authority only watching over their execution and, if they were not properly carried into effect, appealing, according to the nature of the case, to the tribunals to enforce the law, or to the constituencies to dismiss the functionaries who had not executed it according to its spirit. Such, in its general conception, is the central superintendence which the Poor Law Board is intended to exercise over the administrators of the Poor Rate throughout the country. Whatever powers the Board exercises beyond this limit were right and necessary in that peculiar case, for the cure of rooted habits of maladministration in matters deeply affecting not the localities merely, but the whole community; since no locality has a moral right to make itself by mismanagement a nest of pauperism, necessarily overflowing into other localities and imparing the moral and physical condition of the whole laboring community. The powers of administrative coercion and subordinate legislation possessed by the Poor Law Board (but which, owing to the state of opinion on the subject, are very scantily exercised by them), though perfectly justifiable in a case of first-rate national interest, would be wholly out of place in the superintendence of interests purely local. But a central organ of information and instruction for all the localities would be equally valuable in all departments of administration. A government cannot have too much of the kind of activity which does not impede, but aids and stimulates, individual exertion and development. The mischief begins when, instead of calling forth the activity and powers of individuals and bodies, it substitutes its own activity for theirs; when, instead of informing, advising, and, upon occasion, denouncing, it makes them work in fetters, or bids them stand aside and does their work instead of them. The worth of a State, in the long run, is the worth of the individuals composing it; and a State which postpones the interests of *their* mental expansion and elevation to a little more of administrative skill, or of that semblance of it which practice gives in the details of business; a State which dwarfs its men, in order that they may be more docile instruments in its hands even for beneficial purposes—will find that with small men no great thing can really be accomplished; and that the perfection of machinery to which it has sacrificed everything will in the end avail it nothing, for want of the vital power which, in order that the machine might work more smoothly, it has preferred to banish.